FAKING LIT

Literary forgeries are usually regarded as spurious versions of genuine literature. *Faking Literature* argues that the production of a literary forgery is an act that reveals the spurious nature of literature itself. Literature has long been under attack because of its alliance with rh͏   persuasion) rather than with logic and ethics.   :cting such attacks is to demonise literary for   .cquires the illusion of authenticity by being   what are represented as ersatz approximations   g. Ruthven argues that literary forgery is the c   tion of cultural critique. As a powerful indictm   actices in such activities as literary criticism,   and the awarding of literary prizes, literar   serious attention from cultural analysts, and   component of literary studies. This intriguin   interest to all teachers, students and readers of   ..

K. K. RUTHVEN has   ;or of English at the universities of Canterb   d Melbourne, and is a fellow of the Australia   1e Humanities. He has published books on Ez   myth, feminist literary studies, and nuclear criticism. After editing *Southern Review* from 1981 to 1985 he became general editor of *Interpretations*, a series of monographs on recent theories and critical practices in the humanities and social sciences.

FAKING LITERATURE

K. K. RUTHVEN

CAMBRIDGE
UNIVERSITY PRESS

PUBLISHED BY THE PRESS SYNDICATE OF THE UNIVERSITY OF CAMBRIDGE
The Pitt Building, Trumpington Street, Cambridge, United Kingdom

CAMBRIDGE UNIVERSITY PRESS
The Edinburgh Building, Cambridge CB2 2RU, UK
40 West 20th Street, New York, NY 10011–4211, USA
10 Stamford Road, Oakleigh, Melbourne 3166, Australia
Ruiz de Alarcón 13, 28014 Madrid, Spain
Dock House, The Waterfront, Cape Town 8001, South Africa

http://www.cambridge.org

First published 2001

Printed in the United Kingdom at the University Press, Cambridge

Typeset in Baskerville 11/12.5pt   System 3b2   [CE]

A catalogue record for this book is available from the British Library

ISBN 0 521 66015 7 hardback
ISBN 0 521 66965 0 paperback

To
Marion Campbell

Contents

Acknowledgements

I would like to acknowledge my indebtedness to the Australian Research Council for funding, from 1990 to 1992, a related project that developed into this book; Elizabeth Day, Eleanor Hogan, Lisa O'Connell, Dominic Pettman and Ann Vickery, formerly post-graduate students in the University of Melbourne's Department of English with Cultural Studies, who located and obtained copies of the books and articles I requested; Derek Attridge, for his critique of the synoptic proposal for this book and his comments on the penultimate version of it; and Sue Dickinson for copy-editing the final version.

K.K.R.
August 2000

Abbreviations

ASch	*The American Scholar*
AusFS	*Australian Feminist Studies*
BB	*Bulletin of Bibliography*
BrLR	*Brooklyn Law Review*
ECent	*The Eighteenth Century: Theory and Interpretation*
ELH	*English Literary History*
ELN	*English Language Notes*
ESC	*English Studies in Canada*
HisT	*History Today*
LRB	*London Review of Books*
NEQ	*New England Quarterly*
NLH	*New Literary History*
NY	*New Yorker*
NYRB	*The New York Review of Books*
NYTBR	*New York Times Book Review*
OED	*The Oxford English Dictionary* (Oxford, 1989), 20 vols.
PMLA	*Publications of the Modern Language Association of America*
PBSA	*Papers of the Bibliographical Society of America*
PQ	*Philological Quarterly*
RES	*Review of English Studies*
SSL	*Studies in Scottish Literature*
SVEC	*Studies on Voltaire and the Eighteenth Century*
TLS	*Times Literary Supplement*
TSWL	*Tulsa Studies in Women's Literature*

Prologue

For almost one-and-a-half centuries after the British Museum opened its domed Reading Room in May 1857, scholars from all over the world used to assemble there in order to access an incomparable collection of printed and manuscript materials. To study in that circular room lined with books to a height of thirty-odd feet was to experience the encyclopaedic illusion of being at the very centre of knowledge. Not until sections of the wall swung open so that functionaries could retrieve some of the treasures hidden behind them did it become clear to bewildered newcomers that those portals of discovery were lined not with books but with *trompe-l'oeil* imitations of closely shelved volumes. The twenty columns which support the great dome were also 'covered with false book-backs' to the same height.[1]

Fake books are what you expect to find in the mansions of parvenus like the hero of Scott Fitzgerald's *The Great Gatsby* (1925). A sceptical visitor to Gatsby's 'high Gothic library' was surprised to discover, however, that every book housed there was an 'absolutely real' and 'bona-fide piece of printed matter' with 'pages and everything', put there by someone who sustained the illusion of connoisseurship by showing that he 'knew when to stop': that is, he 'didn't cut the pages'.[2] Fake books are not what you expect to find in one of the world's great libraries. Yet the real books on the walls of the British Museum's Reading Room and the false book-spines on its doors and columns constituted a visually seamless space, designed apparently by Antonio (later Sir Anthony) Panizzi, a lawyer and revolutionary who arrived in England in 1823 as a political refugee from Italy, and eventually became the Museum's Principal Librarian.

---

[1] P.R. Harris, *Reading Room*, 16.
[2] Fitzgerald, *Bodley Head Scott Fitzgerald*, 160.

Despised by his English rivals as a 'mountebank', a 'scoundrel Italian' capable of doing what 'no *gentleman* could be found to do', Panizzi had been so well connected as a protégé of the man who became Lord Chancellor, Lord Brougham, that his lack of qualifications in librarianship did not prevent his appointment as a cataloguer in the Department of Printed Books.[3] Unqualified as an architect, he claimed in 1866 to have 'originated' the plan for the Museum's Reading Room, although one of the men responsible for building it, Sydney Smirke, said that what Panizzi originally proposed was 'a flat, low building'.[4] A few years earlier, Panizzi had been accused of piracy in a pamphlet entitled *Some Observations upon the Recent Addition of a Reading Room to the British Museum* (1858), published by the professor of architecture and engineering construction at King's College, London, William Hosking, who had submitted a plan for a circular and domed building on the same site which the Museum's Trustees had rejected in 1849.[5]

The disputed origin and heterogeneous contents of that splendid Reading Room monumentalise various themes in this book, but particularly the imbrication of the spurious with the genuine in literature, that 'strange institution' (as Jacques Derrida describes it) whose history '*is constructed* like the ruin of a monument which basically never existed'.[6] *Faking Literature* is about the power of literary forgeries to disturb the societies in which they are produced, and to do so in ways resented by the guardians of cultural institutions such as literary studies, book-reviewing and the literary awards system. For while the word 'disturbing' is commonly encountered in such quarters as a term of praise, this usage tends to be restricted to the contents of books that are thought of as disturbing us for our own good by unsettling our complacencies about a wide range of personal and social concerns. Writers are also permitted to disturb the conventional forms of literature by developing generic hybridities, provided they avoid the extravagances ridiculed in *Hamlet* as 'tragical-comical-historical-pastoral'. Such transgressive behaviour is described as 'innovative'. But no writer is permitted to disturb those cultural institutions which accredit and mediate literature by demon-

---

[3] Edward Miller, *Prince of Librarians*, 213, 129; Ganzel, *Fortune and Men's Eyes*, 117.
[4] P.R. Harris, *History of the British Museum Library*, 188.
[5] Ibid., 187–88; Fagan, *Life of Panizzi*, vol. I, 368–69, 375.
[6] Derrida, *Acts of Literature*, 36, 42.

strating inefficiencies in their operations and thus questioning the grounds of their existence.

This book treats both 'literature' and 'literary forgery' as categories of writing with much in common. It assumes that since what a society values will show up obliquely in what it rejects, reactions to literary forgeries illuminate perceptions of literariness. It therefore reconsiders the connections between literature and what are variously designated literary 'forgeries', 'frauds', 'fakes', 'hoaxes', 'impostures', 'spuriosities', 'counterfeits' and (more rarely in anglophone accounts) 'supercheries'. No matter which term is used, the relationship between literarity and spuriosity is framed as a binary opposition, in which literature is valorised as the authentic Self and literary forgery disparaged as its bogus Other. The perceived business of literary studies is accordingly to preserve and fortify that distinction by practising a cultural eugenics designed to eliminate the dreck. This is why the outing of a literary forgery is generally admired as a culturally prophylactic event. In my view, however, literary forgery is not so much the disreputable Other of 'genuine' literature as its demystified and disreputable Self. If, then, the 'spurious' and the 'genuine' are consubstantial, how has literature come to be associated with the one by being dissociated from the other? I think that literature is systemically spurious on account of its long-standing association with rhetoric. Consequently, the history of literature is also and inevitably the history of recurrent defences of it against attacks on its epistemological status, the earliest and most influential of which emanate from that arch-enemy of rhetoric, Plato.[7] Furthermore, I think that we ought to revalue literary forgery as an antinomian phenomenon produced by creative energies whose power is attested to by the resistance they engender in those who feel compelled to denounce and eradicate it.

In short, I argue that we should start thinking more positively about literary forgery, and not least because of its opposition to the establishment of no-go areas by cultural police of both the right and the left, who suspend their residual hostilities to one another by jointly condemning it as an unethical practice. Literary forgeries are worth studying because they display even more clearly than those other counterfactual assemblages we call literary works that 'disruptive and capricious power' of the imagination which Edgar Wind

[7] Vickers, *In Defence of Rhetoric*, 83–147.

calls 'anarchic'.[8] They exhibit a carnivalesque irreverence towards the sanctity of various conventions designed to limit what is permissible in literary production. Whenever they succeed they destabilise the fragile economy of literary accreditation by drawing attention both to its conceptual shoddiness and the expediencies that characterise its operations. By doing so they provoke in our cultural gatekeepers anxieties displaced as anger and articulated as opprobrium. Literary forgeries, therefore, constitute a powerful indictment of such cultural practices as literary reviewing and the awarding of literary prizes, especially those which Doris Lessing labels 'razzmatazz'.[9] They are also a serious embarrassment to people who see it as their duty to protect the institution of literature from critiques of it by literary theorists who question received ideas about authorship, originality and authenticity. This is one reason for integrating literary forgeries into studies of cultural values instead of ignoring them as anomalies. Seeing that these supposedly 'irregular' and 'abnormal' literary phenomena occur more frequently than is generally acknowledged, the burgeoning archive of literary forgeries remains an unresolved problem for cultural analysts. Now that English studies is once again reappraising its activities, I think it timely to recall some of its repressed texts, and to consider how the discipline might refashion its agenda in the wake of such a reclamation.

[8] Wind, *Art and Anarchy*, 1.
[9] Lessing, *Diaries of Jane Somers*, [8].

CHAPTER I

Sampling the spurious

Certain times and places are undoubtedly more hospitable than others to the activities surveyed in this book. Britain in the 1760s must have been one such chronotope, when Thomas Percy was tampering with the texts of the ballads he was to publish as *Reliques of Ancient English Poetry* in 1765. That appeared a year after someone called 'William Marshall' translated as *The Castle of Otranto* a book allegedly written by an equally imaginary Italian, 'Onuphrio Muralto', and given the fictive imprint of 'Naples, 1529'. Marketed as 'a Gothic story' in its second edition of 1765, it turned out to be the inaugural manifestation of a literary genre characterised by its 'ghostings of the already spectral' and 'recounterfeiting of the already counterfeit'.[1] Its actual author was Horace Walpole, fourth Earl of Oxford, who transformed his Strawberry Hill residence into a pseudo-Gothic castle. In 1768 a fifteen-year-old called Thomas Chatterton began to retro-fashion himself as 'Thomas Rowley' in order to compose fifteenth-century poetry and other literary muniments. After Walpole had indicated that he was 'by no means satisfied with the authenticity' of Chatterton's 'supposed MSS', Chatterton accused Walpole of having himself 'indulge[d] in such Deceit'. The real foundation of Walpole's double standard, he alleged, was economic: those with 'the Gifts of Wealth & Lux'ry' could get away with literary practices for which the 'poor & Mean' were castigated.[2]

At the beginning of that decade, James Macpherson extrapolated from fragments of Gaelic poetry what he claimed to be English translations of two 'ancient' epics attributed to Ossian: *Fingal* (1761) and *Temora* (1763). The year 1763 was also the date of the first recorded forgery of a document concerning Shakespeare, just a few

---

[1] Hogle, 'Gothic Ghost of the Counterfeit', 295.
[2] Meyerstein, *Life of Chatterton*, 262, 271.

years before he was installed as England's national poet at the belated bicentenary celebrations of his birth, which David Garrick organised for the Stratford Jubilee in 1769. An invented anecdote about Shakespeare was the substance of a letter quoted in an essay about the actor Edward Alleyn and published in the *Theatrical Review.* Written allegedly in 1600 by George Peele (who died in 1596) to Christopher Marlowe (who was killed in 1593), that letter – forged by the Shakespeare scholar, George Steevens – recalled Shakespeare's annoyance at being accused by Alleyn of having plagiarised their conversations when composing the speech about acting in *Hamlet*.[3] The manuscript has not survived, but its 'olde' spellings were designed for a post-neoclassical generation whose antiquarian interests were nurtured by Richard Hurd's *Letters on Chivalry and Romance* (1762), which praises Spenser's *The Faerie Queene* (1596) as a 'Gothic' alternative to those 'Grecian' notions of literary excellence advocated by neoclassical critics.[4] The possibility that Shakespeare was a plagiarist must have occurred a decade earlier to readers of Charlotte Lennox's *Shakespear Illustrated* (1753), which analyses 'the novels and histories on which [his] plays . . . are founded'. It is certainly taken for granted by Herbert Lawrence, whose 'historical allegory', *The Life and Adventures of Common Sense* (1769), demystifies the Bard by representing his plagiarism as symptomatic of behaviour first recorded in Nicholas Rowe's *Life of Mr. William Shakespear* (1709), namely his youthful activities as a deer-poacher.[5] At this iconic moment in the formation of English literature as a source of national pride, Shakespeare is both a transcendent genius and an all-too-human plagiarist. Literary forgery is in Joseph Conrad's sense the 'secret sharer' of literature.

North of the border, James Macpherson had already produced the canonical texts for anybody interested in either committing or studying literary forgery. Like Bardolatry, they too were conscripted for a nationalist agenda. One of their aims was anti-English: to show that, since the Gaels inherited a far more ancient culture than that of the Sassenachs who had defeated them at the Battle of Culloden in 1745, demoralised Highlanders had grounds for feeling culturally superior to their conquerors. The other, however, was anti-Irish: to show that, since the ancient bard who had composed those Gaelic

---

[3] Schoenbaum, *Shakespeare's Lives*, 241–42; Grebanier, *Great Shakespeare Forgery*, 139.
[4] Wellek, *Rise of English Literary History*, 95–102.
[5] Schoenbaum, *Shakespeare's Lives*, 395–96, 68.

ballads 'collected' by Macpherson was a Scot called Ossian rather than an Irishman called Oisean, the originating site of Gaelic culture in the third century AD was not Ireland but Scotland. Macpherson's Ossianic *oeuvre* is as cornucopian a text for analysts of spuriosity as that other 1760s phenomenon, Sterne's *Tristram Shandy*, is for theorists of fiction. As part of a body of writing which 'made use of some fourteen or fifteen Gaelic ballads', *Fingal* is best described as 'a "collage"' of 'reworked authentic material, together with a liberal admixture of pure Macpherson'.[6] Neither wholly Ossian nor wholly Macpherson, but more Macphersonian than Ossianic, that mestizo corpus is the work of a composite figure I shall call 'Macphossian'. Its formal innovation was to develop a generic hybridity which a subsequent generation of French Symbolist poets would know as *poèmes en prose*, but its literary strategy was to market genuine Macpherson in the guise of bogus Ossian.

Macpherson was a native speaker of Gaelic who could not read Gaelic writing, and the ambitious author of an heroic poem in six cantos called *The Highlander* (1758), which failed to attract the attention he had hoped for. In order to satisfy the curiosity of John Home – a friend who had written a successful play called *Douglas* (1756), but who knew no Gaelic – Macpherson 'translated' a poem on the death of Ossian's son, Oscar, which Home showed to a group of Edinburgh literati. Among them was the inaugural professor of rhetoric and *belles lettres* at Edinburgh University, Hugh Blair, who would eventually write but not sign the preface to *Fragments of Ancient Poetry*, and allow Macpherson to rewrite the final paragraph of his also unsigned *Critical Dissertation on the Poems of Ossian* (1763).[7] Persuaded by Macpherson that this book was the pilot study for a major research project – namely, to retrieve the 'lost' epic poetry of the Scottish Highlands – the Edinburgh group funded a couple of field-trips by him between August 1760 and January 1761. This enabled him to collect not only Gaelic manuscripts but also transcripts by his research assistant, Ewan Macpherson, of ballads they heard recited.[8] By January 1761 he was telling a correspondent that he had been 'lucky enough to lay [his] hands on a pretty complete poem, and truly epic, concerning Fingal'.[9] Macpherson made the

6 Thomson, *Gaelic Sources*, 10; Gaskill, ' "Ossian" Macpherson', 129.
7 Chapman, 'Blair on Ossian', 82–83.
8 Stafford, *Sublime Savage*, 116, 121, 123.
9 Thomson, 'Macpherson's *Ossian*', 258.

holistic assumption that he had discovered chips off an old block which, like ancient pots from shards of pottery, could be painstakingly reassembled. By calling the Gaelic ballads 'fragments', he dignified them with the classicising term *fragmenta*, and treated them as parts of a dismembered tradition in need of re-membering into what the preface to *Fragments* calls 'one Work of considerable Length, and which deserves to be styled an heroic Poem'.[10] Like the scattered limbs of Osiris in the Greco-Roman tradition, the reassembled *membra disjecta* of Ossian's ballads might be expected to engender a renascence, this time in Scotland, just as the rediscovery of ancient Greek and Roman texts in the fifteenth and sixteenth centuries had enabled an earlier renascence called the Renaissance. Now that Gaelic was in danger of dying out as a result of the invaders' linguicidal policy of making English the language of instruction in Scottish schools, Macpherson's 'translations' could be praised as a timely attempt to save an endangered species of poetry from extinction.

The theoretical framework for such ambitions derived from contemporary understandings of epic poetry. Macpherson attended the University of Aberdeen at a time when its staff included Thomas Blackwell, the author of *An Enquiry into the Life and Writings of Homer* (1735). Blackwell observed that civil upheavals had been the seedbed of epic poetry not only in Homer's Greece and Dante's Italy but most recently in Milton's England, where *Paradise Lost* (1667) had emerged from a civil war. In traditional hierarchies of literary 'kinds', epic was the pre-eminent genre. Politically, it celebrated the nationhood of an emergent state, and identified national security with a hegemonic family: what Virgil's *Aeneid* had done for Augustus Caesar, Spenser's *The Faerie Queene* (1596) had been designed to do for Elizabeth Tudor, reaffirming her self-legitimating genealogy as a descendant of King Arthur and therefore the rightful ruler of England. Scotland's position in universal history was distinctly anomalous, since although it had experienced turmoil in abundance it appeared not to have produced a Homer. There were two ways of remedying this deficiency. One was to write the missing epic, as William Wilkie ('the Homer of the Lowlands') attempted to do when, taking as his model Alexander Pope's translation of the *Iliad* (1720) into heroic couplets, he published a nine-book epic on the Fall of

---

[10] Mossner, *Forgotten Hume*, 85.

Thebes called the *Epigoniad* (1757), whose heroes were the descendants (*epigones*) of warriors who had participated in an earlier and unsuccessful siege of that city.[11] The other was to discover that 'lost' Scottish epic which, it stood to reason, must once have existed. This was also the preferred option. Since societies of the Enlightenment could no longer believe in either the supernatural 'machinery' or clapped out classical mythology which featured so prominently in the defining examples of the genre, the rediscovery of a Gaelic epic would avoid the problems of inventing one. As the vehicle of northern mythologies, it would revitalise poetry in a manner anticipated by William Collins in his 'Ode on the Popular Superstitions of the Highlands of Scotland, Considered as the Subject of Poetry' (1749), which Collins had given to John Home by 1750. Ossian would emerge as the Homer of the north, his Gaelic language comparable to Homeric Greek, that vivid language of the passions out of which epic arose. After producing English versions of Ossianic poetry declared Homeric by Blair, Macpherson completed the circuit by translating *The Iliad of Homer* (1773) into 'Ossianic' prose-poetry.[12]

Blair admired Macphossian as poetry, although he also wanted it to be revisionist history.[13] Macpherson claimed that the fragments he had collected were vestiges of an oral tradition going back to the third century AD, and a legacy of those indomitable Caledonians who had resisted the Roman invasion of Britain.[14] The legendary chief of the Fenians (called 'Fionn' by the Irish) was actually 'Fingal' (Finn the Gael). The nationalist aim of *Temora*, as set out in the 'Dissertation' which precedes it, is to remove from Scottish culture the stigma of derivativeness from Ireland.[15] Gaelic texts discrepant from Macpherson's 'translations' were denounced as 'spurious fifteenth-century Irish versions' of those earlier Scottish ballads.[16] From an Irish perspective, therefore, Macpherson was guilty not of forgery but of appropriation. Charlotte Brooke's *Reliques of Irish Poetry* (1789) – a title designed to attract readers of Thomas Percy's *Reliques of Ancient English Poetry* (1765) – is in this respect a counter-Macphersonian act of reclamation, despite her 'absolute silence on the Ossian controversy'.[17]

---

[11] Ibid., 68–77.   [12] Stafford, *Sublime Savage*, 85.
[13] Ibid., 99.
[14] Smart, *James Macpherson*, 102–03.
[15] Haugen, 'Ossian and the Invention of Textual History', 312.
[16] Colgan, 'Ossian: Success or Failure?', 346.
[17] Greene, *Makers and Forgers*, 11; O'Halloran, 'Irish Re-creations of the Gaelic Past', 87.

In England the political potential of Macphossian as the lost epic poetry of an heroic but oppressed people could be diffused by discrediting it as a forgery. Published in Edinburgh, and in the language of the invader, Macphossian was far too politicised a text to be assessed in eighteenth-century London solely in terms of those aestheticising criteria which weighed the 'beauties' of a literary work against its 'defects' before passing judgement on it. James Boswell told David Hume that the English had been 'exceedingly fond' of *Fingal* until they learnt 'that it was Scotch', whereupon 'they became jealous and silent'.[18] Samuel Johnson thought that because the Scots 'love *Scotland* better than truth' and certainly 'better than enquiry', they would never admit to the fraudulence of anything which flattered their vanity as much as Macphossian did.[19] The vehemence of such remarks leads Richard B. Scher to argue that those English men of letters who sought to discredit Macphossian – Johnson, Thomas Percy and Horace Walpole – did so because they 'felt threatened by the sudden ascent of their Scottish counterparts'.[20] Their strategy certainly succeeded in England, where for the next couple of centuries Macphossian would be remembered by the arbiters of taste only as a literary forgery, and deployed in support of the Scotophobic view that 'the Teutonic nations' have manifested 'immemorially' a higher 'respect for truth . . . than that acknowledged by the Celts'.[21]

Post-colonial readers figure Macpherson as 'a post-Culloden Highlander' whose retrieval of a national epic offered some consolation for the 'cultural apocalypse of Culloden'.[22] Yet this subaltern interpretation of Macphossian and its supporting 'dissertations' as a declaration of independence, designed to appeal to 'all who feel themselves subjected to an alien cultural hegemony', is qualified by the fact that Macpherson not only defended the 1707 Act of Union in his *History of Great Britain* (1775) but published in 1776 a book on *The Rights of Great Britain Asserted against the Claims of America*.[23] Moreover, Howard D. Weinbrot argues, Macphossian achieved cult status among English readers precisely because its constituent poems were so 'unrevolutionary' as to be 'wholly unthreatening' to a nation

---

18 Mossner, *Forgotten Hume*, 89.   19 Ibid., 94.
20 Scher, 'Percy, Shaw and the Ferguson "Cheat"', 234.
21 Hewlett, 'Forged Literature', 321.
22 Gaskill, '"Ossian" Macpherson', 119; Crawford, 'Post-Cullodenism', 18.
23 Gaskill, 'Ossian in Europe', 666.

convinced that the Jacobites had been so demoralised by Culloden that there would be no further need (as the national anthem had phrased it in 1745) 'Rebellious Scots to crush'.[24] The politics of Macphossian's literary production in Scotland were scaled down to a cultural politics of reception in England, where the principal hegemony it broke was the heroic couplet. The legacy of that prosodic revolution in the realm of the bogus would be seen in the prophetic books of William Blake and subsequently in *Leaves of Grass* by Walt Whitman, who ranked Macphossian in the same class as the Bible.[25] Anglophone admirers read Macphossian, therefore, as a thrilling departure from a late Augustan style of poetry committed, in its fondness for heroic couplets, to the rational pleasures of epigrammatic point and strongly marked closure. Macphossian, by contrast, decomposed poetry-as-product into poetry-as-process, 'hypnotically repetitive, oracular, incantatory, dreamlike'.[26] Its confection of antiquity, sublimity and simplicity both anticipated and helped articulate nostalgia for that mythical age when primitives lived passionately in elemental settings. At a time when nature 'methodised' was losing its allure, Macphossian's evocations of Highland wildernesses – drawn, apparently, not from Ossianic ballads but from the Badenoch landscape around Ruthven, where Macpherson grew up – created a new *frisson* for a generation in transit from a 'Gothick' horror of mountain gloom to a Romantic appreciation of mountain glory as a source of the sublime.[27]

Most importantly, Macphossian was exportable. Against Robert Frost's subsequent dictum that poetry is what gets lost in translation, Macpherson claims in his preface to *The Poems of Ossian* (1784) that any poem which resists a skilled translator must be 'counterfeit'. The favourable reception accorded translations of Macphossian into numerous European languages substantiated his view that the provenance of poetry is less important than responses to it. By presenting himself as a translator whose skills enabled him to 'equal his original' – and how could it have been otherwise, seeing that most of his 'translations' *were* the originals? – Macpherson acknowl-

---

[24] Weinbrot, *Britannia's Issue*, 555; David Nichol Smith (ed.), *Oxford Book of Eighteenth Century Verse*, 302.

[25] Carpenter, 'Vogue of Ossian in America', 413–14.

[26] Frye, 'Defining an Age of Sensibility', 148.

[27] Thomson, *Gaelic Sources*, 84.

edged publicly his talents as a translator and privately his genius as a
poet.[28]

As a 'translator' who was simultaneously an editor and author of
Ossianic poetry, Macpherson was caught between rival modes of
textual transmission, one oral, the other chirographic and more
recently print-specific. The oral tradition sanctioned changes to
traditional tales for the reason given by W.H. Auden in his elegy on
W.B. Yeats, namely that 'the words of a dead man / Are modified in
the guts of the living'.[29] But in the dominant print-culture of the
eighteenth century, which was the first to aspire to a 'correct' text of
Shakespeare's plays, only one form of the words could be authentic.
Macpherson's English 'translations' of both Gaelic manuscripts and
transcripts of oral performances were at varying removes, however,
from their putative originals. Some, like the 1512 *Book of the Dean of
Lismore*, had been preserved in manuscripts which Macpherson was
unable to read on account of their bardic language and old Irish
handwriting.[30] Was Macphossian based on words read or words
heard? When pointing out in 1765 that the Gaelic materials which
underpin *Fingal* had been 'collected from tradition, and some manuscripts', Macpherson seemed to be saying that the Gaelic originals
had been more frequently oral than textual. To represent Ossianic
materials as the oral residue of an oral culture was a strong position
to be in, since critics like Johnson assumed that Macphossian was
based on manuscripts that either did not exist or would not support
Macpherson's translations of them.[31] Macpherson therefore gave
ammunition to his enemies when he abandoned the oral-provenance
argument and proceeded to translate his 'translations' into synthetic
Gaelic.[32] In 1763 he published the Gaelic 'original' of the seventh
book of *Temora*, perhaps put together by his cousin, Lachlan
Macpherson, but in any case 'back-translated' from Macphossian
English.[33] The completion of what Thomson calls 're-fabricated
Gaelic versions' of the whole of Macphossian – the translation of it
into its 'originals' – was a major task still in process when Macpherson
died in 1796. Finished eventually by friends, *The Poems of Ossian, in the*

---

[28] Folkenflik, 'Macpherson, Chatterton, Blake', 388.
[29] Auden, *Collected Shorter Poems*, 141.
[30] Thomson, ' "Ossian" Macpherson and the Gaelic World', 12.
[31] Gaskill, 'Ossian in Europe', 645.
[32] Thomson, 'Macpherson's *Ossian*', 256.
[33] Thomson, ' "Ossian" Macpherson and the Gaelic World', 13; Gaskill (ed.), *Ossian Revisited*,
   13.

Original Gaelic was published in 1807 and accompanied by 'a Literal Translation into Latin'. Far from solving the problem of origins, it merely complicated the textuality of the text by rendering it polyglot.

Macphossian remains the key text for analysts of literary forgery because it generated two quite different phenomena: an 'Ossianic controversy' about the authenticity of the Gaelic materials mediated by Macpherson's 'translation', and an enormous cult readership which felt free to ignore that controversy because it knew what it liked. Macphossian was translated into a dozen languages: Bohemian, Danish, Dutch, French, German, Greek, Hungarian, Italian, Polish, Russian, Swedish and Spanish. The results of that diaspora are traced in such studies as Rudolf Tambo's *Ossian in Germany* (1901), Paul van Tieghem's *Ossian en France* (1917) and Isidoro Montiel's *Ossián en España* (1974).[34] Different countries had different uses for what they imported: for whereas Michael Denis translated Macphossian into German in order to add Ossian to the canon of great writers, Cesarotti's Italian translation was to be ammunition for anticlassicists.[35] By 1805, when the Highland Society of Scotland finally published its *Report* on 'the nature and authenticity of the poems of Ossian', and concluded that Macpherson had merely tampered excessively with genuinely Ossianic poetry, Macphossian was selling better than anything except the Bible and Shakespeare.[36] Critics who assumed that Macphossian could be destroyed by exposing it as a forgery had no influence on a popular readership determined not to let problems of provenance spoil its pleasure in the text. Those who think they are performing a public service by establishing that a popular book is spurious cannot rely on public approval, as is evident from widespread indifference to the revelation in 1999 that the author of *How Green Was My Valley* (1939) was not a Welsh miner's son, Richard Llewellyn, but a Londoner called Vivian Lloyd. What Umberto Eco (recalling Gilles Deleuze) calls 'the force of falsity' makes inaccurate ideas influential, transforms imperfect understandings into creative misprisions and enables fake texts to generate genuine experiences.[37] Mendelssohn-lovers who thrill to the sounds of 'Fingal's Cave' in the *Hebrides* Overture are unlikely to care that it can be sourced ultimately to Macphossian, and was inspired partly

---

[34] Haugen, 'Ossian and the Invention of Textual History', 310.
[35] Gaskill, 'Ossian in Europe', 653.
[36] Smart, *James Macpherson*, 164; Stafford, *Sublime Savage*, 171; Mackenzie (ed.), *Report, passim*.
[37] Eco, *Serendipities*, 1–21; Deleuze, *Cinema 2*, 126–55.

by Mendelssohn's visit in 1829 to the basalt rock formation 'discovered' in 1772 by Joseph Banks on the isle of Staffa off the west coast of Scotland, and identified subsequently as a suitable location to associate for touristic purposes with the hero of *Fingal*.[38]

Macpherson overcame the disappointments of modern authorship provoked by indifference to *The Highlander* (1758) by deciding to become a great ancient poet. This involved foregoing the facile pleasures of fame for the more arcane delights of deception. He did so in the knowledge that he had nothing to lose if he failed (since any 'faults' could be attributed to those Ossianic ballads he had faithfully translated) and everything to gain should he succeed. Publicly, he was merely the talented facilitator of another poet's work; but privately, as the author of Macphossian rather than the translator of Ossian, he could bask in the praise it attracted. Writing as James Macpherson, he would never have been acclaimed as an 'original genius', a phenomenon much discussed after the publication of William Sharpe's *Dissertation upon Genius* (1755). Unlike Macphossian, Macpherson would never have joined that elite group of writers described in William Duff's *Critical Observations on the Writings of the Most Celebrated Original Geniuses in Poetry* (1770), whose other members are Homer, Shakespeare, Spenser, Milton, Ariosto and Tasso. Nor would Hugh Blair have considered Macpherson – as he did Macphossian – the equal of Homer.[39] In such circumstances, the transient satisfaction of showing (by confessing to a forgery) that some of the arbiters of taste at that time were ignorant fools was as nothing compared with the durable delights of knowing that his writings were treated as works of genius. For like Sir Edmund Backhouse, who forged the diary of a Chinese courtier and invented the diaries of a Grand Eunuch in order to authenticate that 'pornographic novelette' he called his 'memoirs' – thus prompting Hugh Trevor-Roper to describe him as 'the T.J. Wise of Chinese manuscripts, the Baron Corvo of Peking' – Macpherson would have relished 'the exquisite private satisfaction of deceiving the elect'.[40] Attacks on his integrity as a translator were unintentional tributes to his excellence as a writer. After Duff had declared Macphossian to be a work of genius, how delightful it must have been to read some five years later Johnson's intended rebuke that those poems 'never

38 Buruma, *Voltaire's Coconuts*, 76, 78.
39 Folkenflik, 'Macpherson, Chatterton, Blake', 384–85.
40 Trevor-Roper, *Hidden Life*, 334, 335, 369, 350.

existed in any other form than that which we have seen'.[41] By the time Macphossian was generally regarded as some sort of forgery, Macpherson had the pleasure of finding himself described as the 'Homer of the Celtic tongue' in an anthology of *Ancient Scottish Poems* (1786) edited by another creative refurbisher of antiquities, John Pinkerton.[42]

The Macphossian affair is a richly foundational episode in the annals of modern spuriosity. Its mixture of Ossianic residues with Macphossianic embellishments results in a textual hybridity which destabilises the commonsense notion that a literary text is either genuine or bogus. For as Macpherson notes in his preface to *Temora*, Macphossian was both inauthentic to English critics (who demanded to see the manuscripts) and authentic to Irish critics convinced that Macpherson had hijacked their own cultural property.[43] The conflictual reception of Macphossian indicates that a literary forgery reveals more about the times it is produced in than about the past it pretends to be part of. By concealing its actual origins and then inventing a factitious source for itself after the event, Macphossian plays havoc with the unidirectional theory of time that underpins diachronic forms of literary scholarship such as *Quellenforschung*, which regards the sources (*Quellen*) of a text as always antecedent to it. But as Borges suggests, 'every writer *creates* his own precursors': anybody who has read Franz Kafka's *The Castle* (1926) will detect Kafkaesque elements in Charles Dickens' description of the Circumlocution Office in *Little Dorrit* (1857).[44] The supersession of Ossian by Macphossian prefigures the postmodern displacement of the real by the simulacrum. The problems posed by Macphossian's historical revisionism is a salutary reminder that literary texts which contain 'history' may not be history. Macpherson's imputation to Ossian of the authorship of Macphossian draws attention to the power of the signature in the creation of textual authority. And the phenomenal success of Macphossian reveals not only the difficulty of establishing authenticity as a criterion of value, but also its unimportance once literary studies redirect attention from the inscrutable origins of a text to the critical history of its reception, and the various uses made of it by those different readerships that constitute its afterlife. In

---

[41] Stafford, *Sublime Savage*, 2.
[42] Haywood, *Making of History*, 117.
[43] Groom, *Making of Percy's* Reliques, 89–90.
[44] Borges, *Labyrinths*, 236.

short, Macphossian seriously challenges the commonsense assumption that 'originality' and 'authenticity' are polar opposites of the fake. Macphossian is an original and authentic fake.

Ballads transmitted in English posed comparable problems in the eighteenth century. The story of how, in 1753, a young Shropshire clergyman called Thomas Percy prevented Humphrey Pitt's maid-servants from continuing to light fires with sheets from a mid-seventeenth-century manuscript collection of ballads ('lying dirty on the floor') is one of the romances of modern scholarship.[45] Encouraged by Johnson to publish his find, Percy selected about a quarter of the texts from what would come to be known as the Percy Folio, and then – compliant with contemporary proprieties – set about making them presentable to readers who thought themselves more refined than the societies that had produced those ballads. By allowing no one to inspect 'his' Folio, Percy avoided the problems Macpherson encountered after publishing a Gaelic specimen in *Temora* (1763).[46] Percy produced an eighteenth-century simulacrum of what his contemporaries considered to be 'ancient' English poems. He did so by not only 'perfecting' them (that is, correcting their 'errors' of style and taste) but also 'restoring' them – rather in the way that ancient sculptures had had their missing limbs prostheticised in Renaissance workshops – by textual additions of varying length, all written in what he took to be the spirit of the originals. Whereas some of the ballads Percy 'improved' were given only a few extra stanzas, others 'were altered beyond all recognition', and emerged with 'scarcely one incident or even one line that might be found in the manuscript version'.[47] Consequently, Percy augmented the thirty-nine lines which comprise the manuscript version of 'Childe of Elle' into a two-hundred line 'Ballad of the Childe of Elle'.[48]

Thirty years after publishing his *Reliques of Ancient English Poetry* (1765), Percy conceded the impossibility of trying to please two different kinds of reader. One was 'the judicious Antiquary' – the kind of person Joseph Ritson turned himself into – who thought that the business of any modern editor of 'strange old stuff' is to reproduce it in a diplomatic text, that is, to print warts-and-all copies

45 Bertram H. Davis, *Thomas Percy*, 24.
46 Groom, *Making of Percy's* Reliques, 102.
47 Walter Jackson Bate, 'Percy's Use of His Folio', 338.
48 Ibid., 345–46.

of the manuscripts, no matter how crude they might appear in spelling, versification or sentiment. The rest were those 'Reader[s] of Taste' who liked to have their exquisite sensibilities caressed by the elegantly melting cadences of Macphossian.[49] By sharing Percy's preference 'to see these old things in a modern dress [rather] than *in puris naturalibus*', they ensured that the *Reliques* were favourably received in the eighteenth century.[50] But in his *Select Collection of English Songs* (1784), Ritson treats Percy's texts as little more than forgeries of the originals.[51] And so in 1794, when Percy was finally goaded into reprinting verbatim the manuscript copy of 'The Marriage of Sir Gawaine', he did so only to show 'how unfit for publication many of the pieces would have been if', instead of 'correct[ing] and amend[ing] them', he had 'superstitiously retained' all of the 'blunders, corruptions, and nonsense of illiterate Reciters and Transcribers'.[52] That argument did not impress the Victorian editors of the Percy Folio, John W. Hales and Frederick J. Furnivall, who describe Percy's editorial treatment of the 'Heir of Linne' as 'sartorial-fartorial'.[53]

Percy's attempt to mediate a text for different readers with incommensurable expectations resulted in the first of many 'scandals of the ballad', as Susan Stewart calls them.[54] Decorousness was an early casuality of the developing taste for 'authenticity'. Allan Cunningham, who faked the materials collected in Robert Cromek's *Remains of Nithsdale and Galloway Song* (1810), thought 'occasional coarseness' necessary if such fabrications were to read like 'fair specimens of the ancient song and ballad'.[55] It was difficult to discern balladry's equivalent of the distinction between antique furniture and the '*faux*niture' described in Herbert Cescinsky's *The Gentle Art of Faking Furniture* (1931). Dense webs of mediation separated modern readers of printed texts from those oral cultures in which ballads were not written and read but sung and heard, and ballad-faking is one of the easier forms of textual factitiousness to master. Symptomatic of such problems is the status of what Sigurd Hustvedt calls 'the *Hardyknute* hoax' as 'a touchstone in ballad criticism'

---

[49] Johnston, *Enchanted Ground*, 81–82.
[50] Bronson, *Joseph Ritson*, vol. II, 605.
[51] Percy, *Reliques*, intro. Groom, vol. I, 53.
[52] Bate, 'Percy's Use of His Folio', 342.
[53] Bronson, *Joseph Ritson*, vol. II, 564.
[54] Stewart, *Crimes of Writing*, 102–31.
[55] Farrer, *Literary Forgeries*, 263.

throughout the eighteenth century.[56] Published in Edinburgh in 1719 as *Hardyknute: A Fragment of an Ancient Scots Poem*, this ballad about 'a Scottish warrior with a Danish name' had been written in contemporary Scots antiqued with old spellings and a few archaic words. Its author, Percy established, was Elizabeth Halkett, Lady Wardlow, one of whose brothers-in-law, Sir John Hope Bruce, circulated it with the provenance myth of its survival as 'a much defaced vellum' found 'in a vault at Dunfermline'.[57] The text of *Hardyknute* reprinted in Allan Ramsay's *The Ever Green* (1724) – a 'Collection of Scots Poems, wrote by the Ingenious before 1600' – had a formative and enduring influence on Sir Walter Scott, who describes it as 'the first poem I ever learnt, the last I shall ever forget'.[58] *Hardyknute* was praised not only by Thomas Warton (as 'a noble old Scottish poem') but also by Thomas Gray, whose judgement that it had been 'retouched in places by some modern hand' did not prevent him from continuing to admire it.[59] Percy, who thought it a 'beautiful poem', was sent by John Pinkerton in 1778 what purported to be the longer second part of *Hardyknute*; and although he thought it 'hardly equal to the first', he offered to publish it in a subsequent edition of his *Reliques*.[60] Pinkerton included it in his own edition of *Scottish Tragic Ballads* (1781), much to the annoyance of Ritson, who in November 1784 informed readers of the *Gentleman's Magazine* that the first part of *Hardyknute* was 'certainly spurious', and that Pinkerton was a literary forger like Macpherson.[61] In his edition of *Ancient Scotish Poems* (1786), Pinkerton confessed that he had composed the second part of *Hardyknute* in 1776 'to give pleasure to the public'.[62] All it gave Ritson, however, when introducing his own edition of *Scotish Song* (1794), was further evidence of Pinkerton's 'palpable and bungling forgery'.[63]

Among the most attentive readers of Macphossian was Thomas Chatterton, who was to write seven Ossianic prose poems and parody 'the high-sounding Ossian' in 'Memoirs of a Sad Dog'.[64] But whereas Macpherson was harassed for failing to produce Gaelic manuscripts of Ossianic material, Chatterton got into more trouble by fabricating the material texts supposedly written in the fifteenth

---

[56] Hustvedt, *Ballad Criticism*, 154, 87.
[57] Masson, *Edinburgh Sketches*, 117, 118, 110.   [58] Ibid., 111–12.
[59] Hustvedt, *Ballad Criticism*, 142, 150.
[60] Ibid., 185, 192.   [61] Ibid., 252–53.   [62] Ibid., 257.   [63] Ibid., 264.
[64] Taylor, *Chatterton's Art*, 273–74; Doody, *Daring Muse*, 229.

century by his imaginary 'Thomas Rowley'. This involved archaising words by writing 'painting' as 'peyncteynge', 'hermits' as 'errm-mietts', and (in a self-reflexive gesture) 'ancient' as 'auntiaunt'.[65] Although Chatterton 'thickened' his diction with redundancies in the course of progressing from his 'Bristowe Tragedie' to 'An Excelente Balade of Charitie', antiquarian tastes demanded even hoarier spellings, which George Catcott furnished when preparing transcripts of Chatterton's poems for eighteenth-century collectors.[66] Such extravagance was imitated with *brio* by a subsequent admirer of stretch-limo spellings, William-Henry Ireland, whose masterpiece in this *Entfremdung* of diction was 'perrepennedycularelye'.[67] Chatterton would also Chaucerise a word by adding a terminal 'e', thus prompting Charles Lamb (parodying Pope on the Restoration poets) to assign Chatterton to that 'mob of gentlemen who wrote with "e's"'.[68] Manuscripts containing such 'worrddes' had to be aged artificially by processes comparable to what is known in the *faux*ni-ture business as 'distressing', which involves 'falsify[ing] the chron-ology of an artefact by fictitious ageing'.[69] Successfully distressed furniture displays features comparable to what the passage of time does naturally when it produces craquelure in oil paintings, *sbulletare* on terracotta garden pots, and the *nobilis aerugo* of patina on bronze.[70] Susan Stewart was the first to apply the word metaphori-cally to 'the phenomenon of the "new antique"', an oxymoron refurbished in Coleridge's admiration for Chatterton's 'young-eyed Poesy / All deftly mask'd as hoar antiquity'.[71] Strictly speaking, Stewart's term is anachronistic, since neither the 'Distrest Lovers' in the subtitle of Lewis Theobald's pseudo-Shakespearean play, *The Double Falsehood* (1728), nor the 'Distressed Poet' depicted in a 1782 engraving of Chatterton is distressed in the *faux*nishings sense. Nevertheless, it usefully labels the literary products of that fashion-able nostalgia which Raphael Samuel calls 'retrochic'.[72] In the eighteenth century an expensive way of indulging such tastes was to

---

[65] Meyerstein, *Life of Chatterton*, 166, 175; Taylor, *Chatterton's Art*, 54.
[66] Chatterton, *Complete Works*, ed. Taylor and Hoover, vol. I, xxviii; Meyerstein, *Life of Chatterton*, 173.
[67] Sergeant, *Liars and Fakers*, 255.
[68] Aldington, *Frauds*, 221.
[69] De Plaen, 'Authenticity', 127.
[70] Nobili, *Gentle Art of Faking*, 186, 51.
[71] Stewart, *Crimes of Writing*, 67; Meyerstein, *Life of Chatterton*, 503.
[72] Samuel, *Theatres of Memory*, 83–118.

erect on one's own estate a picturesque ruin of a building that never existed; illustrated in Batty Langley's *New Principles of Gardening* (1728), they enabled wealthy people to experience pleasurable melancholy from gazing on material evidence of the vicissitude of things.[73] To Stewart, Chatterton's 'Rowley' poems, Macphossian and the ballad 'revival' are all examples of 'distressed genres', the formula for which is 'a counterfeit materiality and an authentic nostalgia'.[74] Distressing is the most difficult deception to get away with, especially if one's resources are merely domestic. Chatterton 'antiquated' his manuscripts (as he put it) by means of 'ochre, candle-flame, glue, varnish, or plain floor-dirt'; even Alexander Howland ('Antique') Smith, who displayed extraordinary calligraphic skills when faking manuscripts by Robert Burns, squandered the advantages gained from using historically authentic paper by staining it with 'weak tea, coffee or tobacco juice'.[75]

At the beginning of the century in which these prodigies of perversity appeared there was published a *Historical and Geographical Description of Formosa* (1704), written originally in Latin by an armchair 'travel liar' who 'pretended not just to have *been* there, but to *come* from there', and thus spoke with the authority of a native informant about Formosan infanticide and cannibalism.[76] Its author, who never revealed his actual patronymic, renamed himself after that Assyrian king who 'came down like the wolf on the fold' in Byron's anapaestic evocation of 'The Destruction of Semnacherib' (1815). Spelled 'Salmanazar' in the Vulgate (2 Kings, 17.3) but 'Shalmaneser' in the 1611 Bible, it became 'Psalmanaazaar' when attached to the *Description of Formosa* before being downsized to 'Psalmanazar' in the *Memoirs* (1764). A Catholic who posed as a pagan before being converted to Protestantism and mistaken for Jewish, Psalmanazar was a Frenchman who masqueraded as Irish in Italy and Japanese in Germany before arriving in England as Formosan. And this was the man whose life, Johnson declared, was 'uniform'.[77] In the second edition of his *Description of Formosa* (1705), and in answer to critics who accused him of having made it up, Psalmanazar observed (with the

---

[73] Baridon, 'Ruins as Mental Construct', 86; Zucker, 'Ruins', 124–25.

[74] Stewart, *Crimes of Writing*, 91.

[75] Browning, 'Essay on Chatterton', 169; Holmes, 'Chatterton: Case Re-Opened', 220; Benjamin, *Autographs*, 99.

[76] Adams, *Travelers and Travel Liars*; Stagl, *History of Curiosity*, 200.

[77] Lee, 'Psalmanazar', 442.

overweening humility later exhibited by Macpherson) that only 'a Man of prodigious parts' could 'invent the Description of a Country, contrive a Religion, frame Laws and Customs, make a Language, and Letters' wholly different from those in 'other parts of the World'.[78] An anonymous *Enquiry into the Objections against George Psalmanaazaar of Formosa* (1710) found him to be 'the Man he pretends to be' and the author of a 'true' history of that island. Some think it was 'inspired' by Psalmanazar, others that he himself wrote it; either way, by the following year he had lost all credibility when the *Spectator* nominated him for the role of Thyestes eating his own children in an opera called *The Cruelty of Attreus*, to be staged on All Fools' Day.[79] His complete retraction was reserved, however, for his *Memoirs* (1764), where he denounces his *Description* as a 'fictitious' or 'fabulous' account, 'hatched in [his] own brain, without regard to truth and honesty', and a 'scandalous imposition on the public'.[80]

Psalmanazar's faith in fakes was still being sustained at the end of the century, when Samuel Ireland published on 24 December 1795 his expensive folio of *Miscellaneous Papers and Legal Instruments under the Hand and Seal of William Shakespeare*. Based on manuscripts allegedly discovered but in fact written by his son, William-Henry Ireland, it included a fragment of *Hamblette* and a holograph of *The Tragedye of Kynge Leare* unblemished by those crudities and ribaldries which mar the surviving texts of that play. Twenty-one at the time, Ireland *fils* – an admirer of Chatterton, who was dead at seventeen – readjusted the date of his birth in order to appear an even more precocious nineteen-year-old, slightly younger than Psalmanazar (who claimed to be 'scarce twenty' when writing his *Description of Formosa*) and much younger than Macpherson, who published *Fragments of Ancient Poetry* at the age of twenty-three.[81] From these eighteenth-century exemplars we derive our association of textual delinquency with youthfulness, although the term 'juvenile delinquency' is not recorded until 1816, when Byron expatriated himself to Italy and mislaid the notebook in which a dozen poems he never wrote would be forged in the 1840s by Major Byron. But before concluding wistfully that fakedom is no country for old men, we should

---

[78] Needham, *Exemplars*, 102.
[79] Ibid., 87; Lee, 'Psalmanazar', 441; Foley, *Great Formosan Impostor*, 43; Stagl, *History of Curiosity*, 185.
[80] Psalmanazar, *Memoirs*, 5, 8, 6, 8.
[81] Sergeant, *Liars and Fakers*, 228.

remember that Daniel L. James was in his seventies when he became 'Danny Santiago' and wrote a prize-winning novel about Latino life in Los Angeles called *Famous All Over Town* (1983) – a title reminiscent, incidentally, of James Payn's fictional treatment of the Ireland affair in *Talk of the Town* (1885).

Miscellaneous Papers prompted the Shakespeare scholar, Edmond Malone, to begin *An Inquiry into the Authenticity of Certain Miscellaneous Papers and Legal Instruments*, which he published as a 424–page volume on 1 April 1796.[82] The timing of Malone's attack was most unfortunate for the young author of a hitherto unknown 'historical tragedy' by Shakespeare called *Vortigern*. Contracted by Richard Brinsley Sheridan, its première was to have preceded in December 1795 the publication of *Miscellaneous Papers*. Instead, it was delayed until 2 April 1796, the day after the publication of Malone's *Inquiry*. The principal actor in *Vortigern*, John Philip Kemble, was the best Shakespearean performer at that time, but a Malonean who wanted the play staged on All Fools' Day.[83] His 'sepulchral' delivery of the phrase, 'this solemn mock'ry', persuaded spectators that it was an apt description of the play itself, whereupon they uttered a 'discordant howl' that went on for ten minutes.[84] Kemble responded to this fiasco by substituting for *Vortigern* an unscheduled revival of Sheridan's comedy, *The School for Scandal* (1777).

The common assumption that *Vortigern* was demolished by Malone's *Inquiry* is not borne out by the text, whose target is not Ireland's play but 'the *farrago* of papers and deeds' exhibited in *Miscellaneous Papers*, which Malone systematically discredits on such historical and philological grounds as their Chattertonian spellings.[85] But in spite of concluding that the manuscript of *Vortigern* was a fake, Malone was so taken with the play as to attend its opening night inconspicuously.[86] Had *Vortigern* not been offered in 'the *pretended* handwriting of Shakespeare', he reasons, it might have passed for 'a genuine old play' by someone other than Shakespeare.[87] Although *Vortigern* 'can be no other than a modern fiction', he concludes, the question of 'whether it is a good or a bad fiction' he will 'leave to others to

[82] Kahan, *Reforging Shakespeare*, 191.
[83] Ibid., 191, 43, 169.
[84] Mair, *Fourth Forger*, 183–84; Grebanier, *Great Shakespeare Forgery*, 223–25.
[85] Malone, *Inquiry into the Authenticity of Certain Papers*, 304, 322.
[86] P. Martin, *Edmond Malone*, 198.
[87] Malone, *Inquiry into the Authenticity of Certain Papers*, 314.

determine'.[88] The most surprising aspect of his *Inquiry*, therefore, is Malone's fascination with a 'Shakespeare' play he knew to be a modern fake. The Chatterton case had aroused in him a similar ambivalence. When objecting in 1782 to the 'Rowleiomania' provoked by Chatterton's attribution of his own 'modern–antique compositions' to a 'fictitious ancient', Malone distinguished those 'spurious productions' from their 'astonishing' author, a teenager who had managed 'to compose, in about eighteen months, three thousand seven hundred verses, on various subjects', and thereby proved himself to be 'the greatest genius that England has produced since the days of Shakespeare'.[89] In that romance of authorship which, towards the end of his *Inquiry*, he weaves around those papers whose factitiousness he has just devoted three hundred pages to exposing, Malone imagines them to have been a joint production. One of the 'artificers of this clumsy and daring fraud' was perhaps an attorney's clerk familiar with legal language and able to counterfeit old handwriting; but the other may well have been a woman, 'for we know not even the sex of the author'.[90] That possibility was to become a certainty for the author of *The Shakspeare Fabrications* (1859), C. Mansfield Ingleby, who declares that 'the elder daughter of Samuel Ireland' wrote *Vortigern* with help from her younger sister.[91] Whoever s/he was, Malone thought that the author was indubitably a poet. This extraordinary fantasia from a Shakespearean scholar who approached the Ireland papers in the manner of a prosecuting counsel indicates that a text whose provenance is demonstrably spurious can retain its allure by displaying those features that even hostile readers will recognise as literary.

Imperfect recollections of some of these scandals were stirred in 1987, when a British feminist press published a collection of short stories by an Asian woman of colour called Rahila Khan. Entitled *Down the Road, Worlds Away*, it appeared in the Virago Press series for teenagers called 'Upstarts'. Set in Britain's urbanised Midlands, several stories concern difficulties experienced by the daughters of Asian immigrants in negotiating cultural differences between life at home and what goes on in those inner-city schools they are obliged

---

[88] Ibid., 315.
[89] Malone, *Cursory Observations on Rowley*, 1, 22, 27, 13, 50, 41.
[90] Malone, *Inquiry into the Authenticity of Certain Papers*, 335, 330.
[91] Ingleby, *Shakspeare Fabrications*, 100–01.

to attend, which may well be located just 'down the road' from where they live but are in other respects 'worlds away' from the domestic ethos provided by their Muslim parents. Three weeks after publishing the book, however, Virago Press learned that its author was a white Englishman called Toby Forward. Currently a parish priest in Brighton, he had been a schoolteacher in both Derby and Peterborough. Unable to find anything 'in fiction to help white and Asian kids understand each other's beliefs, pressures and conflicts', he had decided to fill the gap himself, but to publish his fiction under a pseudonym because he believed that priests are regarded as 'sit-com characters' and not taken seriously.[92]

For several days this episode provoked much anti-feminist hilarity in the media about the vicar and Virago. Its passage from public memory was eased by an embarrassed and angry Virago Press, which increased the scarcity value of Forward's book by withdrawing it. Marking a precarious moment in the segueing of race into British gender politics in the 1980s, this incident shows how literary forgery can double as cultural critique, irrespectively of authorial intentions. Only seven of the twelve stories in *Down the Road, Worlds Away* are about young Asian females; the rest concern male-bonded young white men. Because only one of the female-centred stories ('Daughters of the Prophet') is written in the first person, the earliest readers of 'Rahila Khan' thought she had wasted narrative opportunities to enunciate an Asian-female point of view. According to Forward, both Virago Press and The Women's Press were puzzled by her pronominal reticence, and would have preferred something more direct. But whereas The Women's Press wanted 'Winter Wind' rewritten in the first person before they would anthologise it, Virago Press was more circumspect in dealing with what they took to be cultural alterity. They asked 'Rahila Khan' whether her 'sense of "otherness" was still so great' that she found it impossible 'to write in the first person'.[93] Forward felt she was being manoeuvred into supplying a commodity for which feminist publishers were convinced there was a market. BBC Radio 4, which eventually broadcast the story called 'Pictures', told 'Rahila Khan' early in 1985 'that they wanted things "with a genuine 'ethnic' background" because they didn't get many'.[94] Their conviction that such texts must be out there somewhere was fortified by recent developments in feminist theory. For by

---

[92] Nettell, 'Sex Scandal', 1250.   [93] Forward, 'Diary', 21.   [94] Ibid.

the 1980s second-wave anglophone feminism had undergone substantial critiques of its middle-class and ethnocentric biases, and by facing up to the differences within feminism had begun to refashion itself by cultivating heterogeneity. 'Daughters of the Prophet' proved that 'Rahila Khan' was capable of producing the commodity that First World feminist publishers and broadcasters were determined to find: namely, writing that 'delivered in the unmediated authenticity of first person' narratives the experiences of those Third World women who constituted a significant minority in Britain.[95] 'It wasn't the stories they were buying', Forward concluded, 'it was Rahila Khan'.[96]

Forward seemed unaware of the extent to which, in the 1980s, liberal humanist assumptions about literature had been challenged by various politicising discourses – feminism among them – which collectively went by the name of critical theory. These drew attention to the hidden politics in all cultural practices, including those constructions of the self that we perceive as our identities. Exactly who is entitled to write about them was to become the central concern of an 'identity politics' hostile to procedures considered by Forward to be part of the licence traditionally accorded writers of fiction. One of the critical orthodoxies that underpin his book is that writers have not only a faculty called 'imagination', which they exercise in order to represent lives they themselves have not experienced, but also a capacity to empathise with people who lead such lives. 'Empathy' was coined by Edward Titchener in 1909 to translate a psychological term introduced in 1903 by Theodor Lipps: *Einfühlung*.[97] As an aesthetic concept, however, *Einfühlung* – ' "feeling into", the Germans happily put it' – was first explored in English by a woman (Violet Paget) who wrote as a man, 'Vernon Lee'; broadly speaking, it is the self's capacity for identifying sympathetically with what is other to it.[98] Recognised in antiquity as one of the suasive techniques available to orators, empathy was known to rhetoricians as *ethopoeia*, which Richard A. Lanham glosses as 'putting yourself in the place of another, so as to both understand and express the other person's feelings more vividly'.[99] In courtrooms, this involved 'thinking like a jewel thief, if you are defending one'.[100] And as for

---

[95] Callaghan, 'Vicar and Virago', 195.   [96] Forward, 'Diary', 21.
[97] Wispé, 'History of the Concept of Empathy', 18.
[98] 'Vernon Lee' quoted in Wellek, *Discriminations*, 169.
[99] Lanham, *Handlist of Rhetorical Terms*, 185–86.   [100] Ibid., 71.

speaking like a jewel thief, rhetoricians had a word for that too: *dialogismus*, 'speaking in another person's character'.[101] Ancient historians availed themselves of such devices in order to spice their narratives with what famous people ought to have said on famous occasions. Among them was Thucydides, who felt uneasy about substituting for 'what was actually said' another set of words which 'would express . . . the sentiments most befitting to the occasion'.[102] No such qualms ever disturbed fiction writers, however, who are not bound as historians are by Leopold von Ranke's injunction to tell it how it was (*wie es eigentlich gewesen*) because there is no extra-textual actuality to which their stories are obliged to conform. Indeed, a proven capacity to transcend the self by empathising with others became an indicator of literary merit. Writers took up the challenge in the hope of achieving a *tour de force* like *Memoirs of a Geisha* (1997), a novel by a white American man, Arthur Golden, who enters into the consciousness of a Japanese girl sold at the age of nine to an *okiya* and inducted into the rituals that made her desirable to wealthy Japanese men.[103] Empathy is still valued in literary productions of little interest to identity politicians concerned principally with malfeasances of race, gender and sexualities. Nobody finds it scandalous that the Harry Potter adventure series is the work of a woman, J.K. Rowling; indeed, Paul Jennings gets praised for the transgenerational empathy displayed in his best-selling books about children. And there were no carefully orchestrated expressions of outrage from British bovver boys following the publication of a best-selling novel called *Skinhead* (1970), which struck members of that emergent subculture as the work of an insider, 'Richard Allen', who in fact was not the disaffected youth he appeared to be but an Irish-Canadian professional writer in his mid-fifties called James Moffat.

Some people think that such things ought not to happen, much less succeed. 'The business of authorial identity', Dympna Callaghan warns apropos the 'Rahila Khan' affair, 'can no longer present itself as being about the expansive capacities of human imagination'. Why not? Because a masculinist bias in our culture ensures that 'individual identity and personal experience' are valued in the arts only when the 'universal human nature' they claim to represent is that of

---

101 Ibid., 192.
102 Metzger, 'Literary Forgeries and Pseudepigrapha', 9.
103 Schwartz, John Burnham, 'Masked Memoir', *passim*.

'the privileged white male'.[104] The literary equivalent of 'female drag' is disingenuous, Nancy K. Miller argues, because the men who engage in it do not aim 'to please the Other' – women – but 'to become the Other', thereby drawing attention to themselves as 'the pseudo-Other'.[105] Was Benjamin Franklin guilty of this when publishing in 1747 a much discussed pro-feminist speech by 'Polly Baker' defending her rights over her own body, and specifically her right to have children outside marriage? If so, the satisfactions were private, as Franklin's authorship of this speech was not made public until 1864.[106]

In the reign of identity politics, however, 'empathy' becomes ideologically suspect. If nobody has the right to speak for anybody else, then to do so is an invasive act: 'feeling into' someone else's mode of existence is a molestatory practice akin to feeling them up. In multicultural societies marked by social inequalities between different ethnic groups, 'empathy' is unmasked as a myth of benevolence designed by the powerful to justify their practice of selectively appropriating the cultures of the powerless. 'Speaking for others' is a problem, Linda Martín Alcoff concludes, because it often reveals 'a desire for mastery', and results in self-congratulatory displays of do-goodism by those who, claiming to 'understand the truth about another's situation', present themselves as 'champion[ing] a just cause'.[107] One of Alcoff's exemplary tales concerns the white Canadian author of *Daughters of Copper Woman* (1981), Anne Cameron. This best-selling book relays stories told her by women of the Nootka people, 'members of a secret society' who in 1980 'gave [her] permission to write poetry about Old Woman'.[108] In 1988, however, Cameron acceded to a request from native Canadian women writers to stop producing first-person accounts of the lives of female First Peoples because her work was 'disempowering for indigenous authors'.[109] Four years later, Rosemary J. Coombe reports, the Canada Council's Advisory Committee for Racial Equality in the Arts defined 'the depiction of minorities or cultures other than one's own, either in fiction or nonfiction', as 'cultural

---

[104] Callaghan, 'Vicar and Virago', 197, 196.
[105] Miller, *French Dressing*, 95.
[106] Hall, *Franklin and Polly Baker*, 158–67, 84.
[107] Alcoff, 'Problem of Speaking for Others', 115–16.
[108] Cameron, *Daughters of Copper Woman*, preface (n.p.).
[109] Alcoff, 'Problem of Speaking for Others', 97.

appropriation', and recommended that no writer culpable in this respect should receive a government grant.[110] In such a climate, it was courageous of an African American intellectual, Henry Louis Gates, to argue in 1991 that 'no human culture is inaccessible to someone who makes the effort to understand, to learn, to inhabit another world'.[111]

By masquerading as 'Rahila Khan', who is both female and Asian, Forward collided with the two most sacred cows of identity politics: gender and race. 'It's incredible how some men feel compelled to invade women's space', The Women's Press commented after the event, not knowing that Forward's next collection of stories would be entitled *Feminine Parts* (1992); Virago Press, emphasising race rather than gender in its own post-mortem, was 'distressed that this attempt to represent the Asian community should transpire to be a cruel hoax'.[112] In her judicious assessment of this affair, Rosalind Coward points out that although 'Virago was quite wilfully misled and indeed exploited' by Forward, he was able to succeed in his deception 'because of flaws and weaknesses in attitudes prevalent among publishers towards writers from ethnic minorities'.[113] This resembles Skeat's argument that the 'destitution of philological knowledge' in the 1770s was 'the true secret of Chatterton's success'.[114] The Virago Press editors were complicit in the circumstances that led to their embarrassment, since if they had been better informed about ethnic minorities in Britain they might have been correspondingly more alert to factitious elements in Forward's stories. *Ad hominem* attacks on Forward for his 'insensitivity' were no answer to the damage done by the publication of his book to a particular kind of British feminism in the 1980s. In cases like this, literary forgery is the creative mode of cultural critique.

By the time that the 'Rahila Khan' affair became a news item relished by readers who had had quite enough of feminism, I had already begun to think about writing a book that would modify the terms in which such phenomena get discussed. At that stage, however, I never guessed that another fortunate isle for aficionados of the fraudulent would be Australia in the 1990s. For it was there

---

[110] Coombe, *Cultural Life of Intellectual Properties*, 209, 210.
[111] Gates, ' "Authenticity" ', 30.
[112] Nettell, 'Sex Scandal', 1250.
[113] Coward, 'Looking for the Real Thing', 21.
[114] Skeat, 'Essay on the Rowley Poems', ix.

that Helen Darville, the daughter of English immigrants, Ukrainised herself as 'Helen Demidenko' and published a novel about how Ukrainians who believed that Jews had collaborated with Stalinist Russia in causing the Ukrainian famine of 1932–33 willingly collaborated with Nazis in murdering Jews during the Second World War. Before 'Demidenko' was unmasked, *The Hand That Signed the Paper* (1994) was awarded a Gold Medal by the Australian Literature Society, which has been bestowing them on distinguished writers since 1929, when the inaugural recipient was a woman (Ethel Florence Lindesay Robertson) who published under the name of 'Henry Handel Richardson', and tried to ensure that correspondents who had never met her – including Paul Solanges, the French translator of her novel, *Maurice Guest* (1908) – would never guess she was female.[115] Among the other major literary prizes 'Demidenko' won was the prestigious Miles Franklin Award. This honours the work of another woman (called 'Stella' by her family) who, under the name of the man the award is named after, wrote a now classic Australian novel called *My Brilliant Career* (1901), and bequeathed the funds to establish an annual literary prize – first awarded in 1957 to Patrick White for *Voss* – for a novel 'of the highest literary merit' that 'present[s] Australian life in any of its phases'. In 1993 the 'Demidenko' manuscript had also won the Vogel Literary Award (named after Alfred Vogel, the Swiss naturopath and bread-maker) for an unpublished work by a writer under thirty-five. Analysts of the initial reception of the novel, which was first published in September 1994, describe it as being 'generally favourable' or even 'overwhelmingly enthusiastic'.[116] But on 9 June 1995 the book was denounced as anti-Semitic in the *Australian Jewish News* by Ben Haneman, who thought that 'literary criticism is a load of crap', and could not understand 'why any man or woman would wish to belittle themselves so much as to claim to be a literary critic'.[117] After that, historians found the novel to be historically inaccurate and politically so fascist as to read like 'an apologia for genocide'.[118] Aestheticisers of the novel, who had awarded it literary prizes for its literary merit as 'creative' writing, thus came into conflict with politicisers of it, who castigated the literary establishment for being both culpably ignorant of

[115] Sullivan, 'Regarding Henry', 5.
[116] Riemer, *Demidenko Debate*, 109; Manne, *Culture of Forgetting*, 49.
[117] Jost *et al.* (eds), *Demidenko File*, 35.
[118] Ibid., 56–57.

matters of historical fact and brainwashed by Cold War ideologues
who believe that literature transcends politics. In these exchanges,
the literati were evidently the losers, although not even after the
event did they concede that they might have avoided the difficulties
they got themselves into if only they had deigned to engage with
what left-wing literary theorists had been writing since the 1960s
about the politics of culture. Variously reviled for being anti-Semitic,
fascist and postmodernist (at times these terms seemed interchangeable in the 'liberal' discourse of the moral majority), Darville's first
novel secured for her a permanent niche in Australian cultural
history. It attracted unprecedented media coverage for a young
Australian writer, plus four book-length studies within two years of
its publication, although such figures are modest by comparison with
Ireland's 'Shakespeare', which is calculated to have generated
nineteen books and sixty-one articles while the controversy lasted.[119]

After 'Demidenko' *le déluge*, or so it appeared to spectators of
solemn mockeries in Australia. In 1996 Paul Radley, who in 1980 had
been the inaugural recipient of the Vogel Literary Award, confessed
that his prize-winning manuscript – published subsequently as *Jack
Rivers and Me* (1981) – had been largely the work of his fifty-seven-
year-old Uncle Jack. And then there was the curious case of Colin
Johnson, whose powerful novel, *Wild Cat Falling* (1965), established
his reputation as Australia's first published Aboriginal writer. Coin-
cidentally with Aboriginal protests against bicentennial celebrations
in 1988 of the white 'settlement' of Australia, Johnson changed his
name to Mudrooroo ('Paperbark') Nyoongah. When he was challenged by the Nyoongah community to establish his membership of
it, his genealogising sister, Betty Polgaze, revealed in 1996 that there
were no Aborigines in their family tree, and that Johnson had
inherited his dark skin from an African American grandfather. A
year later we learnt that a white man called Leon Carmen, whose
literary agent was fascinated by literary hoaxes (and especially the
Chatterton case), had published a novel entitled *My Own Sweet Time*
(1994) under the name of 'Wanda Koolmatrie'. The blurb indicated
her affiliation with the wretched of the earth, since her Pitjantjara
mother had been one of that generation of children stolen from their
natural parents when the government implemented its policy that
those who were not 'pure' Aborigines should be either fostered out

---

[119] Marder, 'Shakespearean Frauds', 225.

to white parents or institutionalised and brought up white. Endorsed by an Aboriginal academic who had read the book with 'uncomplicated pleasure', *My Own Sweet Time* was praised in the *Australian Book Review* for its 'sass, intelligence and flair'. Published by a press specialising in indigenous culture, it became the inaugural recipient of the Dobbie Prize for a first novel by a woman. This confirmed Carmen's suspicion that literary gatekeepers committed to affirmative action on behalf of minorities were tacitly operating a double-standard in the form of positive discrimination that made it much easier for 'Wanda Koolmatrie' than for Leon Carmen to get into print. As it happened, the anthropologist Eric Michaels had already drawn attention to a 'curious fact' about Aboriginal paintings, namely 'that almost nothing of this work is ever designated "bad"'.[120] Michaels thought that this was because the collaborative practices of central Australian desert Aborigines who transmit cultural meanings from one generation to the next by means of painted images differ so widely from the signature-fetishism of Western art-dealers who market such paintings as 'art' to well-heeled clients that 'good' and 'bad' are rendered meaningless as evaluative terms.[121] Carmen, whose novel was a creative riposte to the literary consequences of 'political correctness', had a simpler explanation: the literary establishment which ignored him would regard anything written by an Aborigine as 'good'. To sustain that conspiracy theory, however, it was necessary to suppress the fact that his novel had been rejected by both a commercial publisher and a university press before Magabala Books agreed to publish it.

For most Australians, the primal scene of literary forgery – to which I shall return from time to time in what follows – had been staged in August 1944, when two anti-modernist poets, James McAuley and Harold Stewart, cobbled together the seventeen poems of a manuscript called *The Darkening Ecliptic*, the work of an imaginary and recently deceased modernist, 'Ern Malley'. They were sent by his equally imaginary sister, 'Ethel', to Max Harris, who published them in a commemorative issue of his pro-modernist journal, *Angry Penguins*, thus 'proving' that modernist poetry is nonsense published and admired by the critically incompetent.[122] But a more recent episode involved another pseudo-Aboriginal writer with the poly-

---

[120] Michaels, *Bad Aboriginal Art*, 143.   [121] Ibid., 162.
[122] Heyward, *Ern Malley Affair*, 63, 55.

semic name of 'B. Wongar'. In *Walg* (1983) his surname is glossed as 'beginning of the world, spirit world', although *Dingoes Den* (1999) reveals that ('loosely translated') it can also mean 'outsider'; his enigmatic initial was spelled out first as 'Birimbir' ('spirit'), subsequently as 'Banumbir' ('morning star') and eventually as 'Bozic', his Serbian name.[123] Some of his 'Aboriginal' books appeared with white-celebrity endorsements, a strategy he had used in the days when 'B. Wongar' hoped to be mistaken for a Vietnam-war draft-dodger or deserter who had gone bush in northern Australia.[124] This was long before movies like *The Deer Hunter* (1978) and *First Blood* (1982) fuelled nostalgia for a warrior culture, and encouraged bogus 'Vietnam vets' to internalise histories of that war before working the American lecture-circuits in ways deplored by a genuine veteran, B.G. ('Jug') Burkett, in *Stolen Valor* (1999). The contribution by 'Wongar' to this emergent genre, *The Sinners: Stories from Vietnam* (1972), contains a foreword by Alan Marshall, whose auto-biographical account of being permanently crippled by polio at the age of six, *I Can Jump Puddles* (1955), is an exemplary tale of difficulties overcome.

The stories that constitute *The Track to Bralgu* (1978), on the other hand, are introduced by Alan Paton, who wrote that anti-apartheid classic, *Cry, the Beloved Country* (1948); subsequently, Simone de Beauvoir's endorsement of *Walg* (1983) would be displayed prominently on its back cover. Published in both London and Boston, and written in the form of a first-person narrative by an Aborigine, *The Track to Bralgu* appealed to white readers sympathetic to the plight of Aboriginal people by evoking what it is like to be in the victim's position when tribal cultures that regard the land as sacred collide with white racist views of it as an exploitable resource for uranium mining. In this respect, Paul Sharrad observes, 'Wongar' was exactly what left-liberal Australians were looking for: an articulate and politically acute Aborigine, well qualified to become 'the James Baldwin of black Australia'.[125] Not surprisingly, given the intensity with which those who cared about such matters '*wanted* Wongar to be real', *The Track to Bralgu* (1978) was praised in the *New York Times Book Review* as a 'fine book . . . written by an Australian Aborigine'.[126] The reviewer was a white Australian, Thomas Keneally, one of

---

123 'B. Wongar', *Dingoes Den*, 173.   124 Ibid., 113.
125 Sharrad, 'Does Wongar Matter?', 48.
126 Keneally, 'Soul of Things', 14.

whose novels, *The Chant of Jimmie Blacksmith* (1972), fictionalises the unremitting racism experienced by a part-Aborigine, Jimmy Governor, who was hanged in 1901 for murdering some of those whites whose society he tried to assimilate himself into. The film version was released in the same year as Keneally's review of *The Track to Bralgu*. But as Robert Drewe revealed in 1981, the track to Wongar led to a Serbian immigrant called Sreten Bozic, a name which hostile critics like to think is Serb for 'Merry Christmas'.[127] As a refugee from Tito's Yugoslavia, Bozic lived in Paris long enough to become acquainted with Simone de Beauvoir before emigrating to Australia in 1960.[128] Classified there as an 'ethnic' outsider by an Anglo-Celtic hegemony unable to recognise its own ethnicity, he was well placed to empathise with Aborigines, whose incontestable claim to be insiders had not safeguarded them from being treated as pariahs by the whites who 'settled' Australia.[129]

An awareness that history repeats itself – first as tragedy, then as farce – did nothing to moderate the media-fanned outrage that accompanied the efflorescence of spurious literary texts in the 1990s. Their reception demonstrated just how differently literary journalists and literary theorists understand such shenanigans, and therefore why we should reconsider the terms used to describe them.

[127] Drewe, 'Solved: The Great B. Wongar Mystery'; Manne, *Culture of Forgetting*, 56.
[128] Powell, 'Mysterious Case', 12.
[129] Gunew, 'Culture, Gender and Author-Function', 4.

CHAPTER 2

Framing literary forgery

Coming to terms with literary forgery involves thinking about the overlapping descriptors that constitute our understanding of it. In this area of enquiry, prescriptivism is commonplace. Its consequences are illustrated by Bruce M. Metzger, a biblical scholar who seeks to dissociate literary forgeries from those spurious writings sometimes called 'pseudepigrapha', a collective term for texts which either bear 'a false title' or are 'ascribed to another than the true author' (*OED*). In order to do so he decides that 'an intention to deceive' distinguishes a literary forgery from a pseudepigraphon. Furthermore, he thinks that pseudepigrapha are not 'spurious writings' (which is how the *OED* defines them) but 'works wrongly attributed to authors'. That distinction enables him to claim that 'not all pseudepigrapha . . . are to be regarded as forgeries'. Are pseudepigrapha therefore apocryphal ('of doubtful authenticity')? Not according to Metzger, who argues that 'the term "apocrypha" belongs to the history of the canon' rather than to the history of authorship, and that 'the question of false attribution played very little part' in theological discussions about which non-canonical books ought to be included in the Apocrypha. He therefore thinks it 'better' to reserve the term apocrypha for 'all extra-canonical writings, and to use "pseudepigraphic" as a literary category, whether the book is regarded as canonical or apocryphal'.[1] In Metzger's view, theologians create unnecessary problems by their 'lack of agreement on what differentiates literary frauds from innocent pseudonymous impersonations'.[2] He does not consider the possibility that this distinction might be considered tendentious, especially by readers with no vested interest in preserving the Holy Bible as a text

---

[1] Metzger, 'Literary Forgeries and Pseudepigrapha', 4.
[2] Ibid., 21.

unafflicted by problems of authenticity and authority that plague secular writing.

Prescriptive definitions of the terms most commonly encountered in discussions of literary spuriousness are easy to come by. Each tends to be chaperoned by a predictable adjective. Successful 'hoaxes', for instance, are usually called 'amusing', because hoaxing is not regarded as a serious offence. This makes them unlike 'forgeries', which are 'scandalous' or 'outrageous'. And in the nine-teenth century, when such things were called 'impostures', the preferred adjective was 'impudent'. Some attempts at terminological precision in this area, such as Hunter Steele's distinction between 'fakes' and 'forgeries', exhibit that formulaic elegance ('*x* is *y* if and only if *z*') which is one of the pleasures of reading essays in the philosophy of aesthetics. If the work 'falsely purport[s] to have a given history of production', Steele argues, then it is a fake; but if it 'also purports to have the exact history of production which is actually possessed by an original work' then it is a forgery.[3] This is put so well as to appear indisputable. Alice Beckett, however, frames the distinction differently, and without reference to the demarcation proposed by Steele. A fake, in her opinion, is 'a genuine article that has been tampered with', whereas 'a forgery implies fabrication from the start' – although, she concedes, 'there are many grey areas'.[4]

Critics who think about this distinction interpret it differently, and experience similar difficulties when trying to distinguish between other paired terms. Although H.M. Paull considers it 'not altogether easy to draw the line between a hoax and a forgery', he confidently devotes separate chapters to 'the literary forger' and 'the literary hoax'; Giles Constable, on the other hand, who likewise thinks that 'the line between forgeries and hoaxes is often very narrow', wisely decides not to draw it.[5] As the stockpile of incompatible definitions increases, the field of study appears correspondingly more disor-dered, and taxonomists are tempted to sort things out. Indeed, an earlier version of this book aimed to devise, along the lines of Raymond Williams' *Keywords* (1976), a critical lexicography of fakedom, put together by analysing and historicising the discourses used in the description and evaluation of spurious works produced by the great fakemeisters of English literature. It was to have

---

[3] Steele, 'Fakes and Forgeries', 258.
[4] Beckett, *Fakes: Forgery and the Art World*, 37.
[5] Paull, *Literary Ethics*, 141; Constable, 'Forgery and Plagiarism in the Middle Ages', 3.

differentiated literary 'forgeries' from 'hoaxes', 'impostures' and *supercheries*, that 'elegant euphemism' (as E.K. Chambers calls it) which is monumentalised in the four volumes of M.J.M. Quérard's *Les Supercheries littéraires dévoilées* (1847).[6] Anglicised in the early seventeenth century as 'superchery', this word is sufficiently rare to evade the immediately negative associations of the alternatives. For although the English translation of *supercherie* as 'trickery' renders it no less negative, its pedigree in the Italian *superchio* connects it with 'excess'. 'Superchery' therefore has affinities with those definitions of literature which conceive of it in terms of superfluity at the level of the signifier, that is, as superfluous to the requirements of a purely functional mode of communication. Could 'superchery' be the organising term, I wondered, for a study of fake literature? Another possibility was 'spuriosity', described by the *OED* as a lexical rarity first recorded in Charles Kingsley's *The Water-Babies* (1863), where it accompanies 'heterodoxy' as one of those words over four syllables that ought to be taxed. My work-in-progress came to be called 'Spuriosities of Literature' by way of allusion to Isaac Disraeli's *Curiosities of Literature* (1881), a cornucopian book with sections on both 'literary impostures' and 'literary forgeries'.[7] But the prospect of using either 'superchery' or 'spuriosity' as the master-key to those discourses whose own key-terms are 'hoax' and 'forgery' and so forth proved to be yet another misdirected attempt – this time at the metadiscursive level – to abstract from the culture-specific contingencies of varying historical practices an idealising schema with which to contain them. Inevitably, it would have suffered the same fate as other terms designed to taxonomise fake literature, each of which leads a social life quite independently of our Humpty-Dumptyish desire to make it mean exactly (and therefore only) what we want it to mean.

Because everyday usage is promiscuous, lexicographers professionally obliged to be descriptive rather than prescriptive define each word by situating it in a linguistic field which often includes some of the others. Accordingly, the *OED*'s discriminations between 'forgery' and 'counterfeiting' are compromised when it correctly includes 'to counterfeit' among its definitions of 'to forge'. Scholarly usage is equally libertarian. Chatterton is an 'impostor poet' to Louise J.

---

[6] Chambers, *History and Motives of Literary Forgeries*, 6.
[7] Disraeli, *Curiosities of Literature*, vol. I, 132–39; vol. III, 303–15.

Kaplan, a 'hoax-poet' to Marjorie Levinson, but a 'literary forger' to Ian Haywood.[8] A couple of studies of the American poet, Joaquin Miller (the self-proclaimed 'Byron of the Rockies'), exhibit some uncertainty as to whether he was the 'charlatan from the West' described by Nicholas T. Parsons or the 'splendid poseur' and 'fabulous humbug' who feature in the title of M.M. Marberry's book on Miller.[9] This synchronic problem of definition – caused whenever contemporaries choose different words to describe the same phenomenon – is compounded by another and diachronic problem, namely that what is called x or y nowadays may well have been known as a or b in earlier periods. In 1764 a penitent Psalmanazar classified his *Description of Formosa* (1704) as a 'forgery' and himself as an 'impostor'. The latter designation was respected not only by N.M. Penzel (when reprinting the book in 1928 in his 'Library of Impostors' series) but also by Disraeli (1881), Lee (1909), Bracey (1925) and Foley (1968); yet to others he was a 'forger' (Paull, 1928), a 'fraud' (Farrer, 1907; Aldington, 1957), a 'faker' (Sergeant, 1925; Knowlson, 1965), a 'confidence-man' (Needham, 1985) and the author of a 'hoax' (Stagl, 1995).[10] Investigators of literary spuriosity in different historical periods discover that all the available descriptors are tendentious. A classicist, Ronald Syme, thinks that 'imposture' is 'a more helpful designation than "forgery"' when considering ancient examples of the phenomenon.[11] Christopher Brooke, hoping 'to clarify the general context of eleventh- and twelfth-century forgery', finds prescriptive definitions unsustainable in the 'ambiguous territory' constituted by documents produced at a time when 'forgery . . . was an entirely respectable activity'.[12] Although *pia fraus* ('pious fraud') was never endorsed officially by the Church it appeared to be sanctioned by a higher authority than the state. It enabled religious houses to manufacture the documents that established their prior claims to property and privileges, and to

---

[8] Kaplan, *Family Romance of the Impostor-Poet Thomas Chatterton*; Levinson, *Romantic Fragment Poem*, 20; Haywood, *Making of History: The Literary Forgeries of James Macpherson and Thomas Chatterton*.

[9] Parsons, *Joy of Bad Verse*, 234; Marberry, *Splendid Poseur*, 75.

[10] Psalmanazar, *Memoirs*, 8, 12; Disraeli, *Curiosities of Literature*, vol. III, 136; Lee, 'Psalmanazar', 439; Bracey, *Eighteenth-Century Studies*, 77; Foley, *Great Formosan Impostor*; Paull, *Literary Ethics*, 32; Farrer, *Literary Forgeries*, 83; Aldington, *Frauds*, 33; Sergeant, *Liars and Fakers*, 201; Knowlson, 'Psalmanazar: Fake Formosan'; Needham, *Exemplars*, 75; Stagl, *History of Curiosity*, 178.

[11] Syme, 'Fraud and Imposture', 13.

[12] Brooke, 'Approaches to Medieval Forgery', 100–01.

justify such activities on the grounds that one has 'to fight the world with the world's weapons'.[13] In such circumstances, T.F. Tout remarks, 'it was almost the duty of the clerical class to forge', and they could do so with impunity because they were protected by 'benefit of clergy' from civil prosecution.[14]

The problems posed by semantic instabilities in the lexicon that defines literary 'forgery' and its cognates are illustrated by the *OED*'s entry for 'forge' as a verb. From the fourteenth to the sixteenth centuries, most of the usages recorded are non-pejorative: 'to make, fashion, frame, or construct (any material thing)'. For instance, the question God asks Moses in the 1611 text of Exodus 4.11 ('Who maketh the dumb?') appears in the earlier Wycliffite translation as 'Who forgide [forged] the dowmbe?' God is here a non-duplicitous forger, 'the heavenly Maker' (in Sidney's phrase) 'of that maker' whom the Scots call a 'makar' and the English a 'poet', from the Greek *poiein*, 'to make'.[15] In the same period, however, 'forge' was used in the opposite, pejorative and subsequently more familiar sense of 'to make (something) in fraudulent imitation of something else'. The confusion between positive and negative nuances of this word is exploitable by ironists like Lee Siegel, whose *Love in a Dead Language* (1999) quotes from an imaginary letter in which Chatterton asks Sterne, 'Is not God the forger of all creation?'[16] This slippage between benign and malign uses of the same word constitutes for Barbara Johnson evidence of a crisis in signification, because it instantiates 'difference' as a difference *within* the word 'forge', rather than as a difference *between* 'forge' and some other word, such as 'fake'.[17] Instead of assuming a difference *between* 'literature' and 'literary forgery', therefore, we might consider each term as marking a difference *within* the category of the literary. A similar slippage in the Welsh *prydydd* persuades David Greene that there is 'a general semantic tendency for any verb meaning "make" to move into the field of "make up", which can mean "to embellish" or "to concoct with intent to deceive"'.[18] Culturally, the most important consequence of this endogenous difference is confusion about the

---

13 Clanchy, *From Memory to Written Record*, 148.
14 Tout, 'Mediæval Forgers and Forgeries', 208, 209.
15 Sidney, 'Apology for Poetry', 9.
16 Siegel, *Love in a Dead Language*, 139.
17 Johnson, *Critical Difference*, 4.
18 Greene, *Makers and Forgers*, 4.

ontological distinctions between 'literature' and 'literary forgery'. A non-discriminatory history of this dissociation would begin by revisiting that moment when 'forge' was still the site of what Barbara Johnson calls 'warring forces of signification', and when forging-as-making was in conflict with forging-as-fraudulence. 'A forgery is still a making', Ian Haywood reminds us; 'its condemnation is a matter of interpretation and law'.[19]

When Umberto Eco revisited the semiotic problem of the fake in 1989 he drew attention to the ways in which Reformation attitudes to biblical pseudepigrapha play havoc with the formalism advocated by taxonomists like Metzger and Steele, whose definitions are designed to prevent slovenly commentators from perpetuating confusion by misdescribing texts. The most inclusive text of the Old Testament of the Holy Bible is a Greek version, the Septuagint, so called because seventy-two (*septuaginta*: 'seventy') translators allegedly worked on it. Fourteen of the books contained in the Septuagint are regarded by Protestants as non-canonical and designated the Apocrypha. In the Roman Catholic canon, however, only three of those fourteen books are deemed apocryphal; the remaining eleven are considered to be of 'secondary' importance and therefore deutero-canonical. Clearly, not even the most scrupulous lexicographical formalism can control the effects of historical upheavals on taxonomic systems. 'For Protestants', Eco concludes, 'the Catholic deuterocanonical books are usually called apocrypha and the Catholic apocrypha are called pseudoepigrapha'.[20] Seeing that carefully discriminated senses of such interrelated terms become distinctions without differences in the entropy of usage, the working definition of fake literature in this book privileges inclusiveness: 'any text whose actual provenance differs from what it is made out to be'. Within that broad definition, the common terms for denoting various sorts of textual spuriousness become interchangeable with one another, not on account of procedural slovenliness, but because that is what histories of their usage show to be the case. I also think that agency should be ascribed to a spurious text rather than to its author, whose inscrutable motives have to be divined before it can be classified as a 'hoax' or 'forgery' or whatever. Speculations about authorial intentions are important to biographers but irrelevant to analysts of the

---

[19] Haywood, *Faking It*, 6.
[20] Eco, 'Forgeries, Originals and Identity', 606.

cultural life of a spurious text misrecognised by the institutions that
process it. Whether or not Chatterton intended to subvert what Nick
Groom calls 'the print ideology' of eighteenth-century scholarship,
his 'Rowley' manuscripts (which proliferated as other people transcribed them) indubitably challenged – only a decade or so before
Thomas Warton published the first *History of English Poetry* (1781) –
'the assumption that typography [is] the fundamental medium of
literature and the empirical unit of literary history'.[21]

The quest for suitable terms with which to distinguish between
different kinds of literary spuriousness indicates what might be called
the 'conscious' component of such enquiries. By contrast, 'unconscious' assumptions about literary forgery are revealed in the
metaphors or tropes it attracts. Each of these represents the production of fake literature as analogous to some other activity, such as
counterfeiting. The organising tropes of any discipline enable its
practitioners to explain what they do by describing it as if it were
something else with which people are familiar. In the more positivistic purlieus of textual editing, for instance, textual variance is
treated as evidence of textual error. A desire to establish the one true
text derives from an unarticulated but monotheistic mind-set, which
aims to replace the Many by the One. An equally unconscious but
pervasive moralism is implicit in the designation of rejected textual
variants as 'corrupt'. And those diagrammatic stemmata which
represent both the blood-line of the true text and its filiations with
bastardised versions look very much like a displacement on to textual
editing of a characteristically patriarchal anxiety about legitimacy of
descent and the inheritance of property. In the family romance of
patriarchal scholarship, the legitimacy of textual heirs is confirmed
by publicly disclaiming textual bastards. 'The old school of teachers',
Quintilian recalls in his vade-mecum for budding orators, used to
'reject books whose titles they regarded as spurious, as though they
were expelling a supposititious child from the family circle'.[22] The
political unconscious of monistic editorial theory is a Romantic
ideology of literary authorship, which conceives of the text as an
autonomous object produced by an individual genius. Scholars who
internalise such tropes in the course of their professional training,
and reproduce them unselfconsciously in their own practice, are not

---

[21] Groom, 'Chatterton Was a Forger', 278, 289.
[22] Quintilian, *Institutio Oratoria*, i.iv.3.

really thinking about what they are doing. Instead, they themselves are being 'thought' by those foundational metaphors which constitute the broadly political unconscious of their discipline.

Each of the principal tropes applied as a heuristic device to literary forgery treats it as a textual irregularity. But in so far as every trope is merely an analogy, and therefore a type of 'aspect seeing', it frustrates attempts to perceive the distinctive features of fake literature; for by seeing it 'as' something else, we end up merely apperceiving it as a construct. ' "Seeing as" ', Wittgenstein observed, after pondering that famous drawing which (depending on how you look at it) resembles either a duck or a rabbit, 'is not part of perception'.[23] In this respect, any analogy designed to illuminate something may have opprobrious consequences for it. Certainly, the tropes commonly used of literary forgery reinforce negative attitudes. If seen as comparable to other and unequivocally deplorable kinds of fraudulence – such as the practice of scientific fraud in medicine, or the industrial counterfeiting of aircraft parts from inferior materials – then literary forgery will be judged by the company it keeps, and classified as a punishable misfeasance. Although theoretically the major tropes are all equally viable, at different times one will be preferred to others. We therefore learn something about a community of readers from its favourite trope, if only because consumer-choices are constrained by assumptions that pre-select them. Whenever literary studies takes an ethical turn, for example, as it did in the early 1990s, critics are likely to trope literary forgery as an ethical malpractice. In the 1980s, on the other hand, when law, critical theory and literary studies formed an interdisciplinary conjuncture, literary forgeries could be perceived as offences against intellectual property and troped as crimes of writing.

To sample various books which have appeared on this topic since 1907, when J.A. Farrer published the results of his forays in *Literary Forgeries*, is to encounter the dominant ways of figuring its relation to literature. The trope of forgery is no more problematic for Farrer than it was for Isaac Disraeli, whose *Curiosities of Literature* (1881) prompted Farrer to produce his own 'comprehensive or bird's-eye view of literary forgery'.[24] Andrew Lang likewise takes it for granted when, introducing Farrer's book, he observes that an exhaustive

---

[23] Wittgenstein, *Philosophical Investigations*, 197.
[24] Farrer, *Literary Forgeries*, vii, v.

treatment of the subject 'might begin with the Homeric poems', most of which, 'if we accept a prevalent theory' – first broached in F.A. Wolf's *Prolegomena ad Homerum* (1795) – are 'a sort of literary forgery', in so far as 'Homer' is merely a name attached to compendia of traditional and thus multi-authored materials labelled the *Iliad* and the *Odyssey*.[25] As proof that literary forgery still goes on, Lang confesses that in order to provide documentary support for the narrative in his own historical novel, *A Monk of Fife* (1896), he 'even went so far as to forge extracts in Old French, from the chapel register of St. Catherine of Fierbois'. But that misdemeanour took place in the legitimately duplicitous realm of fiction, and was different from the 'open forgery' he would have been guilty of had he attempted to infiltrate into Francis James Child's collection of *English and Scottish Popular Ballads* (1882–98) convincingly distressed manuscripts of a couple of his own poems, 'Simmy o' Whythaugh' and 'The Young Ruthven'.[26]

When H.M. Paull reconsidered in 1928 some of the materials covered in Farrer's survey, he was aware that 'no fault in criticism is so frequent and unfair as the judgment of the past by the standards of the present'.[27] Farrer had likewise advocated a non-judgemental study of literary forgeries, because 'suspense of judgement is one of the highest and most difficult of the intellectual virtues', and has 'many affinities with charity in the moral sphere'.[28] Paull's equanimity was shaken, however, by the profusion of 'ecclesiastical forgeries', the Christian authors of which exhibit a 'moral obliquity of vision' that he finds 'incomprehensible'. His humanistic permissiveness – sanctioned by the adage, *nihil humanum a me alienum* ('nothing human is alien to me') – turns out to be merely skin-deep: 'one's natural attitude' towards literary forgery, he declares, is 'condemnation'.[29] By 'natural', of course, he means 'cultural'. As Loyal Rue shows, the cultural tradition of deploring deceptive behaviour is at odds with the natural history of deception as a survivalist and evolutionary strategy: 'man' is therefore not (*pace* Auden) 'the only creature ever made who fakes', although humans appear to be better at it than other species.[30]

---

25 Ibid., xiii; Turner, 'Homeric Question', 125.
26 Farrer, *Literary Forgeries*, xv, xxv.
27 Paull, *Literary Ethics*, 24.
28 Farrer, *Literary Forgeries*, vi.
29 Paull, *Literary Ethics*, 24, 39.
30 Rue, *By Grace of Guile*, 125; Auden, *Collected Shorter Poems*, 317.

The key issue for Paull is exhibited in the title of *Literary Ethics* (1928). Whatever else literary forgeries might be, he argues, they are the product of unethical practices, and the only justification for spending time on them is to acquire data for a study of what the subtitle of his book calls 'the growth of the literary conscience'. Paull is especially irritated by 'a dubious licence in fiction', namely the practice of including in a novel 'a preface, or note, on the title-page, in which the author, speaking in his own person, gives a misleading account of the origin of the story'.[31] The 'advertisement to the first edition' of *Rob Roy* (1817), for instance, presents what follows as 'a parcel of Papers' sent to the anonymous editor of them by an 'unknown and nameless correspondent' with a request that they 'be given to the Public'. When Scott reprinted *Rob Roy* in 1829, however, he confessed that 'the communication alluded to' in that advertisement had been 'entirely imaginary'.[32] Such mock-provenances are a legitimate convention in fiction, popular because they allow novelists to distance themselves from their own narratives by presenting them ironically as someone else's. Paull finds this procedure ethically suspect because it provides a *carte blanche* for literary forgers. If the title-page of *Journal of the Plague Year* (1722) declares that the book was 'written by a Citizen who continued all the while in London', then we have a right to expect an eye-witness account of events in 1665, and not something made up over fifty years later by a novelist called Daniel Defoe.

Paull's argument here is not with the fictional text *per se* but with what Gérard Genette calls its 'paratext'.[33] The *explicit* paratext is constituted by the title-page, prefatory materials and information on the cover or dust-jacket; the most important of the *implicit* paratexts is the genre of the work, which (as in the Defoe example) may not be identical with the genre specified on the title-page or deducible from it. Theoretically, the function of paratextual features is to indicate exactly what sort of book confronts us, and thus prevent misreadings that arise from misidentification. Paull wants the paratext to remain 'outside' the text it contains in order to avoid being contaminated by it: *Robinson Crusoe* (1719) would thus be identifiable as a novel by Daniel Defoe, and not Crusoe's autobiographical account of his life on a desert island. Writers, on the other hand, see fictional opportu-

---

[31] Paull, *Literary Ethics*, 153.
[32] Scott, *Rob Roy*, ed. Duncan, 3–4, 456.
[33] Genette, *Paratexts*, 1–2.

nities in the paratext, and not least for the pleasure of teasing readers like Paull, who thinks that books should be labelled as correctly as other commodities are legally required to be in the interests of consumer protection. But writers are not obliged to regard their paratexts as statutory declarations about their texts. Paull would like fiction to be regulated by something like that tacit contract which underwrites the publication of autobiographies. Labelled by Philippe Lejeune 'the autobiographical pact', its function (as formulated by Laura Marcus) is to 'affirm the " 'identity' between the names of the author, narrator and protagonist" and guarantee the non-fictive status of the autobiography to the reader'.[34] It achieves this by aspiring to the same referential status as historical discourse, which likewise 'claim[s] to provide information about a "reality" exterior to the text, and so to submit to a test of *verification*'.[35] But of course no work of fiction is 'referential' in this sense. 'In the compact between novelist and reader', Cynthia Ozick declares, 'the novelist promises to lie, and the reader promises to allow it'.[36] That trust-based contract between writer and reader which Paull yearns for is absent from the market-place where such transactions take place, and whose motto is not 'trust me' but *caveat emptor*. Paratextual liberties are anathema to Paull because literary forgers capitalise on them, thus violating the fiduciary basis of publication, which obliges writers to behave responsibly instead of playing games with us.

The intellectual pedigree of this commonly held view that literary forgeries instantiate ethical malpractice is that moralism which informs Matthew Arnold's view of the high seriousness of literature and the concomitant responsibilities of authorship. It was because literature is 'serious' that forgeries of it had to be castigated, especially at a time when exponents of the nascent academic study of English literature were trying to convince sceptics that their activities would engage with matters much less frivolous than chatter about Shelley. This was not the right moment for the Ossianically named Oscar Fingal Wilde to record, in *The Portrait of Mr W.H.* (1889), 'a long discussion about Macpherson, Ireland, and Chatterton', during which he had remarked that 'to censure an artist for forgery [is] to confuse an ethical with an aesthetical problem'. Chatterton's 'so-called forgeries', Wilde added, 'were merely the result of an artistic

---

[34] Marcus, *Auto/biographical Discourses*, 196.
[35] Lejeune, *On Autobiography*, 22.
[36] Ozick, *Portrait of the Artist as a Bad Character*, 93.

desire for perfect representation'.[37] That argument would have had no force at the trial of 'Antique' Smith, who in 1893 was sentenced to one year's imprisonment for his forgeries of unpublished poems and letters by Robert Burns and Sir Walter Scott.[38] Nor was the jury at Wilde's own trial two years later impressed by his claim that the assessment of literature should be based on aesthetic rather than moral criteria. In the spirit of the *Pall Mall Gazette*'s 1867 articles on textual finagling by 'Our Naughty Novelists', Emily Lawless tried unsuccessfully to trouble-shoot the ethical issue by infantilising literary forgery in 1897 as 'the very superfluity of naughtiness'.[39] A few years earlier she had displayed her own aptitude for such naughtiness as the 'editor' of *With Essex in Ireland* (1890), a work of fiction that purports – successfully as far as W.E. Gladstone was concerned – to be 'extracts from a diary kept in Ireland during the year 1599 by Mr. Henry Harvey'. *With Essex in Ireland* has affinities, therefore, with fake diaries designed to deceive historians into thinking them part of the archival record. One such example is *The Diary of a Farmer's Wife 1796–1797* (1964) by 'Anne Hughes' (Jeanne Preston), which was televised by the BBC and screened as an educational programme to show British schoolchildren what everyday life used to be like in rural Georgian England.[40] Another is Mary Chestnut's *A Diary from Dixie* (1949), which Edmund Wilson read as a contemporary account of the American Civil War (1861–65) by the wife of a Confederate official, although eventually it was shown not to have been written until the early 1880s.[41] Ethical critics could not accept Lawless' tolerant view of these matters because her own literary practice showed her to be part of the problem.

With the teaching of literature defended in terms of its efficacy in developing the moral sensibilities of those who studied it, the scapegoating of fake literature became a means of shoring up the correspondingly real thing while also displaying one's own probity by occupying the moral high ground. The co-option of literature for moral education in the twentieth century is evident in the published

---

[37] Quoted in Höfele, 'Originalität der Fälschung', 75.

[38] Roughead, *Riddle of the Ruthvens*, 122–43.

[39] 'Olphar Hamst', *Handbook of Fictitious Names*, 170–71; Lawless, 'Ethics of Literary Forgery', 90–91.

[40] Tolstoy, 'Diary of Nobody at All', *passim*.

[41] Lynn, *Air-Line to Seattle*, 50–59.

criticism of Lionel Trilling (whose doctoral dissertation was on Matthew Arnold) and F.R. Leavis, who regarded the close study of literary texts as especially valuable in providing students with opportunities to confront and vicariously work through some of those ethical choices they would have to make in their own lives. Since reading with discrimination was deemed propaedeutic to living a morally responsible life, moral evaluation is central to Leavisite criticism of literature. Although Leavis positioned himself against belletristic dilettantism, his sense of the mission of literary studies accorded with the traditional view that the humanities are worth studying because they make humans more humane than they might be otherwise. That humanistic faith was shaken in the 1960s by George Steiner, whose meditations on the cultivated tastes of those in charge of the Nazi death-camps led him to conclude that the humanities do not necessarily humanise anybody.[42] And it was to be questioned also by neo-Marxist and post-colonial critics, who interrogated humanism to reveal its complicity in the barbarism displayed by 'civilised' nations in their colonial encounters. But the major assault on Leavisite humanism in literary criticism came first from structuralist critical theory in the late 1960s, which decentred 'the human' as the source of knowledge by focusing instead on those cultural systems and deep structures that determine our perceptions of the way things are. Reconfigured as an unstable category formed at the interstices of conflicting discourses and ideologies, 'the human' could no longer be regarded as a free agent from whom all meaning and value emanate.

The post-structuralism which followed engaged in a systematic deconstruction of the categories that constitute humanism, on the grounds that they were never more than logocentric constructs in the first place, whose primary function has been to consolidate and advance the interests of a particular type of human subject, namely one which is white, male and European. This anti-foundationalism proved immensely liberating to people oppressed by the status quo, who were encouraged to believe that the world could be reconstructed more equitably if those metaphysical structures which make it the way it is were to be dismantled. Oppressive regimes perceived as overdue for deconstruction included the racism of white supremacists, the sexism of male suprematists, and the Eurocentrism which

[42] Steiner, *Language and Silence*, 15.

marginalises and inferiorises people from other cultures. In this respect, therefore, the post-structuralist agenda could claim to be 'ethical', although it certainly was not perceived as such by those whose reading habits had been shaped by Arnoldian moralism filtered through Leavisite practical criticism. Early readers of Derrida's *Of Grammatology* (1967) were given the impression that everything is deconstructible because nothing is sacred. Hostile critics found it symptomatic of a disturbing anti-humanism, which was destroying literary studies. The very idea of literary 'theory' was repellent because Leavis himself always argued – much to the bewilderment of historians of literary criticism like René Wellek – that no literary criticism worth reading exhibits extractable 'theories'. Late in 1989, however, Derrida admitted that some things – 'justice' in particular – are beyond the reach of deconstruction. He had now decided that while the 'law (*droit*) is essentially deconstructible', justice 'in itself, if such a thing exists, outside or beyond law, is not'.[43] This marked a return to the metaphysical reassurance that *Of Grammatology* had set about demolishing. Derrida's about-face on justice is the hinge of what came to be called 'the turn to ethics' in the 1990s, the significance of which is argued about by participants whose intellectual pedigrees differ widely but who have comparable views on the uses of criticism.[44] Epigones of Leavis saw the turn to ethics as a backlash against post-structuralism so severe as to signal its demise; resilient post-structuralists, on the other hand, claimed that their concerns have always been ethical and continue to be so, as is evidenced by their interest in the philosophy of Emmanuel Levinas.[45] Either way, Paull's view of literary forgery as an ethical malpractice is likely to find more supporters nowadays, when interest centres once again on the moral competence of both writers and their readers, than it would have done in the 1980s, when attention focused predominantly on the textuality of verbal artefacts. Yet if we simply reject as unethical the products of literary agendas that are programmatically unethical, such as literary forgeries, we will never get beyond the banalities of recognition and denunciation. And we will pass up the opportunities they provide to explore the cultural significance of our fascination with the fraudulent.

[43] Derrida, 'Force of Law', 14.
[44] Parker, 'Turn to Ethics', *passim.*
[45] Critchley, *Ethics of Deconstruction, passim.*

A common trope for literary forgery, 'counterfeiting', is encountered
in both strong and weak versions: the strong ones foreground the
fiscal analogy between writing and the illicit production of banknotes
or coins, whereas the weak explore counterfeiting as a striking
synonym for anything not genuine. A fine example of the weak usage
is Hugh Kenner's *The Counterfeiters* (1968), which addresses postmodern readers who find themselves 'deep . . . in the counterfeit'
because they have 'long since had to forego easy criteria for what is
"real"'.[46] Kenner argues that the cult of facts since the late seventeenth century, and their aggregation into statistical data, have
produced a simulacrum of the human he calls 'counterfeitable man',
the fictional matrix in which both Gulliver and Macphossian
materialise. Recognising that we are more complex than such quanti-
fying systems assume, writers become counterfeiters whose most
serious work is easily mistaken for a hoax. One of Kenner's examples
is *Ulysses* (1922), which Joyce himself refers to in *Finnegans Wake* (1939)
as 'an epical forged cheque on the public', and which thematises
spuriousness in its Eumaeus episode, where 'money and narratives
are counterfeit', and 'identities are genuine forgeries'.[47] An equally
interesting example, however, is T.S. Eliot's *The Waste Land* (1922),
which a *Time* reviewer of the first edition thought was a hoax. That
possibility intrigued Herbert Palmer, who parodied Eliot's *Ash Wed-
nesday* (1930) as *Cinder Thursday* (1931) before Eliot published *Burnt
Norton* (1936), parodied in turn by Henry Reed as *Chard Whitlow* (1941).
Vacillating between the genuine and the parodic, this sequence of
calcinatory titles reproduces a disturbing characteristic of *The Waste
Land*, a poem in which 'hoax and earnest are strangely, hypnotically,
and bafflingly blended'.[48] Such betwixt-and-betweenness typifies the
indeterminacy of avant-garde writing like Gabriel Vicaire and Henri
Beauclair's *Les Déliquescences: Poèmes décadents* (1885). Published as the
work of an imaginary writer, 'Adoré Floupette', this book is both an
homage to and parody of French Symbolist poetry.[49] 'The counter-
feiter's real purpose', Kenner argues, 'is to efface himself, like the
Flaubertian artist, so that we will draw the conclusion he wants us to
draw about how his artifact came into existence'.[50] Defoe's most

---

[46] Kenner, *Counterfeiters*, 20.
[47] Ibid., 72; Osteen, 'Money Question in Joyce's "Eumaeus"', 821–22.
[48] Palmer, *Post-Victorian Poetry*, 312–13.
[49] Weiss, *Popular Culture of Modern Art*, 147.
[50] Kenner, *Counterfeiters*, 30.

famous book is counterfeit in Kenner's sense, because 'our knowledge that *Robinson Crusoe* is fiction, not memoir, alters *Robinson Crusoe*
profoundly'.[51]

Such subtleties do not trouble Sonia Cole as she ranges across
various 'fields' of forgery in her book entitled *Counterfeit* (1955). She
takes this as her key-term because the making of counterfeit money is
'the most pernicious of all types of forgery', which is why the English
made it a statutory offence in 1562 and a capital offence in 1634.[52]
Cole overlooks the fact, however, that counterfeiting is a well-
established trope in 'genuine' literature produced by canonical
authors. Charles Baudelaire, for instance, wrote a piece on counterfeit money called 'La Fausse monnaie', in which a man first impresses
his companion by giving a silver coin to a beggar, and then shocks
him by confessing that the coin was counterfeit. This self-evidently
parabolic tale can be read as an allegory of the counterfeitness of any
text transmitted by a donor-writer to beggar-readers. 'La Fausse
monnaie' provoked a lengthy commentary by Jacques Derrida, who
reads 'the narrative [a]s a fiction and a fiction of fiction, a fiction on
the subject of fiction, the very fiction of fiction'.[53] For Cole, on the
other hand, 'counterfeit' is an unexamined term, useful only as a
vituperative catch-all for a broad spectrum of spuriosities. She never
considers the metaphorical implications of a word whose etymology
(*contrafactio*, 'setting in opposition') opens up the possibility of
refiguring the relationship between counterfeit and genuine as
oppositional.

The 'counterfeit' trope is used negatively whenever comparisons
are made – explicitly or tacitly – between linguistic reciprocity and
monetary exchange. Words then come to be seen as gold 'coins'
whose qualities must be assayed in order to guarantee their exchange
value. This is especially true of poetry, which is believed to contain a
greater concentration than other literary genres of this valuable
coinage, as F.T. Palgrave understood when compiling *The Golden
Treasury of Songs and Lyrics* (1861). Not surprisingly, the introduction of
paper money into societies accustomed to coinage provokes unease.
The gist of *Paper Money Lyrics*, which Thomas Love Peacock wrote
between 1815 and 1826, is that real money becomes as unreal as the
counterfeit whenever gold and silver are replaced by paper currency,
because all we get then is a 'series of paper promises', structured by

---

[51] Ibid., 31.   [52] Cole, *Counterfeit*, 14–15.   [53] Derrida, *Given Time*, 85.

the circular proposition 'that the promise shall always be a payment, and the payment shall always be a promise'.[54] The analogy between fiscal value and literary value is most visible in the designation of neologisms as 'coinages'. Whether such verbal 'minting' is authorised is generally a moot point. Marc Shell argues that Plato disparaged those expert rhetoricians, the sophists, as 'money-coiners of words' because he regarded both 'money (wage earning) and language (sophistry)' as 'finally in necessary opposition to the Good (philosophy), which must overcome them'.[55] In view of literature's alliance with rhetoric rather than philosophy, and considering its second-rateness in remaining content to produce mere imitations of imitations of the real, Plato considers it unqualified to be a purveyor of the truth. Yet 'if that which is imitated has no ontological status', Shell observes, 'then literature cannot ever be counterfeit, for there is no original for it to copy'.[56] In that case, the troping of literary forgery as counterfeit literature becomes correspondingly problematic, and loses its force as a strategy of disparagement once it is acknowledged that literature itself is treated in Plato's *Republic* as a counterfeit product.[57] From that perspective, the counterfeiting (by literary forgery) of the counterfeit (literature) may cause perturbations among the benighted inhabitants of Plato's cave. But it will not trouble philosophers in pursuit of that genuine knowledge which is *sophia*.

The counterfeit as a literary problem looks quite different when removed from ethical surveillance and relocated in a noetic domain created by theorists in both economics and literary studies, who share an interest in Karl Marx's speculations about the links between value and capital. The confluence of monetary theory with literary theory informs Jean-Joseph Goux's 1984 book on the 'coiners' (*monnayeurs*) of language, which investigates 'the structural homology between money and language'.[58] Goux is particularly interested in the supersession of 'real' money (especially gold) by the kind of paper money which is called 'representative' if its convertibility is fully guaranteed, but 'fiduciary' if not.[59] He finds it significant that 'the crisis of realism . . . coincided with the end of gold money'.[60] André

---

[54] Peacock, *Paper Money Lyrics*, 100.
[55] Shell, *Economy of Literature*, 38–39.
[56] Ibid., 126.   [57] Ibid., 141.
[58] Goux, *Coiners of Language*, 4.
[59] Ibid., 15.   [60] Ibid., 3.

Gide's 1926 novel, *Les Faux-Monnayeurs* (*The Counterfeiters*), was written in the aftermath of the First World War, when 'gold money disappeared in France', shortly after which 'England began to circulate banknotes without gold backing'.[61] In Goux's reading, *Les Faux-Monnayeurs* 'fictionalises the shift from a society founded on legitimation by representation' (the gold standard) 'to a society dominated by the inconvertibility of signifiers' (paper money). Paper currencies cause problems because they 'refer to one another like tokens in infinite slippage, with no standard or treasury to offer the guarantee of a transcendental signifier or referent'.[62] The comparable 'slippage' in literary production is marked by the difference between realist fiction and those fictions about fiction that are known as metafiction. Realist fiction attempts to represent reality as successfully as Upton Sinclair did in *The Jungle* (1906), a novel which described the appalling conditions of turn-of-the-century Chicago stockyards so well as to prompt an official enquiry into them. Metafiction, on the other hand, is driven by a different agenda; for instead of trying (like a realist novel) to conceal what Goux calls 'the imposture of all fiction', it revels in its own fictiveness.[63] The principal character of *Les Faux-Monnayeurs* is an imaginary novelist who keeps a journal while writing a novel (also called *Les Faux-Monnayeurs*) about another imaginary novelist – just as Gide himself, while writing *Les Faux-Monnayeurs*, kept a journal published subsequently as *Journal des Faux-Monnayeurs* (1927). Lacking a real foundation for its baroque superstructures, Gide's novel is modelled on the potentially infinite regressions of a *mise en abyme* in an economy in which money has merely a token status. 'By revealing the duplicity that founds his own "counterfeit" novel', Jonathan Romney argues, 'Gide reveals the duplicity present, and concealed, in all literary production'.[64]

This view is not dominant in the literary world, where the withdrawal of fake literature from circulation is justified by appealing to a distinction between 'good' and 'bad' money epitomised as Gresham's Law. Formulated by a Scottish economist, Henry D. Macleod, and attributed by him to Queen Elizabeth I's financial adviser, Sir Thomas Gresham, this law maintains that bad money drives out good money, because, whenever both are in circulation,

---

[61] Ibid., 20.   [62] Ibid., 4.   [63] Ibid., 10.
[64] Romney, 'Forgery and Economy in Gide's *Les Faux-Monnayeurs*', 196.

people pass on the bad and hoard the good. Transferred to literary studies, this provides the grounds for categorising literary 'counterfeiting' as something not in the public interest. Technically, therefore, scholars are obliged to identify and cast out the counterfeit. If they were to do so systematically, however, literature would disappear from libraries, because the literary practice of imitation has canonised the counterfeit. Gresham's own lifetime, for instance, coincided with the literary cult of the *Anacreontea*, those Alexandrian imitations which were far more influential than the surviving fragments of poems by the ancient Greek Anacreon; yet nobody has proposed applying Gresham's Law to a belated English example of the genre, Robert Herrick's *Hesperides* (1648).[65] Internalised as part of the mental equipment of literary scholars, Gresham's Law tends to be appealed to whenever the authenticity of a text is questioned: hence Arthur Johnston's remark that 'Macpherson's forgeries inevitably drove out of circulation the rude originals' of the Ossianic ballads.[66] Such formulations rest on the assumption that economics can never provide anything more substantial than metaphors for the production, circulation and consumption of literature. But the relationship between literature and economics is neither ancillary nor ornamental in Sandra Sherman's account of finance and fictionality in the writings of Daniel Defoe, whose 'texts instantiate the homology between financial credit and literary credibility, and engage both the discourse of emerging capitalism and the theory and practice of fiction'.[67] In Sherman's analysis, the deceptive truth-claims made in Defoe's fiction are unstable because they replicate the characteristic instability of economic discourse in the early eighteenth century, whose most public show of insubstantiality was that speculators' nightmare, the South Sea Bubble of 1720. In this period, Sherman argues, 'fiction proliferates fiction to hide fictionality, [and] palimpsest promises pile up against no visible, originary Fund'.[68] Whenever that happens, the presumed gap between genuine text and counterfeit text disappears.

By far the most common way of writing about literary forgery is to trope it as playfulness, as Dwight Macdonald does when describing the eighteenth century as 'the golden age of literary

---

[65] Aldington, *Frauds*, 186.
[66] Johnston, *Enchanted Ground*, 79.
[67] Sherman, *Finance and Fictionality*, 8.
[68] Ibid., 2.

hanky-panky'.[69] Entertainment is the organising principle in John Whitehead's book, *This Solemn Mockery* (1973), whose title derives from the show-stopping line in Ireland's *Vortigern* (1796). Whitehead offers an anecdotal account of some of the most famous cases from Chatterton to Thomas J. Wise, who in the late nineteenth century damaged the credibility of the rare books trade by co-operating with H. Buxton Forman in the business of bibliographical forgery. This involved meddling creatively with printed books as physical objects in order to fabricate (by means of type-facsimiles) hitherto unsuspected first editions of works by well-known nineteenth-century authors. The most famous is a bogus 1847 text of love poems written by Elizabeth Barrett Browning to her husband, *Sonnets from the Portuguese* (1850), which Forman and Wise printed some time during 1893–94.[70] 'Not So Wise!' is the title of Whitehead's chapter on this episode in bibliographical history, the ramifications of which did not become clear until the 1930s, when two booksellers, John Carter and Graham Pollard, published their findings in *An Enquiry into the Nature of Certain Nineteenth Century Pamphlets* (1934), an initial draft of which they entitled 'Wise-cracking'.[71] *This Solemn Mockery* reads like a companion to Lawrence Jeppson's book about fakery in the fine arts, *The Fabulous Frauds* (1970), which is subtitled 'fascinating tales of great art forgeries'. Whitehead treats his case studies as the literary equivalent of confidence tricks, performed by rogues whose successful gulling of people who ought to have known better is a continuing source of *schadenfreude*, especially when the victims of such high jinks include 'experts'.

Whitehead shows no interest in relating his material to those 'ludic' theories of cultural practices whose point of departure is Johan Huizinga's *Homo Ludens* (1938). The title of Huizinga's book reconstitutes *homo sapiens* as a creature whose defining characteristic – as formulated in the fourteenth of Friedrich Schiller's letters *On the Aesthetic Education of Man* (1795) – is an 'impulse' or 'instinct' to play (*Spieltrieb*), which enables Schiller to claim that 'man . . . is only fully a human being when he plays'.[72] Observing 'western civilization *sub specie ludi*', Huizinga draws attention to the ludic structures of many of its cultural institutions, some of which, such as 'the domain of law,

[69] Macdonald, Dwight, 'Annals of Crime', 169.
[70] Jones, M., *Fake?*, 224.
[71] Collins, *Two Forgers: Forman and Wise*, 251.
[72] Hutchinson, *Games Authors Play*, vii; Schiller, *Aesthetic Education*, 107.

justice and jurisprudence', are not usually thought of in these terms.[73] How the *Spieltrieb* affects our relations with one another was the subject in 1964 of a best-selling book on *Games People Play* by a transactional psychologist, Eric Berne, who acknowledges Stephen Potter's humorous treatment (in *Theory and Practice of Gamesmanship*, 1947) of the requisite 'ploys' for achieving and maintaining the pleasurable state of 'one-upmanship' among friends and colleagues.[74] Berne's title incorporates the two key-terms which in ludic analysis constitute opposite poles in a behavioural spectrum that ranges from the spontaneities of play (fooling around for fun) to those rule-bound activities characteristic of games like chess or tennis and verbal games like sonnets.

For cultural analysts, the most provocative account of this phenomenon is the contested taxonomy developed by Roger Caillois in *Man, Play and Games* (1961), which classifies all games in four major categories: *agon* (competitive games), *alea* (games of chance), simulation, and *ilinx* (dangerous games which induce the 'voluptuous panic' of vertigo).[75] A typology of fake literature could easily be devised from Caillois' schema. *Agon* is familiar already in literary studies through the work of Harold Bloom, whose book on *The Anxiety of Influence* (1973) is a Freudian interpretation of the Oedipal problems experienced by male writers obliged to engage agonistically with their literary forefathers. Anthony Grafton imagines the two sets of players identified in the title of his book, *Forgers and Critics* (1990), as involved in a never-ending *agon* in which literary forgers perform the socially useful function of stimulating scholars to devise increasingly sophisticated methods for detecting the activities of textual mischief-makers.[76] This is something of a *topos* in the annals of literary spuriosity: in 1796, for example, the *Gentleman's Magazine* observed that one good outcome of Ireland's Shakespeare forgeries was that they had 'drawn forth a detection' from that 'able master', Edmond Malone.[77] Grafton's hypothesis is strengthened by the agonistic relationship in the electronics industry between hackers and their twin adversaries, hacker-trackers and the developers of anti-hacking software. Hacker and hacker-tracker re-enact in cyberspace the

---

[73] Huizinga, *Homo Ludens*, 198, 97.
[74] Berne, *Games People Play,* 58.
[75] Cailloix, *Man, Play and Games*, 12–13, 23.
[76] Grafton, *Forgers and Critics*, 6, 123.
[77] P. Martin, *Edmond Malone*, 199.

games played by Grafton's forgers and critics, improving one
another's performances until they become superstars like the
German Marcus Hess (who retrieved military secrets from Western
computers and then sold them to the KGB) and his American
nemesis, Clifford Stoll, who describes the hacker-tracking of Hess in
The Cuckoo's Egg (1989). Anybody upset by the continuing production
of literary fakes will therefore find *Forgers and Critics* reassuring,
because it situates them in a narrative of containment.

As for Caillois' other categories, *ilinx* is a game that attracts people
addicted to their own adrenalin, and was probably being played in
the early 1970s by Clifford Irving, when he wrote (and almost
succeeded in publishing) a book which he claimed was the autobiography of the reclusive but still very much alive billionaire,
Howard Hughes.[78] 'Simulation', on the other hand, is the game
played whenever writers – genuine or fake – choose to write under
pseudonyms in the belief that their actual names will prejudice either
the publication or reception of their books. And those who maximise
the risk of being found out doing so are engaged in games of *alea*.
Sometimes, like Asa Earl Carter, they gamble and win. A former
speechwriter for Governor Wallace of Alabama ('Segregation now!
Segregation tomorrow! Segregation forever!'), Carter refashioned
himself retrospectively by acquiring a Cherokee upbringing and
changing his first name to 'Forrest'. The silvan associations of his
new name are evoked in the title of his best-selling Native American
'autobiography', *The Education of Little Tree* (1976), a book which
immediately embarked on a new and successful career as fiction after
its exposure as fraudulent in 1991.[79] Clearly, story-tellers content
merely to entertain readers with accounts of their recent trips to the
lexical playgrounds of fake literature could learn from Huizinga and
Caillois how to present such writings in ways that would bring them
into the mainstream of cultural critique.

Writers on literary forgery often refer to it in passing as a crime,
even when their own treatments of it are conducted almost exclusively in terms of some other trope: Whitehead, describing it as 'a
criminal field', concurs in this respect with Grafton, for whom
literary forgery is ultimately 'a sort of crime', the 'criminal sibling' of
critical scholarship.[80] To think about it like that became more than

---

[78] Fay *et al.*, *Inside Story of the Hughes-Irving Affair*, *passim*; Irving, *The Hoax*, *passim*.
[79] Gates, 'Authenticity', 26–7.
[80] Whitehead, *This Solemn Mockery*, 4; Grafton, *Forgers and Critics*, 37, 127.

metaphorical after 1710, when the Statute of Queen Anne brought to
bear on literary production the legal fiction of copyright, and thus
enabled the courts to consider the immateriality of printed words as
material property with economic value. Although it inaugurated
judicial processes for dealing with breaches of what later would be
called intellectual property rights, the 1710 Copyright Act contains
no definition of 'literary property'.[81] 'Based on the modern notion of
the individualised, inimitable act of literary creation', Ian Haywood
observes, it marked 'the birth of the author-owned text'.[82] Others
are more wary, however, of assuming that the copyright-owning
person as defined by the 1710 Act is identical with the aesthetic
personality predicated by a later and Romantic conception of
authorship. The purpose of the legislation which resulted in that Act,
David Saunders argues in his book on *Authorship and Copyright* (1992),
was neither 'to recognise a writer's subjectivity in a written work' nor
'to give legal recognition to an inalienable human right inherent in
the writer'.[83] On the contrary, by determining 'the regulation of
printed books as printed commodities', it was designed to protect the
business interests of booksellers, and specifically their 'right to trade
in mechanical duplicates of the work'.[84] Saunders confirms John
Feather's observation that the booksellers regarded the legislation 'as
being for their [own] protection, not for the protection of authors
and certainly not to encourage authors to enjoy the profits of their
work after publication'.[85] The Romantic conception of aesthetic
authorship was thus not an ideal to which the Act of 1710 falteringly
aspired. Since it was common in the early eighteenth century for an
author to relinquish ownership of a work to the bookseller who
published it, the principal beneficiaries of that Act were booksellers,
not authors, despite the booksellers' argument 'that authors' interests
were booksellers' interests'.[86] In other words, the 1710 copyright law
protected the investment of capital by booksellers rather than of
labour by authors.[87]

The key trope of Susan Stewart's stimulating enquiries into
eighteenth-century literary forgeries is displayed in the title of her

[81] Saunders, *Authorship and Copyright*, 54.
[82] Haywood, *Faking It*, 21.
[83] Saunders, *Authorship and Copyright*, 10.
[84] Ibid., 213, 212.
[85] Feather, 'Book Trade in Politics', 36.
[86] Saunders, *Authorship and Copyright*, 52.
[87] Frow, 'Repetition and Limitation', 10.

book, *Crimes of Writing* (1991). This sophisticated analysis of 'problems in the containment of representation' sees them as in various ways a consequence of the Copyright Act, which enabled the development of a recognisably modern conception of literary forgery. By treating the famous cases as exemplary 'cruxes in the notion of literary or intellectual property', Stewart makes the study of literary impostures central to eighteenth-century notions of authorship and therefore to our understanding of eighteenth-century literary culture.[88] Her book is itself both a function of and a contribution to an interdisciplinary conjuncture in the 1980s between literary studies and law, or more precisely between the critique of literary studies by critical theory and of law by critical legal studies. The discursive construction of literary forgery by academic critics is a more volatile affair than it is for those who write for a popular readership because it is susceptible to changing fashions in the metadiscourse of literary studies. *Crimes of Writing* was enabled institutionally by a different interdisciplinary formation from the one in which Ian Haywood (working at the interface between literary studies and history) undertook his doctoral research on Macpherson and Chatterton. Published in 1986 as *The Making of History*, Haywood's book historicises their practices without much reference to the 1710 Act, although it was to feature more prominently in his subsequent study of the 'art and politics of forgery', *Faking It* (1987). The principal strength of *Crimes of Writing* is to historicise current confusions about literary forgery by sourcing them to that moment in eighteenth-century Britain when codificatory categories such as 'authority, genealogy, precedence, application, specificity, and transcendence' began to be understood as 'qualities of a literary realm that it bec[ame] the task of the law . . . to regulate'.[89]

To trope literary forgery as a 'crime' of writing involves seeing it as symptomatic of behaviour designated criminal by the law, and reproducing the teleology of William Hogarth's engravings of 'The Rake's Progress' (1733–35) when speculating about *The Fake's Progress* (1977), which is the title of Tom Keating's autobiography as an art forger. Joseph Ritson observed in 1790 that 'a man who will forge a poem, a line or even a word will not hesitate, when the temptation is greater & the impunity equal, to forge a note or steal a guinea'.[90]

---

[88] Stewart, *Crimes of Writing*, 16.
[89] Ibid.
[90] Bronson, *Joseph Ritson*, vol. II, 548.

Equally convinced that 'all in the house of forgery are relations',
Walpole insinuated that if the indigent Chatterton had not died so
young he might well have adapted his 'ingenuity in counterfeiting
styles' to the forging of 'promissary notes'.[91] Psalmanazar was in this
respect anomalous, since before publishing his orientalising fantasy
about Formosa he had already forged a passport in order to establish
his 'Japanese' identity in Germany. To criminalise literary spuriosity
involves refashioning the critic as detective, and popularising the
painstaking scholarship required if literary detection is to match, say,
the achievement of Richard Bentley, who established in 1697 that *The
Epistles of Phalaris* were fraudulent, and thought that 'the chief
Province of a Critick' is 'to detect Forgeries'.[92] To operate successfully as the kind of critic Thomas Hoving calls a 'fakebuster', your
qualifications must include the 'mental makeup of a detective'.[93]
That opinion is encountered less frequently in literary studies than in
the world of fine arts, where the stakes are higher because of the vast
sums of money exchanged in the sales of 'authentic' artefacts by a
few acknowledged masters. In the world of books, nothing has
outclassed the detective work done by those self-styled Wise-crackers,
Carter and Pollard. The famous photograph of them standing
outside the British Museum shows Carter looking like a senior
detective in pre-war British films.[94] Their now classic investigation of
Wise's bibliographical malpractices reads like a detective story,
which the *New York Review of Books* renamed 'The Case of the
Crooked Bookman'.[95] This genre is high on the list of narrative
options whenever literary forgery is troped as crime, and is used
effectively by Robert Harris in his book on the forged Hitler diaries,
Selling Hitler (1986).

Narratives of literary forgery tend to be triumphalist, because the
'crime' is always identified and usually solved. But what of those
cases – the existence of which is statistically feasible – which are not
even identified, let alone solved? Whereas histories of most human
achievements chronicle successes, a history of literary forgeries is
restricted to recording failures, that is, those instances which have
been detected. For as Edward C. Banfield reminds us, 'there is no

91 Meyerstein, *Life of Chatterton*, 277.
92 Haywood, *Faking It*, 45.
93 Hoving, *False Impressions*,17, 235.
94 Barker and Collins, *Sequel to 'An Enquiry'*, frontispiece.
95 Ricks, 'Case of the Crooked Bookman', 34.

record of a forgery that has deceived everyone'.[96] A phenomenology of the fake, therefore, would have to be a largely theoretical enterprise, based on extrapolations from examples which are known about only because their attempted deception failed, whether through confession by their authors or detection by someone else. Another problem is the hyperbole of Stewart's phrase, 'crimes of writing', in so far as the literary activities she describes were not punishable offences even in the eighteenth century. One reason for this, Paul Baines argues, is that 'criminal forgery . . . was itself undergoing economic and cultural change' in that period, and therefore did not constitute 'a stable domain with which literature could sometimes engage'.[97] Significantly, and in spite of the fears voiced by Ritson, Baines finds no instance of 'a literary forger cross[ing] the boundary into defined criminal behaviour'.[98] Just as well for Macpherson and Chatterton, one might add, given the savagery with which people convicted of forgery were punished: John Ward, for instance, was sentenced to have his head and hands secured in a wooden pillory, both ears cut off with a pruning knife, and both nostrils slit with scissors before being cauterised with a red-hot iron.[99] So although the Act of 1710 turned literature into a property protected by law, literary 'forgery' seems to have been understood as more of a metaphor than a malpractice. 'He in poetry no forgery fears', wrote an anonymous contributor to the *Grub Street Journal* in 1731, 'That knows so well in law he'd lose his ears'.[100] That remark was occasioned by *The Double Falsehood* (1728), which the *Grub Street Journal* writer thought should be regarded as a Shakespeare forgery by Lewis Theobald, and not (as Theobald himself claimed), an original play by Shakespeare merely 'revised and adapted' by Theobald in the way that John Dryden had renovated Shakespeare's *Antony and Cleopatra* (1606–07) for Restoration audiences as *All for Love* (1678).

The principal difficulty faced by anybody who chooses to write about these matters is a metacritical problem: is each literary forgery so culture-specific as to render cross-cultural comparisons invalid? From a universalist perspective, this question is superfluous: all such

---

96 Banfield, 'Art versus Collectibles', 31.
97 Baines, 'Literary Forgery and the Ideology of Detection', 599.
98 Baines, 'Macaroni Parson and Marvellous Boy', 96.
99 Baines, ' "Ward in Pillory" ', 209.
100 Marder, 'Shakespearean Frauds', 215.

instances are merely cultural variants of a unitary phenomenon to which various names are attached. But from a localist perspective the question is crucial, since literary forgery – like literature itself – is not a transhistorically stable essence but a culturally variable construct. Much depends, therefore, on whether the organising term for such enquiries is 'similarity' or 'difference'. Similarity-seekers, whose motto is *plus ça change, plus c'est la même chose*, operate on the assumption that phenotypal differences are less significant than those archetypal similarities which occur synchronically across contemporary cultures and diachronically throughout history. No matter what their cultural origin, all literary forgeries are equally intelligible because they derive from deceptive modes of human behaviour that are both timeless and universal. As a mode of intellectual enquiry, similarity-seeking enables an extraordinarily wide variety of texts to be assembled under a common rubric for comparative purposes. By surveying the field in this way we deepen our understanding of our common humanity, which comprises *inter alia* our common duplicity and gullibility. But this homogenisation also entails disadvantages. These include the erasure of particular differences in the interests of generalisation, and the de-contextualising and de-historicising of local practices in the course of universalising such phenomena.

The business of remedying such deficiences preoccupies a rival group of enquirers, the difference-seekers, who operate under the banner of *autres temps, autres moeurs*. Accustomed to expect unfamiliarities when encountering alterity in the historical sites they visit, they are suspicious of anything that looks familiar, and handle it with as much caution as we learn to treat those linguistic *faux amis* ('false friends') which result from the fortuitous coincidence of grammatological sameness ('gift' and *Gift*) with semantic difference (*Gift* is German for 'poison').[101] Difference-seekers think that because what is called literary forgery covers an enormous range of historically and culturally variable phenomena, we should abandon both the hubristic ambitions of the overview and the grand narratives it encourages in books with titles like Frank Arnau's *Three Thousand Years of Deception in Art and Antiques* (1961). Instead, we should pay scrupulous attention to the specificities of particular works which congregate within the same chronotope, and knuckle down to the task of producing archivally based 'thick descriptions' of them which

---

[101] Thody *et al.*, *Faux Amis and Key Words*, *passim*.

will enable their microhistories to be written.[102] Such a procedure will vastly improve our understanding of the cultural conditions in which a particular literary forgery was produced, the distribution networks through which it circulated, the socio-political affiliations of its earliest readers and critics, and the different agendas for which they appropriated it. A disadvantage of such discursive fissiparousness, however, is a tendency to heighten the discontinuities between one thing and another and thus make comparisons between them correspondingly more difficult. For eclectic readers, therefore, the principal problem with the culture-specific model of literary spuriosity is that it fails to account for what appear to be similar phenomena in different periods. The argument that each text is fully intelligible only in terms of its own genealogy is methodologically impeccable to differentiators. But to others this rationale makes the culture-specific model of enquiry unavoidably and regrettably myopic.

Every writer on literary forgery I have read is attracted primarily to one of these models, although such allegiance does not exclude an occasional bit of the other. Furthermore, whenever difference is privileged (as it is nowadays) as a means of recognising and tolerating diversity, sameness-seekers are given a hard time. Anthony Grafton, for instance, clearly ranks similarity and continuity more highly than differences and discontinuities. In *Forgers and Critics* (1990) he treats literary forgery as a transhistorical phenomenon whose various manifestations exhibit a family resemblance to one another; and while conceding that literary forgers are 'diverse in their personalities and interests', he concludes that they have similar motives because the range of possibilities is so small.[103] Anybody familiar with 'the *longue durée* of literary fraud', he argues, will find 'little radically new' in the writings of Chatterton and Ireland.[104] Grafton's universalist position on these matters is based on evidence which is partly psychological (readers in all ages exhibit a 'basic willingness . . . to be deceived') and partly formalist (literary forgers use the same 'basic techniques and topoi').[105] Paul Baines, on the other hand, sees no point in treating eighteenth-century literary forgeries Grafton-like as mere 'repetitions of an unvarying schema'.[106] He prefers to situate

[102] Geertz, *Interpretation of Culture*, 7.
[103] Grafton, *Forgers and Critics*, 49.
[104] Ibid., 56, 54.　　[105] Ibid., 35.
[106] Baines, 'Literary Forgery and the Ideology of Detection', 600.

literary forgeries in those socio-political contexts from which aestheticising critics seek to 'rescue' them. The distinctive feature of Macphossian, he finds, is not so much its elegiac grandeur as its 'barely concealed' Jacobitism; and literary forgery in the eighteenth century is fully intelligible only in terms of such matters as 'intense debate about the nature of paper currency and its value' and the juridical upgrading of forgery from a crime punishable by ear-cropping to a capital offence.[107] As formulated by Nick Groom, the rationale for this kind of enquiry is first 'to demonstrate that immediate context is so fundamental to the construction of a forgery that the forgery is clearly determined by it', and then to show how '[t]he narratives of forgery are plotted around a pre-existing set of co-ordinates'.[108] Whereas Grafton exhibits a uniformitarianism which enables him to establish continuities between historically discrete cultural phenomena, Baines and Groom are by contrast discontinuist in arguing for the uniqueness of an eighteenth-century socio-economic formation, whose discursive manifestations include those textual transgressions we call literary forgeries.

[107] Ibid., 597, 599.
[108] Groom, 'Forgery or Plagiarism?', 51–52.

CHAPTER 3

Cultivating spuriosity

Two intellectual developments in the final decades of the twentieth century made it possible to reconsider the relationship between 'genuine' and 'fake' literature. The more important was post-structuralist critical theory, which seriously challenged commonsense assumptions about such key components in traditional literary studies as authorship, originality, authenticity and value. And the other was the continuing anatomy of what Jean-François Lyotard labelled in 1979 'the postmodern condition', which enables us to see literary forgeries as in some ways normalised by the spuriosities of everyday life. Together they provide the tools with which to critique traditional strategies for concealing the scandal of literature as a cognitive mode. And by doing so they reveal how the ritual scapegoating of those caught perpetrating literary forgeries distracts attention from the spuriosity of literature itself.

An appropriate place to start is with the post-structuralist critique of binary oppositions in thought processes, the aim of which is to demonstrate that each of the terms paired as opposites in the structuring of knowledge is never wholly autonomous but always and already implicated in the other. The notion that knowledge can be advanced by arranging phenomena into paired sets of opposites is a venerable mode of analysis perpetuated in media representations of public debate. Aristotle attributed the method to the Pythagoreans, whose categories included right/left, male/female and good/evil; and a recent book on 'core sociological dichotomies' describes over twenty of them, including fact/value, public/private, relative/absolute, and work/leisure.[1] Etymologically, a 'dichotomous' practice merely cuts something in half; but in logic, the two components which result from division-by-dichotomy are deemed mutually ex-

---

[1] Jenks (ed.), *Core Sociological Dichotomies, passim.*

clusive: x and *not-x*. Common sense treats 'literature' and 'literary forgery' as logically dichotomous. As an analytic method, dichotomising underwent a revival in the structuralism that developed in the 1960s out of Ferdinand de Saussure's descriptive linguistics, which views language as structured by permutations of minimal units of sound called phonemes, each standing in binary opposition to the rest: m versus *not-m*, for instance, makes 'mat' *not* 'bat'/'cat'/'hat', etc. In structuralist analysis, these microstructures of language are assumed to be replicated homologously in the macrostructures of culture, whose dynamics are intelligible in terms of such binary oppositions as self/other (in the formation of subjectivity), white/ black (in the articulation of racial difference), west/east (in the construction of Eurocentrism), and above all nature/culture, which is the difference between the way things are and what we make them out to be, that is, how we 'construct' them.

In literary studies, misgivings about the heuristic efficacy of binary oppositions have come from various quarters, but notably from post-structuralist emphases on the slippages and seepages between the terms which constitute such pairs. The analytic ideal of mutual exclusivity degenerates in practice into interdependency, and notoriously in the distinction between 'self' and 'other', where each is so implicated in the other as to be compromised by it. As oppositionality gives way to varying degrees of interactivity, the preservation of binary oppositions comes to appear suspect at best and at worst harmful. It is seen as particularly invasive in the treatment of genital indeterminacy in babies classified as neither male nor female but intersexual. Since genitalia are treated as markers of sexual difference in a world made up of males and females, culture (in the form of gender assignment by corrective surgery) intervenes to reshape the neither-norisms produced occasionally by nature into that corporeal either-orism insisted upon by a culture whose gender practices are predicated on the existence of bodies fully compliant with the principle of sexual dimorphism. The construction of literary forgery as the binary opposite of literature depends similarly on the preservation of an either-orism which misleads Murray Warren into introducing his annotated bibliography of Chatterton's writings with the question, 'literary impostor or poet?'[2] How would traditional literary studies cope if the answer to that question were that Chatterton was

---

[2] Warren, *Descriptive and Annotated Bibliography of Chatterton*, 13.

both? Walpole, for instance, concluded from his textual encounters with Chatterton that 'a complete genius and a complete rogue can be formed before a man is of age'.[3] They wrote at a time when various binary oppositions – such as imitation/originality, history/fiction and authenticity/inauthenticity – were still in flux. The texts which occupied the spaces created by these emergent categories constituted intermediate cases whose terms were negotiable and whose effects were guaranteed to disturb either-orists. Donald S. Taylor observes that some of the sixty-odd documents Chatterton fabricated in order to authenticate his 'Rowley' poems constitute 'imaginary history'. But when he argues that this obliges us to read Chatterton as '*some* kind of historian', he is likely to alarm historians like Gordon S. Wood, who thinks that 'the discursive conventions of history' differ from those of 'historical novellas', and that the 'speculations' Simon Schama articulates and defends in his ficto-history, *Dead Certainties* (1991), are indeed 'unwarranted' in a historian.[4]

Critics who work with interactionist models of cultural analysis are more responsive to the toing-and-froing that goes on between those autonomous domains created by binary oppositions. The American currency artist, J.S.G. Boggs, aroused much interest with his one-side-only drawings of banknotes which are so realistic that in 1986 he was prosecuted for having reproduced British currency without the permission of the Bank of England. The products of his liminal activities were neither circulated as counterfeit money nor sold as art. By attempting to 'spend' his drawings in return for goods and services, Boggs drew attention to the arbitrariness of those cultural conventions that uphold the binary opposition between fiscal and aesthetic value.[5] A recognition that distinctions proposed by the analytic mind become permeable in particular circumstances is a recurrent theme in Philip J. Deloria's *Playing Indian* (1998), a book which shows how Native Americans and white 'Indian hobbyists' have interacted with one another to construct a shared notion of Indian 'authenticity'.[6] Henry Louis Gates likewise warns against drawing too sharp a distinction between 'authentic' narratives

---

[3] Meyerstein, *Life of Chatterton*, 282.
[4] Donald S. Taylor, *Chatterton's Art*, 46, 48; Schama, *Dead Certainties*, 322; Wood, 'Novel History', *passim*.
[5] Weschler, *Boggs*, 62.
[6] Deloria, *Playing Indian*, 148.

produced by African American slaves and the inauthenticities contributed to that genre by white Abolitionists. 'Many authentic slave narratives', Gates reports, 'were influenced by Harriet Beecher Stowe', who in turn included such narratives among her 'primary sources for her own imaginative work, *Uncle Tom's Cabin* [1852]'.[7] Such hybridities destabilise the dualism which represents the fake as a nefarious singularity, whose virtuous adversary is another putative singularity called the genuine. In these circumstances, an Hegelian oppositionalism which requires things to be either the 'same' or 'other' is less helpful than that same-and-different model developed by Gilles Deleuze, which assumes that because the structural relationship between x and y is formed by 'divergence' (*différenciation*) rather than 'negation' (*différentiation*), it results in a series of 'both-ands' rather than 'either-ors'.[8]

Various contexts are proposed for the postmodern obsolescence of binary opposition as a heuristic device. Some politicise it as replicating the global demise of Cold War dualism after the collapse of the USSR, and the consequent emergence of a new world order in which various 'Third' World countries participate; others see it as figured in Anthony Giddens' conception of a 'third way' in politics, which seeks to transcend the stand-off between left and right by making capitalist society more humane.[9] Whatever the logic of the grand design, the collapse of binary opposition is not only rationalised by post-structuralist critical theory but registered lexically by a proliferation of oxymora and portmanteau-words. Each of these describes a betwixt-and-betweenness which challenges the either-orism of prescriptive categorisation. The aestheticist opposition between 'art' and 'politics', for instance, has been weakened by the emergence of 'representation' as a critical term, which refers not only to what is depicted but also to the political right to be included and have one's say. Hybrid terms like 'faction' were devised to describe the kind of writing exemplified in Tom Wolfe's *The New Journalism* (1973) or Norman Mailer's *Armies of the Night* (1968), which resist categorisation as either factual or fictional. A generic meltdown of comparable magnitude is marked by the use of such terms as 'critifiction' or 'ficto-criticism' to describe writing which programmatically questions the distinction between 'primary' texts produced

[7] Gates, ' "Authenticity" ', 29.
[8] Deleuze, *Difference and Repetition*, xi-xii.
[9] Arac, 'Future of English after the Cold War', 10.

by creative writers and those 'secondary' texts which critics and scholars assemble around them.[10] Although Umberto Eco expressed his disapproval in 1986 of 'theoreticians [who] behave like writers of fiction', Norma Bouchard describes *Foucault's Pendulum* (1989) as 'a critifictional text, since it partakes of the same epistemological concerns informing Eco's latest theories of reading and interpretation'.[11] Geoff Dyer's *Out of Sheer Rage* (1997) presents itself as a novel which was 'intended to be a sober, academic study of D.H. Lawrence'. But because its narrator suffered a breakdown it ended up being only 'intermittently about Lawrence', although nevertheless sufficiently so to justify the inclusion of ten pages of end-notes which source episodes in Dyer's novel to Lawrence's own published writings.[12] Such *métissages* exert considerable pressure on cultural institutions whose taxonomies rest on the assumption that the maintenance of differences between one thing and another ensures the preservation and integrity of them all. Defenders of such institutions are as suspicious of Brian Matthews' ficto-biography of Henry Lawson's mother, *Louisa* (1987), as they are of Serge Doubrovsky's attempt to replace 'autobiography' by 'autofiction' in order to recognise the fictive component in every attempt at writing a self.[13]

In romanticised accounts of such phenomena, binary oppositions collapse under the pressures of desire, and specifically the desire of each component to experience its opposite. In a poem called 'News for the Delphic Oracle', W.B. Yeats – who had learnt from William Blake's *The Marriage of Heaven and Hell* (1790) that 'eternity is in love with the productions of time' – presents the relationship between mortality and immortality as a two-way traffic. For while the neo-Platonist philosopher Plotinus yearns to escape from the world of dying generations into a timeless realm of pure forms, the goddess Thetis is so attracted by the sensuality of our world as to marry a mortal, Peleus.[14] A much discussed postmodern example of the collapse of binary opposition has been that amalgam of the *cyb*ernetic and the *org*anic, the cyborg, 'a creation whose hybridity represents the fusion and confusion of pre-existing dichotomies, including those

---

[10] Federman, *Critifiction, passim*; Muecke and King, 'On Ficto-Criticism', *passim*.
[11] Bouchard, ' "Critifictional" Epistemes in Contemporary Literature', 500, 501.
[12] Dyer, *Out of Sheer Rage*, 170.
[13] Lejeune, *On Autobiography*, xii.
[14] Yeats, *Collected Poems*, 376–77.

surrounding race, gender, sexuality and class'.[15] As developed by
Donna Haraway in 'A Cyborg Manifesto' (1991), the cyborg func-
tions as 'a model of alterity with no sense of dualistic difference and
therefore no subordinated other'.[16] Media commentators complain
about the iniquities of hybridising information and entertainment as
'infotainment', or information and commercials as 'infomercials'.
Fiction and documentary entropise into 'mockumentary' or 'fictu-
mentary', a hybrid whose dramatic equivalent is the 'docudrama'.
The heritage industry routinely ignores distinctions between the
'authentic' and the 'reproduction' in the process of fabricating for
tourists 'authentic reproductions' of historically famous places, such
as colonial Williamsburg. Although Ada Louise Huxtable dislikes
such oxymora – because 'authentic is the real thing, and a reproduction, by definition, is not' – she herself distinguishes the 'real fake' of
Las Vegas from the 'fake fakes' of theme-parks.[17] In Williamsburg,
she complains, 'the blend of new and old, real and fake, original and
copy, even in the best of these restorations, defies separation or
analysis'.[18]

Yet the ubiquity of oxymora such as 'real fake' suggests that the
distinctions Huxtable seeks to preserve among artefacts are now
obsolescent. Singers who perpetuate country music in the guise of
various stock characters (such as 'old-timer', 'hillbilly' and 'cowboy')
are described by Richard A. Peterson as 'fabricating authenticity'.[19]
Original oil paintings in the distinctive styles of various modern
masters are available from a Manhattan gallery that trades under the
name of True Fakes Ltd.[20] In its London counterpart, Susie Ray sells
'hand painted Old Master and Impressionist paintings' to clients
who want an original of their own.[21] Such paradoxes cannot be
dismissed as merely postmodern chic. For when Amy G. Remensnyder assesses the influence of legendary information on the contents
of medieval reliquaries like the one at Conques – supposedly given to
the abbey by Charlemagne, and one of many such objects believed at
that time to contain Christ's foreskin – the term she uses to describe
such practices is 'imaginative memory', which again collapses the

---

[15] Armitt, *Theorising the Fantastic*, 9.
[16] Ibid., 76.
[17] Huxtable, *Unreal America*, 18, 75.
[18] Ibid., 17.
[19] Peterson, *Creating Country Music, passim.*
[20] Honan, 'Into an Age of Fake', C14.
[21] Beckett, *Fakes: Forgery and the Art World*, 118; Jones, 'Do Fakes Matter?', 11.

distinction between fiction and history.[22] In the writerly arts, a taste for what the *Monthly Review* was calling in September 1784 'modern antiques' was exemplified not only by ballad forgeries like *Hardyknute* (which elicited that remark) but also by Chatterton's distressed manuscripts.[23] Eric Hebborn used his extraordinary technical expertise to paint 'new Old' masters, and a study by Egbert Haverkamp-Begemann and Carolyn Logan of 'interpretative drawings from Michelangelo to Picasso' is called *Creative Copies* (1988).[24] This oxymoron is used also to describe the practice of medieval artists who transformed the models they followed into the style of their own time; and in post-medieval art the term 'creative copy' labels what results when Dürer imitates a Mantegna or Degas a Ucello.[25]

Societies which attempt to confer meaning on their activities by structuring behaviour in terms of binary opposites are plagued by the figure folklorists call 'Trickster', whose 'power derive[s] from his ability to live interstitially, to confuse and to escape the structures of society and the order of cultural things'.[26] Literary forgeries contribute to the mayhem created by representatives of this liminal figure. Although common sense has naturalised the distinction between 'literature' and 'literary forgery' so successfully that we regard it as a substantive difference, Trickster-theory makes it possible to think counter-intuitively of the 'spurious' and the 'genuine', and to see them not as opposites but rather as allotropic states of one another. Does this mean, then, that the term 'literary forgery' is itself an oxymoron, like 'gentleman publisher'?[27] I think it is described more accurately by the astronomical term 'syzygy'. Whereas the earliest citations of this word preserve the etymological sense of a 'yoking' or 'conjunction', subsequent usage incorporates the disjunctive sense of 'opposition'. Like the prefix 'key' in 'keyword' – which instantiates the contradictory activities of both opening and closing a lock – the word 'syzygy' incorporates a concealed antithesis, in this instance between conjunction and disjunction. Historically, 'literary forgery' has been understood solely

---

[22] Remensnyder, 'Legendary Treasure at Conques', 894–95.
[23] Hustvedt, *Ballad Criticism*, 252.
[24] Hebborn, *Drawn to Trouble*, 122.
[25] Caviness, 'Medieval Conservation, Restoration, Pastiche and Forgery', 205; Haverkamp-Begemann and Logan, *Creative Copies*, 15.
[26] Babcock-Adams, 'The Trickster and His Tales Reconsidered', 148.
[27] Lessing, *Diaries of Jane Somers*, [9].

as a disjunctive syzygy; this book, by contrast, puts a case for considering its conjunctive aspects.

The received wisdom of literary studies is that a fake literary text is merely supplementary to those genuine ones which make up the corpus of literature. Sometimes amusing, sometimes outrageous, but always deemed to be 'outside' literature, literary forgeries are classified as optional extras which right-minded readers will reject. Fake literature can therefore be dispensed with as easily as purists jettison sequels to the novels of Jane Austen or films of them. But if the notion of 'supplementing' is inflected by the ambiguity in the French *supplier*, it becomes possible to conceive of it as a syzygy which incorporates an endogenous difference between *adding to* something (by making good its deficiency) and *taking the place of* something. This distinction between the 'supplementary' and 'sub-stitutional' senses of the word 'supplement' clarifies the relationship between, say, *Pride and Prejudice* and a film of that novel, as well as the way in which literary forgeries relate to literature. It enables us to articulate more clearly a commonly encountered objection to the publication of texts designed to stand alongside such classic witness-narratives by Holocaust survivors as Primo Levi's *If This Be a Man* (1947). In claiming to be no more than modest additions to that massive archive of Shoah testimony whose function is to counter the prevailing amnesia in postmodern conditions, such bogus but well-written 'memoirs' – which may result from copycat behaviour induced by the heroisation of disaster – circulate more widely than the cruder texts of non-writers who actually experi-enced the events they narrate. In that respect they are substitu-tional supplements masquerading as supplementary supplements. A successful example by a 'wannabe' witness is Binjamin Wilkomirs-ki's *Fragments: Memories of a Wartime Childhood* (1996), which purports to reproduce its author's horrific experiences as a Latvian Jewish boy who miraculously survived the Polish death camps. Jewish readers were not alone in finding Wilkomirski's book offensive as soon as its classification was changed from supplementary to substitutional. Wilkomirski's rhetorical control of the genre, however, is masterly: if you did not know that *Fragments* is a substitutional text then you would praise it – as most people did initially, Jewish readers included – as a moving supplement, written in 'the hope that perhaps other people in the same situation would find the necessary support and strength to cry out their own traumatic childhood memories'.[28] That must have seemed a noble sentiment to all those Jewish literary judges who awarded Wilkomirski's book the Prix de Mémoire de la Shoah in France, the *Jewish Quarterly*'s Literary Prize in Britain, and the National Jewish Book Award in the United States. The substitutional supplement occupies as anomalous a position in the historical record as the counterfactual, which enables us to speculate about what might have taken place if what actually happened had not eventuated.[29] Understandably, most professional historians are inclined to treat counterfactuality as a problem merely 'supplementary' (in the usual sense) to the important business of establishing what happened. But creative writers and other explorers of 'heterologies' – the logics of othernesses – will continue to regard the production of substitutional supplements as worth taking risks for.

Speculations like these go against the grain of a commonsense conviction that because the structure of temporality is unilinear, the genuine always precedes the spurious. Yet the possibility that what common sense treats as posterior to something may well be anterior to it is exemplified in the history of the word 'heterosexuality', which was devised not (as heterosexuals assume) before the delineation of 'homosexuality' but after it. Thus the genuine may not be the origin from which spuriosity deviates or lapses. Instead, it may be a wholly imaginary state, like utopia, produced by the mechanism known to lexicographers as 'back-formation': that is, the genuine may be something extrapolated from the spurious as its imagined opposite, and then retrojected as its equally imagined antecedent – in the way that 'couth' and 'gruntled' are jokingly imagined to be the antecedent opposites of 'uncouth' and 'disgruntled'. The problem with such reversalism, however, is that it perpetuates the conundrum of priority. Furthermore, it is thought preposterous to claim that what comes naturally 'before' (*prae*) something – as a book precedes a book review – could ever be said to 'come after' it (*posterus*). Yet Stanislaw Lem's *Imaginary Magnitude* (1985) is 'pre-posterous' in precisely this sense, since it contains introductions to books not yet written, such as *A History of Bitic Literature* (2009), which includes any work of literature 'whose *real* author is not a human being' but a computer.[30]

I think it more productive to defer the problem of priority and

---

28 Wilkomirski, *Fragments*, 155.
29 For 'counterfactuals' see Ferguson (ed.), *Virtual History*, *passim*.
30 Lem, *Imaginary Magnitude*, 41.

proceed instead on the assumption that the 'genuine' and the 'spurious' are consubstantial, rather in the way that both Petrarchanism and anti-Petrarchanism are contemporaneous and interdependent in Renaissance English love poetry. What we learn from Freud's 1919 report on 'The "Uncanny" [*Unheimlich*]' is that spuriosity is always likely to be present in the genuine, *unheimlich*, if only as a return of the repressed, *nachträglich*.[31] Melancholy, as John Keats claims in his famous ode on that indisposition, is not external to happiness but already immanent in it, which explains why 'in the very temple of Delight / Veiled Melancholy has her sovran shrine'. The probability that spuriosity and genuineness are implicated in one another inextricably is supported by the theory of constitutive alterity, which holds that we discover what something is by understanding what it is not. In *Powers of Horror* (1980), for instance, Julia Kristeva argues that the expulsion of 'the abject' enables the subject to define itself in relation to what consequently is deemed 'other' to itself. Whatever has been 'abjected', however, will always return as the repressed: hence the abject becomes a spectral presence or 'secret sharer' in the subject which abjects it. A corollary of such speculations is that so-called 'genuine' literature is founded on the expulsion of precisely that which returns to haunt it, namely literary forgery.

The post-structuralist critique of essentialism enables us to understand that both literature and literary forgery are cultural constructs rather than discrete and autonomous essences. As categories of writing within specific traditions, they are therefore susceptible to reclassification without textual alteration. When someone called 'Our Nig' published in 1859 a book called *Our Nig* – 'sketches from the life of a free black' subjected to white racism, and copyrighted to 'Mrs. H.E. Wilson' – its author was assumed to have been white until Henry Louis Gates established that Harriet Wilson was 'most probably the first Afro-American to publish a novel in the United States'.[32] Not a word of *Our Nig* changed, however, since the evidence adduced to effect its reclassification was not intrinsic but circumstantial. Various benefits ensue from regarding cultural phenomena as constructs rather than essences. For a start, we can demystify received traditions by conducting historical enquiries into who

---

[31] Freud, *Standard Edition*, vol. XVII, 217–56.
[32] Harriet E. Wilson, *Our Nig*, intro. Gates, xxxiii, xiii.

constructed or 'invented' them, which is the procedure adopted by various contributors to Eric Hobsbawm and Terence Ranger's book, *The Invention of Tradition* (1983). Furthermore, since anything constructed is capable of being deconstructed, literary forgery can be shown to have many components in common with literature. Family resemblances are obscured if we treat literature and literary forgeries as sovereign domains, as different from one another as chalk from cheese.

An especially important development from the critique of essentialism has been a shift of critical emphasis from origins to effects. This is exemplified in Roland Barthes' essay on the 'reality-effect', but more particularly by Michel Foucault's account of how every text produces an 'author-function', which differs distinctively from those biographical traces that give us our impressions of its author as a historical personage.[33] This is worth remembering when people get upset by the work of writers who either confess to be or are outed as literary cross-dressers, such as William Sharp, who masqueraded so successfully as 'Fiona Macleod' (whose Christian name he took from *Fingal*) that he was able to contribute an entry on 'her' to *Who's Who*.[34] In terms of the theory of discursive effects, the appropriate question to ask of such texts is not who wrote them, which refers to an origin and a sex, but what author-effect they produce in their readers, which signals a destination and a gender. Any text marked by those discursive features which are recognised as 'feminine' will be read as feminine, even if its author happens to be biologically male, and whether or not he claims to be pro-feminist. The same principle holds for the gender-reversed case of Alice Sheldon, who in 1968 began publishing science fiction under the pseudonym of 'James Tiptree, Jr', and would have continued to be regarded as a male writer if she herself had not confessed eight years later to being female. Her most appreciative critic, Robert Silverberg, felt there was 'something ineluctably masculine about Tiptree's writing', and therefore found 'absurd' the suggestion that 'Tiptree' might be the pseudonym of a woman.[35] Ironically, one of the stories which convinced him that 'Tiptree' was a man is 'The Women Men Don't See [1973]', the title of which probably alludes to Ralph Ellison's

---

[33] Barthes, *Rustle of Language*, 141–48; Foucault, *Language, Counter-Memory, Practice*, 130–31.

[34] Gaskill, '"Ossian" Macpherson', 138; Drabble (ed.), *Oxford Companion to English Literature*, 892.

[35] 'James Tiptree, Jr', *Warm Worlds and Otherwise*, xii.

famous novel about the blacks whites don't see, *Invisible Man* (1952), and the oppressive consequences of that wilful aversion of the hegemonic gaze. Silverberg thought this story remarkable for being both 'profoundly feminist' and told in the 'entirely masculine manner' of a man whose 'obviously first-hand acquaintance with the world of airports and bureaucrats' substantiated the rumour that he was 'some sort of government agent involved in high-security work'.[36] On the evidence of these 'muscular' stories by an author who had an 'equally keen knowledge of the world of hunters and fishermen', Silverberg produced his identikit picture of 'Tiptree': 'a man of 50 or 55' – Sheldon was fifty-two when she became 'Tiptree' in 1968 – 'possibly unmarried, fond of outdoor life, restless in his everyday existence, a man who has seen much of the world and understands it well'.[37] After his essay had been reprinted as the introduction to a selection of stories by 'Tiptree' called *Warm Worlds and Otherwise* (1976), Sheldon wrote to tell Silverberg the correct answer to the Shakespearean question posed in his whimsical title, 'Who Is Tiptree, What Is He?' When her book was reprinted in 1979, Silverberg generously allowed his introductory essay to remain, adding in a postscript that Sheldon had 'called into question the entire notion of what is "masculine" or "feminine" in fiction'. This incident reveals just how easy it is to perform a gendered identity when the rhetorical techniques for doing so produce texts that confirm those stereotypical assumptions which mistakenly code human behaviour as either masculine or feminine.

The phenomenon most closely related to the concerns of this book is the 'authenticity-effect', without which the heritage industry would collapse. Any text – verbal or otherwise – which reproduces those effects which normally signify authenticity will be read as authentic, even if its provenance turns out to be bogus. Such effects do not (as they pretend) reproduce an antecedent reality, but instead produce the illusion of its existence, retroactively. How they succeed in doing so is revealed occasionally by operatives of a comparable feat of legerdemain, the 'erudition-effect'. Amusingly illustrated in Michael Kerrigan's vade-mecum, *Bluff Your Way in Literature* (1987), the 'erudition-effect' has some distinguished practitioners, including the twentieth-century's most respected poet-critic, T.S. Eliot. While lecturing in adult education courses, Eliot learned how to appear 'a

---

[36] Ibid., xvi, xii.　　　[37] Ibid., xv, xii, xiv.

prodigy of information'; and as a London reviewer working to tight deadlines he developed what he describes as 'a certain cunning in avoiding direct bluff', principally by 'only hinting at [his] pretended knowledge'. Some of this is displayed in his notes to *The Waste Land* (1922), which in 1957 he was to dismiss as 'bogus scholarship', thus inviting speculation as to whether the same can be said of his essay on 'The Metaphysical Poets' (1921), which was to become the most influential account of seventeenth-century English poetry for the next forty years.[38] If Lyotard is to be believed, an equally impressive gallery of erudition-effects is on display in his now classic study, *La Condition postmoderne* (1979), a 'report on knowledge' commissioned by the government of Quebec. Three years after the English translation of this book in 1984, Lyotard was quoted as saying that it was 'all a bit of parody', because in preparing it he had 'made up stories' and 'referred to a quantity of books [he]'d never read'.[39] In the absence of such confessions, however, skilfully deployed erudition-effects may create a reputation for learnedness that lasts well beyond the lifetime of their perpetrator. In Sir Thomas Browne's *Religio Medici* (1643), for instance, information garnered on a wide range of topics related directly or tangentially to religion is franked with the pronoun 'I' and then recirculated as Browne's own thoughts in what consequently is taken to be an intellectual autobiography. And another successful self-fashioner as a polymath was Browne's contemporary, the diarist John Evelyn, whom Guy de la Bédoyère describes as 'adept at making it appear that he was better-read than he actually was', instancing Evelyn's raids on St Augustine's *Confessions*, Montaigne's *Essais* (1580–88) and compendiums like Erasmus' *Adagia* (1500) for out-of-the-way references and quotable quotes.[40] Sound advice on infusing 'an air of erudition' into one's writing is given in an essay on 'How to Write a *Blackwood* Article' (1838) by Edgar Allan Poe, who similarly demystifies poetry into an ensemble of contrivances for producing calculable effects when using his best-known poem ('The Raven') as an example of 'The Philosophy of Composition' (1846).[41]

The Foucauldian theory of language that underpins the discursive theory of effects views words as constituting rather than reflecting our sense of the real. A corollary of this position meets with

38 Ruthven, *Ezra Pound as Literary Critic*, 37–38.
39 Anderson, Perry, *Origins of Postmodernity*, 26.
40 Bédoyère, 'Evelyn and the Art of Quoting', 16.
41 Poe, *Complete Tales*, 126–32.

considerable resistance: namely, that since our understanding of events in the world is constructed discursively, those events are spectral by comparison with the immediacy of the verbal and visual media used when reporting them. The *reductio ad absurdum* of this argument is epitomised in the much maligned title of Jean Baudrillard's *The Gulf War Did Not Take Place* (1991), which argues that people who sought news of that war had to make do instead with a media-massaged and disinformational simulacrum of it. No such difficulties attend the claim that, in fiction, reality is discursively constructed, since there is no reality outside the text for a work of fiction to 'reflect'. The point of departure for such speculations is Ferdinand de Saussure's atomisation of the linguistic 'sign' (the word) into a 'signified' (what it refers to) and a 'signifier' (the sound, rhythm and other material properties of the word). This distinction enables signification to be privileged over reference in the economy of language, and especially the language of literature. Thus Barthes describes the literary text as a 'galaxy of signifiers' rather than a raft of referents.[42] In a literary work, none of these signifiers has a complementary signified except in the eyes of literary tourists and the businesses that cater for their interests by converting the signifiers of fiction into referents. Admirers of *Wuthering Heights* (1847), for instance, can be induced to visit Haworth in order to see a ruined Elizabethan farmhouse – formerly called 'Top Withins', but now renamed for their benefit 'Wuthering Heights' – and to experience for themselves what it is like to be wuthered on the Yorkshire moors.

Whether or not fictional characters and incidents refer to people and events in the real world is a question of interest not only to readers and literary critics but also to legal theorists, who debate whether imaginative writing can be actionable under the law of defamation. Proponents of the theory that literature is characterised by 'irreference' (the term introduced by Mary Kinzie apropos the non-referential properties of John Ashbery's poetic diction) seek to disclaim liability for fiction by producing variations on the formula that any resemblance between the characters in a novel and persons living or dead is purely coincidental.[43] Opponents of this view, however, usually base their case on the evidence of realist fiction, which they take to be typical of all literary production. The fictional

---

[42] Barthes, *S/Z*, 5.
[43] Kinzie, ' "Irreference" ', 267.

representations in John Steinbeck's *The Grapes of Wrath* (1939), writes
Frederick Schauer, 'are hooked onto the real world': that novel
would never have received the laudatory attention it did in the
absence of such extra-textual realities as 'real dust bowls, real
hunger, and real "Okies"'.[44] Schauer's confidence that *The Grapes of
Wrath* represents an intransigent real was to be contested a decade
later by Charles J. Shindo, whose *Dust Bowl Migrants in the American
Imagination* (1997) reveals the mismatch between the historicity of the
rural Depression in America and mythopoeic treatments of it in both
Steinbeck's novel and John Ford's film (1940), as well as in Dorothea
Lange's documentary photograph of a *Migrant Mother* (1936) and
Woody Guthrie's *Dust Bowl Ballads* (1940). Schauer concludes that
because novelists are given extraordinary privileges they should
behave responsibly. As 'intentional user[s] of falsehood', licensed to
ply their trade in societies that place a higher value on truth-telling
than on tale-telling, they should not expect to be exempt from
prosecution when what they write is judged defamatory.[45] Other
contributors to the symposium at which Schauer delivered this
judgement disagreed. 'Libel claims based on fiction should be lightly
dismissed', Garbus and Kurnit argue, 'because they tread so heavily
on something so delicate and so valuable'.[46] A striking feature of this
exchange between legal theorists is their common assumption that
all imaginative works are ultimately referential. That conviction is
bolstered by books like William Amos' *The Originals* (1985), whose
subtitle promises to reveal 'who's really who in fiction', and M.C.
Rintoul's *Dictionary of Real People and Places in Fiction* (1993). Authorial
denials of referential specificity are equally common, however. When
accused of having based his characterisation of Miss Birdseye in *The
Bostonians* (1886) on Nathaniel Hawthorne's sister-in-law, Miss
Peabody, Henry James replied that Miss Birdseye was drawn not
from life but from his 'moral consciousness'.[47] Such answers do not
impress victims in such cases, who find themselves in the awkward
position of having to argue that the fictional character they take
exception to not only represents them (since everybody will recognise
'Miss Birdseye' as a portrait of Miss Peabody) but also *mis*represents
them (because 'Miss Birdseye' is a travesty of Miss Peabody).

---

[44] Schauer, 'Liars, Novelists, and Defamation', 261.
[45] Ibid., 266–67.
[46] Garbus and Kurnit, 'Libel Claims Based on Fiction', 423.
[47] Vivian Deborah Wilson, 'Law of Libel and the Art of Fiction', 38.

According to the speech-act theory pioneered by J.L. Austin in *How to Do Things with Words* (1962) and developed by John Searle in his book on *Speech Acts* (1969), language is better understood in terms of performativity than reference. We use it not merely to denote things but to perform certain actions, in the way that a literary forgery performs authenticity. Austinian performativity was appropriated for gender studies by Judith Butler, who introduced it in *Gender Trouble* (1990) before developing 'a politics of the performative' in *Excitable Speech* (1997). In a famous essay on 'womanliness as masquerade', Joan Riviere argues that women are obliged to perform femininity in patriarchal societies: here 'identity' is not an immutable essence but an unstable amalgam of fictions performed for calculated effects in the *theatrum mundi*. Riviere's essay was published in 1929, the same year as Nella Larsen's novel, *Passing*, which takes as its title the term first used in the 1830s of runaway slaves whose skin-colour was pale enough for them to pass as white and thus trespass in white society. The term has broadened as a result of being adopted by people hoping to avoid the consequences of being stereotyped by their social class, ethnicity, sexuality or gender; various contributors to Elaine K. Ginsberg's book on *Passing and the Fictions of Identity* (1996) present it in performative terms as a means of escaping subordination and oppression in racist and homophobic societies.[48] Helen Darville was under no such pressure when she decided to perform a different ethnicity by literally performing Ukrainian dances in order to display the cultural heritage she had souvenired by masquerading as 'Helen Demidenko'; nor indeed was George Psalmanazar, when he performed oriental 'savagery' in cultivated London by being seen to eat raw meat.[49] Such activities are never condoned on the grounds that some people are 'transculturals' in the way that others are transsexuals. On the contrary, putting on the style of cultural otherness is disparaged as equivalent to whites donning 'blackface' when performing in minstrel shows. One example is the 'yellowface' used by Kenneth Rexroth when inventing 'Marichiko', a Japanese woman whose poems he claimed to have translated when publishing them in 1978; but a more complex phenomenon is the 'redface' adopted by Sylvester Long (whose parents were classified as black in North

[48] Ginsberg (ed.), *Passing and the Fictions of Identity*, 3.
[49] O'Connell, 'Demidenko and the Performance of Difference', 44; Lee, 'Psalmanazar', 439.

Carolina) in order to acquire a professional identity in journalism and the movies as 'Buffalo Child Long Lance', the first two names having been conferred on him at a Blackfoot ceremony.[50] In the Scarlet Pimpernel version of performativity, you present yourself as too stupid to be capable of forging the text you are associated with: William Squire, for instance, 'played the role of daft provincial' so well that Thomas Carlyle never suspected him of having forged the thirty-five letters by Oliver Cromwell that Carlyle published as genuine in 1847.[51] But you can be protected equally well by the unwarranted presumption of your stupidity: thus Johnson could no more believe that 'a vulgar uneducated stripling' called Chatterton had written the 'Rowley' poems than Ireland *père* could accept that his feckless son was the author of *Vortigern*.[52]

Performative gestures are structured by a desire to escape entrapment by experiencing those identitarian freedoms promised by the pursuit of alterity. Armand Schwerner, for instance, registered his disaffection from his Jewish identity by becoming that imaginary 'scholar-translator' who 'transmitted' through him English versions of non-existent Sumerian texts collected as *The Tablets* (1999). Because psychiatry appears to hold the key to such activities, some of the syndromes it has identified promise scientific explanations of why literary forgers behave as they do. Yet the objectivity of such models is questionable when they themselves turn out to have literary sources. During the 'Demidenko' scandal, the term 'Munchausen's syndrome' was bandied about as if it were a scientific description of what was wrong with Helen Darville. Yet the term itself is literary in origin: it derives from a collection of tall stories written in English by a German mineralogist called Rudolph Erich Raspe, who went to England disguised as a Dutchman to avoid accusations of embezzlement back home. Issued anonymously under the title of *Singular Travels, Campaigns and Adventures of Baron Munchausen* (1785), it satirised the *Narrative of Marvellous Travels and Campaigns in Russia*, published the same year by Baron Karl Friedrich Hieronymus von Münchhausen, whose legal action against Raspe's lampoon was unsuccessful.[53] Furthermore, 'Munchausen's syndrome' may well have been a

---

[50] 'Marichiko', 'Love Poems' 103; Smith, Donald B., *Long Lance*, 76–77, 102.
[51] Ryals, 'Carlyle and the Squire Forgeries', 517.
[52] Meyerstein, *Life of Chatterton*, 466; Grebanier, *Great Shakespeare Forgery*, 241.
[53] Haddy, 'Münchhausen of Munchausen Syndrome', 142; Blumenthal, *False Literary Attributions*, 16–17.

facetious coinage when Richard Asher introduced it in 1951 (and in a medical, not a psychiatric, journal) to describe the behaviour of people who turn up at hospitals with scarred bodies and tall tales about how they acquired them. For after quoting Pooh Bah from Gilbert and Sullivan's *The Mikado* (1885), and defining the condition as an 'intense desire to deceive everybody as much as possible', Asher compares it with the 'Walter Mitty syndrome', which he names after a short story by the American humorist, James Thurber, called 'The Secret Life of Walter Mitty [1942]'.[54] Such accounts are inflected generically by a tradition of medical humour. Moreover, Chris Amirault reports that the literariness of Munchausen's syndrome has been so contagious among those who describe instances of it that it is on its way out as a psychiatric term, and is being replaced in medical discourse by the term 'factitious disorder', whose purpose is to redirect attention from tale-telling – what J.C. Barker characterised in 1962 as *pseudologica fantastica* – to the simulated behaviour that characterises sufferers from the syndrome.[55]

These developments have taken place in what Guy Debord designated in 1967 'the society of the spectacle', which he regards as an inevitable consequence of 'modern conditions of production'.[56] As a result, 'everything that [once] was directly lived has moved away into a representation'.[57] That 'immense accumulation of *spectacles*' which saturates our everyday lives alienates us by transforming our lived sense of reality into 'a pseudo-world *apart*', and therefore 'an object of mere contemplation'.[58] In this respect, notes Sadie Plant, people have become 'spectators of their own lives'.[59] Social life experienced a major casualty when industrial capitalism stimulated a desire for commodities, since this resulted in the 'degradation of *being* into *having*', one sign of which was the phenomenon described in 1899 by Thorstein Veblen as 'conspicuous consumption' and displayed in the mansion of the great Gatsby.[60] But now that social life is dominated completely by the economics of production, Debord argues, there has been 'a generalized sliding of *having* into *appearing*'.[61]

[54] Asher, 'Munchausen's Syndrome', 339.
[55] Amirault, '*Pseudologica Fantastica* and Other Tall Tales', 175, 183.
[56] Debord, *Society of the Spectacle*, n.p., no. 1.
[57] Ibid.   [58] Ibid., nos. 1, 2.
[59] Plant, *Most Radical Gesture*, 1.
[60] Debord, *Society of the Spectacle*, no. 17; Veblen, *Theory of the Leisure Class*, 43–62.
[61] Debord, *Society of the Spectacle*, no. 17.

In the course of this totalisation of 'appearing', an earlier society of conspicuous consumers has metamorphosed into the society of the 'spectacle', which – by substituting intangible images for tangible commodities – signals the triumph of commodity fetishism. A decade or so later, when Debord revisited *la société du spectacle*, he had not been persuaded by Michel Foucault's argument that modern society is characterised by 'surveillance' rather than 'spectacle'.[62] Instead, the 'tendency' he had observed 'to replace the real with the artificial' had since become 'ubiquitous'.[63] And as an example of how, in the society of the spectacle, 'what is genuine is *reconstructed* . . . to resemble the false', he instances the repristination of the Sistine Chapel ceiling by experts at work 'restoring' to Michelangelo's frescoes 'the fresh, bright colours of a cartoon strip', thus ensuring that they will attract the attention of those mechanical agents of spectacularisation, 'the tourists' cameras'.[64] In the cultural conditions of late capitalism, sport is similarly spectacularised. 'The "real" football is now the spectacle of football', Plant observes: 'the televised match becomes better than "being there"'.[65] And one of the things which makes it better is that indispensable adjunct to the pleasures of watching sport at two removes, the slow-motion action-replay, which offers an infinitely repeatable micro-spectacle in the virtual spectacle of a real-time sport called football.

Six years before this *marxisant* elegy for the way we were before commodification and spectacularisation set in, the American sociologist, Daniel J. Boorstin, published a book called *The Image* (1961), the subtitle of which was renamed in the paperback reprint of 1964 'a guide to pseudo-events in America'. 'Pseudo-event' is Boorstin's term for a 'new kind of synthetic novelty which has flooded our experience'.[66] Unlike events, which happen unpredictably before they are reported (if at all), a pseudo-event is created precisely in order to be 'reported or reproduced', in the way that press-agents of out-and-about politicians stage photo-opportunities for journalists.[67] The structuring of pseudo-events as news creates the illusion that they are newsworthy; indeed, 'it is the report that gives the event its force'.[68]

---

[62] Foucault, *Discipline and Punish*, 217.
[63] Debord, *Comments on Society of the Spectacle*, 51.
[64] Ibid., 50–51.
[65] Plant, *Most Radical Gesture*, 68.
[66] Boorstin, *The Image*, 9.
[67] Ibid., 11.   [68] Ibid., 10.

The contents of such reports are not facts but what Norman Mailer
had already called (apropos Marilyn Monroe) 'factoids': 'facts which
have no existence before appearing in a magazine or a newspaper'.[69]
Pseudo-events are not only 'more dramatic' than actual events but
'easier to disseminate and to make vivid', because they are 'planned
for dissemination'.[70] Being 'more intelligible and hence more reassuring' than real events, they are 'more persuasive than reality
itself'.[71] Not surprisingly, therefore, 'whenever . . . a pseudo-event
competes for attention with a spontaneous event in the same field, the
pseudo-event will tend to dominate'.[72] When news 'gathering' is
obliged to compete with news 'making' in the limited space available
for news 'reporting', we witness the operation of a 'new Gresham's
law': 'counterfeit happenings tend to drive spontaneous happenings
out of circulation'.[73] The fate of 'real' news in such conditions is
symptomatic of many other 'new varieties of unreality' catalogued
and analysed by Boorstin.[74] These include the supersession of
travellers by tourists and of heroes by celebrities, who are famous
merely for being famous. Boorstin's anecdotal style and mass of
empirical data make *The Image* a very different kind of book from *La
Société du spectacle* (1967), whose theoretical positionings render it less
accessible for anglophone readers unaccustomed to Gallic abstraction
in social analysis. Nevertheless, both books assume that the real is
readily at hand as a touchstone when critiquing various kinds of
unreality. Debord retains his faith in an authenticity that Situationists
like himself thought they could restore by deconstructing the factitiousness of the spectacle. Boorstin likewise never questions the
existence of an 'underlying reality' to which he himself has unmediated access.[75] Despite the saturation bombing of his intelligence
and sensibilities by media outlets and advertising corporations with
vested interests in marketing the spurious, Boorstin presents himself
as somebody who has resisted being brainwashed because his own
sense of reality is not a cultural construct but the gift of a natural
common sense.

Such confidence is treated as illusory by most analysts of the
postmodern condition, and especially by Jean Baudrillard in his
study of *Simulacra* (1981). This book, which describes the gradual

[69] Mailer, *Marilyn*, 18.
[70] Boorstin, *The Image*, 39.
[71] Ibid., 36.   [72] Ibid., 39.   [73] Ibid., 40.
[74] Ibid., viii.   [75] Ibid., 21.

evacuation of the real from representation as a fourfold process, can be used to model the fate of representation in the history of literature.[76] In the course of this trajectory, representation begins as 'the reflection of a basic reality', which is the condition literature aspires to whenever a taste for realist fiction dominates. Subsequently, representation 'masks and perverts a basic reality', as fiction tends to do by means of its invented characters and counterfactual scenarios, which collectively constitute those secondary worlds or heterocosms that refugees from reality resort to for private pleasures. At the third stage in this Baudrillardian schema, representation 'masks the *absence* of a basic reality'; literature achieves this by privileging the signifier over the referent, a manoeuvre which enables French Symbolist poets to refine a *poésie pure* uncontaminated by reference to the real. And by the time that postmodern novelists develop self-reflexive metafictions that avoid contact with the real – which they do partly by concentrating on the fictive processes that bring their texts into existence, and partly by positioning those texts primarily in relation to other works of fiction – we reach the terminal phase of Baudrillard's *trajectoire*, at which representation 'bears no relation to any reality whatever', because it has become 'its own pure simulacrum'. When it is no longer possible to dissociate the signifier from the signified, or representations from realities, reality becomes redundant. Its place is occupied by 'hyperreality', whose constituent simulacra distinguish themselves from other kinds of representation by *preceding* the real instead of following it. In this 'precession' of simulacra – to quote the *franglais* encountered in English translations of Baudrillard's *précession* ('precedingness') – images without any grounding reference to the real interact meaninglessly with one another in an empire of signs.

Spuriosity is thus normalised in Baudrillard's postmodern world, symptoms of which – such as the Disneyfication of the global real in the wake of cocacolonisation, and the transformation of the actual into theme parks and tourist destinations – are recorded amusingly in Umberto Eco's 1975 report on his encounters with the hyperreal in the USA. *Travels in Hyperreality* is the 1987 title of the book published in 1986 as *Faith in Fakes*, which focuses on tourist spectacles that exemplify the 'America of furious hyperreality'.[77] A semiotician

---

[76] Baudrillard, *Simulations*, 11.
[77] Eco, *Travels in Hyperreality*, 7.

masquerading as a tourist, Eco searches for 'the Absolute Fake' as passionately as pilgrims seek vestiges of the true faith in sacred places, and finds himself in various new-world locations guaranteed to affront his old-world sensibilities.[78] These include museums which translate Leonardo da Vinci's *The Last Supper* into a waxwork display, complete with symphonic background music and portentous voice-overs; the mansion of William Randolph Hearst ('the Xanadu of *Citizen Kane*'), which not only erases both temporal and geographical distance by enabling *objets d'art* from different times and places to congregate on the same site, but segues the genuine acquisitions seamlessly into their fake settings; and 'absolutely fake cities', from Disneyland in California to Disney World in Florida, with their similarly eclectic reconstructions of historically diverse moments in places globally distant from one another. For Baudrillard, the manifest unreality of Disneyland is strategically important to America's image of itself. Its function is to persuade 'us' – the implied consensus here includes both sophisticated Europeans like himself and Americans acculturated into European sophistication – that the rest of America is real, 'when in fact all of Los Angeles and the America surrounding it are no longer real, but of the order of the hyperreal and of simulation'.[79] Eco went there to confirm his hunch that whereas 'the American imagination demands the real thing', it is obliged paradoxically to 'fabricate the absolute fake' in order to attain it.[80] To 'see Tom Sawyer immediately after Mozart', or to 'enter the cave of *The Planet of the Apes* after having witnessed the Sermon on the Mount with Jesus and the Apostles', is to become convinced that 'the logical distinction between Real World and Possible Worlds has been definitively undermined'.[81] This kind of criticism, however, tends not to be directed against those high-brow modernist texts which bring time past and time present into the timeless present of a *musée imaginaire*. Nobody complains, for instance, about the hyperreality of T.S. Eliot's *The Waste Land* (1922), in which the Great War of 1914–18 is contemporaneous with the Punic Wars of the third century BC, and London occupies the same textual space as the Ganges in India and Lake Leman in Switzerland. To admirers of Eliot's poetry, such collocations evince an admirable sense of what

---

[78] Ibid., 40.
[79] Baudrillard, *Simulations*, 25.
[80] Eco, *Travels in Hyperreality*, 8.
[81] Ibid., 14.

he himself called 'tradition'; but if anyone were to build something along the lines of Gary Hallgren's drawing of *The Waste Land* as a theme park, its contents would be regarded as a tasteless assemblage of postmodern kitsch.[82]

In most cultural commentary, 'simulacrum' is a derogatory term. Ada Louise Huxtable, for instance, deplores the way in which, in turn-of-the-millennium America, 'the replica is accepted as genuine and the simulacrum replaces the source'.[83] Distinctions between the real and the false are not only not made nowadays but no longer deemed necessary in a culture that prefers accessible and user-friendly simulacra to the aura and resonance of authentic artefacts and locations. 'Simulation', she observes, 'has a logic and special attraction for those who like their jungles plastic and their heroes animatronic'; and the fact that 'those who do are legion' is regrettable.[84] Even when such goings-on provoke amusement rather than outrage, and the critique undergoes a correspondingly generic switch from polemic to comedy, as it does in Julian Barnes' novel, *England, England* (1998), simulacra continue to be regarded as deplorable. *England, England* describes how some of the randomly distributed sites of English cultural capital come to be replicated and relocated more accessibly for tourists on the Isle of Wight. This operation is marketed as a quintessentialising gesture designed to do for England what *poésie pure* aspired to do for poetry, which is to eliminate the superfluities. Its effect is to make England obsolete and therefore redundant, since it cannot compete in either attractiveness or convenience with its simulacrum. The entrepreneur who oversees this simulacrisation of England hires a 'French intellectual' to explain the theory behind it. In the course of telling the developers 'that in the modern world we prefer the replica to the original because it gives us the greater *frisson*', the Frenchman quotes – but does not name – Guy Debord on how, in the twentieth century, mere representations became substitutes for the former practice of living a life.[85] He expresses astonishment, however, that Debord intended this 'profound truth' to be taken 'as criticism not praise'.[86] At this moment, a Nietzschean 'transvaluation' of the simulacrum appears

[82] Hallgren, 'Eliot's *Wasteland*', 126–27.
[83] Huxtable, *Unreal America*, 2.
[84] Ibid., 9.
[85] Barnes, *England, England*, 54.
[86] Ibid., 54–55.

imminent. But *England, England* is not interested in thinking 'other-wise' about the problem of the simulacrum: the French intellectual is given a cameo-role merely to reassure theorophobic readers that such people are purveyors of dangerous nonsense.

England, England would have been a very different novel if Barnes' French intellectual had been modelled on Gilles Deleuze, whose enquiries into the philosophical origins of the simulacrum led him back to Plato's *Sophist*, which identifies two different sorts of repre-sentation: the 'good' icon and the 'bad' simulacrum. In Platonist accounts, the icon is tolerable because – as a copy of an original – it at least attempts to reproduce an ideal reality, and can be judged by the proximity of its resemblance to it. The simulacrum, by contrast, is pernicious because it reproduces mere appearances, and is allied with the sophistry and rhetoric to which Plato's philosophy was opposed. In its determination to ensure 'the triumph of the copies over simulacra', Deleuze argues, Platonism was committed to 're-pressing simulacra'.[87] Consequently, the fulfilment of Friedrich Nietzsche's ambition ' "to reverse Platonism" ' can be achieved only by going against the grain of a culture whose ways of thinking have been thoroughly Platonised. In this case, it involves first perceiving that 'the simulacrum is not a degraded copy', and then recognising its subversive potential in 'harbor[ing] a positive power which denies *the original and the copy, the model and the reproduction*'.[88] This redemptive manoeuvre puts a positive spin on the much despised simulacrum by redefining it as the site of creativity rather than the absence of reality. It valorises the ability of art to unmoor itself from reference to the real and to flourish in a realm of pure signs. Photorealist paintings, for instance, which strive to look like photographs of the things they depict (rather than the things themselves), are simulacral in this positive and Deleuzean sense. So too are those ecphrastic passages in Sidney's *Arcadia* (1590) and Spenser's *The Faerie Queene* (1596), which read like descriptions of paintings or tapestries of the scenes they describe. Instead of striving towards translucency, and creating the illusion of an unmediated and therefore immediate contact with the real, the authors of such texts distance themselves from it by thickening the layers of mediation, thus liberating themselves from the tyranny of reference to the real. In this way they exhibit what

---

[87] Deleuze, 'Simulacrum and Ancient Philosophy', 257.
[88] Ibid., 262.

Deleuze had called in his earlier book on *Nietzsche and Philosophy* (1962) 'the power of the false', which he glosses as that '*will* to deceive . . . which alone is capable of competing with the ascetic ideal and successfully opposing it'. This is why art is so important: it 'invents the lies that raise falsehood to this highest affirmative power'.[89]

A key exhibit in Deleuze's demonstration of 'the power of the false' is *F for Fake* (1975), a mockumentary film by Orson Welles about two well-known fakemeisters. One is the Hungarian artist, Elmyr de Hory, who specialised in faking canvases by modern masters such as Matisse and Picasso. The other is Clifford Irving who, before he was imprisoned for having fabricated the 'autobiography' of the movie-mogul, Howard Hughes, had published a biography of de Hory – 'the greatest art forger of our time' – called *Fake!* (1969), which Welles thought 'might be a fake about a fake faker'.[90] De Hory's portrait of Irving (labelled 'con man of the year') appeared on the cover of *Time* on 21 February 1972, when its lead-story was 'the fabulous hoax of Clifford Irving'. According to Deleuze, however, forgers like de Hory do not exhibit the full 'power of the false' because, lacking 'the power of metamorphosis', they cultivate instead an 'exaggerated taste for *form*'. It takes a creative artist to exercise 'the power of the false to a degree which is realized, not in form, but in trans-formation'.[91] The simulacrum, in Deleuze's contribution to the reversal of Platonism, achieves its full potential only in 'genuine' art.

An influential agent in the simulacrisation of the real in post-modern conditions has been the computer, whose ability to conjure up the virtual reality of a world without origins – 'copies of things that no longer have origins' – is the subject of Sherry Turkle's study of *Life on the Screen* (1995), which investigates the virtualisation of subjectivities in a culture of simulation.[92] The computerisation of financial transactions enabled corporate fraud to become 'the growth industry' of the 1980s, according to the subtitles of a couple of books on the topic: Harry West's *Fraud* (1987) and Mihir Bose and Cathy Gunn's *Fraud* (1989). Its manufacturing counterpart has been so successful that the industrial counterfeiting of brand-name pro-ducts is a global practice now considered ineradicable.[93] Meanwhile,

---

[89] Durham, *Phantom Communities*, 8.
[90] Combs, 'Welles's *F for Fake*', 221.
[91] Deleuze, 'Powers of the False', 146.
[92] Turkle, *Life on the Screen*, 47.
[93] Warneminde, 'Fakes: The Futile Fight', 36.

the digitalisation of images and the undetectable manipulation of them by a process called 'morphing' has effected the demise of claims made on behalf of photography as a veridical medium. 'Photographic' is no longer an honorific adjective to attach to 'realism' as it was when Theodore Dreiser published *Sister Carrie* (1900).[94] Furthermore, one by one the twentieth century's iconic photographs, which immortalise as epic images what appear to be moments of spontaneous human behaviour, are being shown to have acquired their evocative powers by calculated artfulness. Among them are Dorothea Lange's *The Migrant Mother* (1936) and Robert Capa's Spanish Civil War masterpiece, *Death of a Republican Soldier* (1937). In Alfred Stieglitz's *The Steerage* (1907) the working-class Europeans who gaze apprehensively from the lower decks of a ship at the New World which offers liberty to the oppressed were photographed in fact on a vessel bound for Europe; and Alfred Eisenstaedt's *Life* magazine photograph of a nurse and a sailor spontaneously celebrating the end of the Second World War with a passionate embrace had been rehearsed and shot months earlier in readiness for VJ Day. If seeing is no longer believing, neither is hearing. The audio equivalent of morphing enabled the actor playing the hero of Gerard Corbiau's film, *Farinelli* (1995), to be praised for lip-synching a castrato voice with a range of three-and-a-half octaves, digitally created by seamlessly melding the recorded voices of a soprano and a counter-tenor. Only five years earlier, however, a male duo marketed as Milli Vanilli had been stripped of their Grammy award when it was discovered that instead of singing in live performances they had merely lip-synched the voices of a less photogenic trio, one of whom was female.[95]

Bogus quotations are remembered because they ought to have originated with the people they are attributed to. The fact that no ancient text corroborates Shakespeare's certainty that Caesar said to one of his assassins, *Et tu, Brute* ('you too, Brutus'), has not impeded the circulation of these words as a familiar quotation. Most of the bogus quotations collected by Paul F. Boller and John George in *They Never Said It* (1989) are the product of a communal revisionism misnamed misquotation. Nobody wants to know that it was Charles Dudley Warner and not Mark Twain who remarked that 'everybody

[94] Orvell, *Real Thing*, 125.
[95] Posey *et al.* (eds.), *Hoaxes and Deceptions*, 35–36.

talks about the weather but no one does anything about it', even though Warner collaborated with Twain on the novel whose title was to name the era of Reconstruction following the Civil War in America, *The Gilded Age* (1873).[96] Jeffrey Burton Russell has not eliminated the misconception that nobody knew the earth was round until Christopher Columbus sailed to America in 1492.[97] The myth persists because a triumphalist narrative of Enlightenment requires there to have been a preceding age of superstitious ('monkish') ignorance in which people believed that the earth is flat. Another ineradicable misconception provides the title of Geoffrey K. Pullum's *The Great Eskimo Vocabulary Hoax* (1991), a book which popularised Laura Martin's exposure of the myth that the Inuit and Yukik languages (homogenised as 'Eskimo') exhibit scores of words for different types of snow, when in fact 'Eskimo has about as much differentiation as English does for "snow" at the monolexemic level: snow and flake'.[98] Literary testimonies to the power of the false include James Whitcomb Riley's pseudo-Poe poem called 'Leonainie', which its admirers refused to accept as fake even after Riley had admitted to writing it.[99] Literature makes such misrepresentations memorable. Popular perceptions of Richard III are still determined by Shakespeare's characterisation of him in *Richard III*, and Shakespeare's Owen Glendower in *Henry IV, Part One* represents English prejudices against the Welsh far too well to allow that characterisation to be discredited by what is known about the historical Owain Glyndwr.

Pleasure in the spurious helps perpetuate it, as is evident in the commercial success of drag-shows and all-in wrestling. Re-enactments of historical events for the entertainment of tourists who visit heritage sites elicit the same pleasure in the bogus as other products of retromania, such as mock'n'roll performed by Elvis Presley lookalikes, and tribute bands with names like The Rolling Clones. Some of these – like Bjorn Again, the group which impersonates Abba – have become as famous as their originals through enabling audiences embarrassed by the musical tastes of their youth to re-experience the pleasure of such music guiltlessly in having it recycled as parody. Anybody can enjoy sham without shame by cultivating a camp

[96] Blumenthal, *False Literary Attributions*, 9.
[97] Russell, *Inventing the Flat Earth, passim.*
[98] Laura Martin, ' "Eskimo Words for Snow" ', 422.
[99] Joel S. Schwartz, 'Alfred Russel Wallace and "Leonainie" ', 4–5.

attitude towards it. People who associate the Middle Ages with tournaments and revels rather than with squalor and disease can experience the joys of jousting, dancing and medieval cuisine while retaining the comforts of modern society by joining the Society for Creative Anachronism.[100] 'The public appears disposed to be amused', wrote the maestro of humbug, P.T. Barnum, 'even when they are conscious of being deceived'.[101] The popular culture of our time confirms his observation. But because high seriousness remains the dominant value of literary pundits, literature is expected to manifest higher ambitions, and to resist the spuriosities which characterise both everyday life and literary forgeries. If the future of that illusion is to be sustained, however, the binary opposition on which it is based will have to be reaffirmed to the satisfaction of sceptics, and authorship will need to become a more respectable institution than it has been in the past.

---

[100] Ball and Ellsworth, 'Emperor's New Clothes', 80.
[101] Lindberg, *Confidence Man in American Literature*, 187.

for instance, authorial collaboration was routine, and not least because writers were regarded as merely one component in the ensemble which tried to make a living by staging public perfor- mances of plays. Collaboration ranged from professional partner- ships like Francis Beaumont's with John Fletcher to the practice of hiring a writer to refurbish an old play written by somebody else.[5] Thomas Heywood evidently mastered the requisite skills to survive in such conditions, for a molestatory metaphor in his preface to *The English Traveller* (1633) indicates that he had 'either an entire hand, or at the least a maine finger' in 220 plays.[6] As a professional collaborator in the production of scripts for playhouses, Heywood engaged in what Jeffrey Masten calls 'textual intercourse', an activity 'predicated on *erasing* the perception of any differences that might have existed . . . between collaborated parts'.[7] Modern critics, on the other hand, have put their knowledge of such practices to a different end by attributing to their preferred author those parts of the work they admire, and then relegating the rest to an inferior collaborator. An early example of this disintegrationist procedure is displayed in Edward Ravenscroft's preface to his 1687 adaptation of *Titus Andronicus* (1594), a play he regards as 'a heap of Rubbish' because it was written by somebody other than Shakespeare, who 'only gave some Master-touches to one or two of the Principal Parts or Characters'.[8]

Before collaboration can be viewed more positively, it must be thought of as providing opportunities for synergies that facilitate diversity. The greater the range of experiences represented in some- one's collected works, the more likely it will appear that no single author could possibly have written them all. This explains the emergence of 'groupist' theories about the composition of Shake- speare's plays. One such example is Thomas W. White's *Our English Homer* (1892), which redistributes the Shakespeare canon to other Elizabethan dramatists.[9] As White's title suggests, disintegrationism as a critical practice had been pioneered in Homeric studies a century earlier by F.A. Wolf, who did not think that a single author was responsible for either the *Iliad* or the *Odyssey.*[10] If you cannot believe with Coleridge that Shakespeare was 'myriad-minded', then

[5] Albright, *Dramatic Publication in England*, 202–03. [6] Ibid., 210.
[7] Masten, *Textual Intercourse*, 17.
[8] Wadsworth, *Poacher from Stratford*, 9. [9] Ibid., 61.
[10] Turner, 'Homeric Question', 128.

you may well incline to the view that 'Shakespeare' was the brand-name used by a syndicate like the one Gilbert Slater describes in *Seven Shakespeares* (1931), which includes Francis Bacon and Christopher Marlowe as well as an assortment of aristocrats, including Sir Walter Ralegh, the Countess of Pembroke and the earls of Derby, Oxford and Rutland.[11] And if you are desperate enough for evidence you may even resort to séances, as Percy Allen did before publishing his *Talks with Elizabethans* (1947), which reveals that Shakespeare was good at plots, villains, comedy and theatrical know-how; Oxford supplied loveable characters and lyrical writing, whereas Bacon was merely a consultant whose advice was rarely taken.[12]

More down-to-earth theorists see collaboration as a means of subverting that agonistic model of textual production which envisages writers as solitary performers locked in competition with one another. Collaboration enables those who practise it to reap the benefits of exploring the spaces between sovereign subjectivities, and to do so without risking long-term damage: the collaboration of Ford Madox Ford with Joseph Conrad – which Henry James found 'inconceivable' because 'their traditions and their gifts are so dissimilar' – did not prevent them from going their separate ways after working together successfully to produce *Romance* (1903).[13] Nevertheless, as Wayne C. Koestenbaum reveals in *Double Talk* (1989), the homosocial contract which sustains male–male collaboration can be fraught with anxieties and homoerotic entanglements. Especially interesting are the psychodynamics that led T.S. Eliot to gender himself 'feminine' and stereotypically passive to Ezra Pound's actively 'masculine' role in the literary obstetrics which delivered the poem we know as *The Waste Land* (1922) from the manuscripts that preceded it.[14] By contrast, in feminist practice as described by Lisa Ede and Andrea Lunsford, writing collaboratively mobilises a sexual politics designed to reveal 'the ways in which our society locates power, authority, authenticity and property in an autonomous, masculine self'.[15] They encourage women writers to escape a restrictively masculinist notion of authorial singularity by engaging in 'a dialogic collaborative mode', whose fluidities are such that 'one

---

[11] Hope and Holston, *Shakespeare Controversy*, 179–80; Schoenbaum, *Shakespeare's Lives*, 428–29.
[12] Allen, *Talks with Elizabethans*, 40.
[13] Alan Judd, *Ford Madox Ford*, 70–71.
[14] Koestenbaum, *Double Talk*, 112–39.
[15] Ede and Lunsford, *Singular Texts / Plural Authors*, 234.

"person" may occupy multiple and shifting roles as the project progresses'.[16] What they have in mind is not the mother-and-daughter activities of Rosa and Amalia Panvini, who jointly crafted thirty volumes of Benito Mussolini's private diaries, but something along the lines of Sara Maitland and Micheline Wandor's anti-Noachian novel, *Arky Types* (1987), which is composed of letters written in their own persons as well as in several personae, including a pair of radical separatist lesbian tortoises.[17] By co-operating only with other women writers, Cary Kaplan and Ellen Cronan Rose argue, women can avoid 'the customary hierarchy and competitiveness of heterosexual interaction'.[18]

Heterosexual interaction becomes even more complicated in cross-cultural collaborations, which fissure the ideology of authorship along the faultline of race as well as gender. A couple of once popular collections of Native American stories illustrate the innocence of such practices before identity was theorised as a politics of the personal. The content of both books was the work of Ohiyesa, a Sioux ('Lakota people' was not yet recognised as the preferred designation) so well acculturated into white society that in 1890 he graduated with a medical degree from Boston University, where he was known as Charles A. Eastman. He married Elaine Goodale, a poet who 'edited' his writing so extensively that both *Wigwam Evenings* (1909) and *Smoky Day's Wigwam Evenings* (1910) were published under their joint authorship.[19] Since this working relationship seems to have been more interdependent than competitive, it may be more accurate to describe heterosexual competitiveness as 'common' rather than 'customary'.

Trouble arises whenever one partner tries to calculate exactly what s/he has put into a joint venture. In this respect, an unusually modest male disclaimer which invites contradictory responses is W.B. Yeats' admission that only a couple of the eleven plays which bear his name were entirely his own work. The others, he said, resulted from varying degrees of collaboration with Lady Augusta Gregory, and so much so that in the case of *Cathleen ni Houlihan* (1902) – which Yeats refers to in his poem 'The Man and the Echo' as 'that play of

---

[16] Ibid., 240, 235.
[17] Maitland and Wandor, *Arky Types*, 222, 48–49.
[18] Kaplan and Rose, 'Strange Bedfellows: Feminist Collaboration', 550.
[19] Carol Lea Clark, 'Charles A. Eastman (Ohiyesa) and Elaine Goodale Eastman', 273, 279.

mine' – he thought that 'the authorship should be ascribed to her'.[20] If you think that Yeats was a great poet but an indifferent dramatist, then Lady Gregory's contribution to *Cathleen ni Houlihan* will be evidence that collaboration with a minor writer lowered the quality of his work. If you remember that Lady Gregory was also Yeats' patron, then what he says about her input into his plays may strike you as self-serving pseudo-humility. But if you believe that male dramatists are notorious for exploiting the creative abilities of women who associate with them – which is John Fuegi's criticism of Bertolt Brecht, '*at least* 80 percent' of whose most famous play, *The Threepenny Opera* (1928), was the work of Elisabeth Hauptmann – then you're likely to conclude that heterosexual 'collaboration' is a benign misnomer for a sinister male activity more correctly labelled exploitation.[21] As the literary equivalent of not sleeping with the enemy, female–female co-operation is designed to avoid not only heterosexual exploitation but the adverse political associations of 'collaborator' with *collabo*, the term used by the French Resistance during the Second World War to describe anybody who 'collaborated' with the Nazis, if only sexually (*la collaboration horizontale*). The slide from a textual to a military sense of 'collaboration' is exemplified in the writing career of Colette. After claiming that she herself wrote the 'Claudine' novels published by her first husband, Henry Gauthier-Villars, under his professional name of 'Willy', Colette eventually collaborated with the *collabos* by writing for Nazi-authorised papers during the German occupation of France in the 1940s.[22]

By that time, collaboration was already an avant-garde practice among the French Surrealists, whose attempts to break with the Romantic ideology of authorship included a game of consequences called *cadavre exquis*, which involves writing one or two words on a piece of paper, folding it blank, and then passing it on to the next person in the compositional chain. Named after a striking outcome of one such game ('The exquisite / corpse / shall drink / the young / wine'), the *cadavre exquis* mobilises arbitrariness, chance and discontinuity against those purposeful, selective and concatenating

---

[20] Pethica, ' "Our Kathleen": Yeats's Collaboration with Lady Gregory', 3, 15; Yeats, *Collected Poems*, 393.

[21] Fuegi, *Life and Lies of Bertolt Brecht*, 196.

[22] Meltzer, *Hot Property*, 90–91; Spender, Dale, *The Writing or the Sex?*, 147–49; Brunazzi, 'Question of Colette and Collaboration', 284, 287.

features that critics expect to find in single-authored texts. Theoretically, these 'composite productions', as André Breton described them in 1948, were to substitute 'a uniquely collective authority' for the individual authority associated with the Romantic model of authorship, and thus reaffirm Lautréamount's dictum that 'poetry must be made by all. Not by one'.[23] Yet whenever Romanticism rules in the public sector, risks are involved in abandoning an autonomous 'I' for a consensual 'we'. These are acknowledged by the authors of *A Thousand Plateaus* (1987), Gilles Deleuze and Félix Guattari, who named their propensity for thinking as a twosome *pensée à deux* in the expectation that this phrase would evoke a psychiatric condition first identified in 1877 by another couple, Charles Lasègue and J. Falret, as *folie à deux* ('shared delusion').[24]

That some co-operative ventures are executed less easily than they are planned is illustrated by the composition of *The Whole Family* (1908), a novel designed to portray a typical American family 'in middling circumstances, [and] of average culture and experiences'. At William Dean Howells' suggestion, Harper's contracted eleven other writers to collaborate with him in writing it, most of whom found it hard to filter individuality out of authorship. Consequently, just as 'the family' turns out to be a unitary fiction whose purpose is to trouble-shoot intra-familial factions, so too the ideology of composite authorship was at odds with the realities of professional rivalry among Howells' co-contributors, whose disagreements in the course of creating what John W. Crowley calls 'the whole famdamnily' were replicated in a plot that 'increasingly focused on family misunderstandings and family rivalries'.[25] No such problems troubled the twenty-four *Newsday* journalists (three-quarters of them men) who became 'Penelope Ashe' for the purposes of contributing one chapter each to a 'BM' ('Big Money') novel inspired by two examples of the genre published in 1966: Jacqueline Susann's *The Valley of the Dolls* and Harold Robbins' *The Adventurers*.[26] Their communal achievement – put together on the understanding that no chapter would be acceptable unless it manifested 'an unremitting emphasis on sex', and that 'excellence in writing [would] be quickly

---

[23] McCabe *et al.*, *Artistic Collaboration*, 31–32; Plant, *Most Radical Gesture*, 50.
[24] Stivale, *Two-Fold Thought of Deleuze and Guattari*, xi.
[25] Bauer, 'Politics of Collaboration in *The Whole Family*', 107; Crowley, 'The Whole Famdamnily', 106.
[26] McGrady, *Stranger Than Naked*, 2, 6.

blue-pencilled into oblivion' – was published in 1969 as *Naked Came the Stranger*, and remained on the best-seller lists in New York for almost four months of that year.[27] By confirming (immediately after publication) speculations that the book was a hoax, the *Newsday* collective manipulated the media coverage so well that 'an estimated sixty-five thousand reviews, articles, columns, and editorials' came to be written about the affair.[28] Responses were overwhelmingly favourable to the hoaxers for having demonstrated what both the arbiters of taste and the *Newsday* collective knew already, namely that best-selling fiction is junk-food consumed by the tasteless. This successful deception did not engender media outrage because its target was 'merely' popular fiction. Cultural vigilantes, who attract favourable attention by being seen to castigate duplicitousness, have nothing to gain by defending books devoid of literary merit. Antipathy to literary forgery is reserved principally for the products of high culture.

The case for distinguishing 'authentic' from 'spurious' writing is weakened by the fact that widely accepted textual practices contravene the Romantic ideology of authorship. Whenever 'authorship' is defined in terms of 'authorisation' rather than 'authoring', writing is no longer a necessary condition of authorship. *Profiles in Courage*, published 'by' John F. Kennedy in 1956, was in fact drafted largely by his speechwriter, Theodore C. Sorensen, from materials supplied by researchers.[29] Kennedy authored it by authorising its contents: the Pulitzer Prize was awarded to Kennedy in 1957 as the authorising 'author' of this book, not to Sorensen and others who merely researched and wrote it.[30] This kind of textual production is resorted to habitually by busy public figures, and is commonly encountered in bureaucracies, where people are paid to write documents they do not sign and sign documents they do not write. When required to speak at length in public, politicians depute the production of an appropriate speech to a subordinate, who is briefed on what needs to be said and has the rhetorical skills to say it well. Such speeches are authorised when the politician who commissions them delivers them *ex officio*. Some regard this practice as unethical. It cannot be condoned, writes Ernest G. Bormann, on the grounds that 'every-

---

[27] Ibid., 12, 13, 213.
[28] Andreas Schroeder, *Cheats, Charlatans, and Chicanery*, 15.
[29] Parmet, *Jack: The Struggles of John F. Kennedy*, 332–33.
[30] Hellmann, 'JFK: The Author and the Text', 745.

body knows that the speeches are ghostwritten anyway', because this is not something known to everybody.[31] Speechwriting was already problematic in antiquity, although not necessarily for ethical reasons. Cicero remarks in his *Brutus* that the ancient Greek rhetorician Isocrates eventually stopped writing 'speeches for other people to deliver' after being 'often prosecuted for assisting, contrary to law, to circumvent one or another of the parties in judgment'.[32] The objection here is to the outsourcing of 'forensic' rhetoric, which was the kind used in courts of law. Writing something for someone else to deliver was not perceived as a problem in the production of either 'demonstrative' rhetoric (as displayed in laudatory speeches on ceremonial occasions) or the 'deliberative' rhetoric encountered in a 'political speech . . . in which the speaker recommends or warns against an action'.[33] The speechwriters of politicians are much less conspicuous than their bodyguards. If what they have written comes to be collected as the speeches of the person they have worked for, the most they can expect is to be cited as an editor, as Sorensen was when Kennedy's speeches (of which the president was declared 'the true author') were collected in 1988.[34]

Other evidence of 'dispersed' authorship includes ghostwriting, in which books 'by' someone 'as told to' someone else are published with titles like *The Confessions of a Con Man, as Told to Will Irwin* (1909). This genre is widely accepted as a way of soliciting 'autobiographies' from famous or infamous people who have neither the time nor the talent to write them. As a term that evokes a distinctly spooky process, 'ghost' was not used in connection with such writing until the early 1880s, when members of the newly founded Society for Psychical Research began examining spiritualistic phenomena such as 'automatic writing', on which they published a paper by Frederic Myers in their 1885 *Proceedings*.[35] Rationalistic contempt for spiritualism is responsible for the derogatory associations of ghostwriting. Hence its ironic use by Marjorie Garber, who investigates 'literature as uncanny causality' in *Shakespeare's Ghost Writers* (1987), a title which itself seems uncannily caused (since she never mentions it) by George and Bernard Winchcombe's *Shakespeare's Ghost-Writer(s)* (1968).

[31] Bormann, 'Ethics of Ghostwritten Speeches', 262.
[32] Nichols, *Rhetoric and Criticism*, 36.
[33] Lausberg, *Handbook of Literary Rhetoric*, 33, 32.
[34] Kennedy, *'Let the Word Go Forth'*, 2.
[35] Armstrong, *Modernism, Technology, and the Body*, 188.

Unlike translators, who sometimes gain considerable respect for their work, ghostwriters are usually ignored. An exception is Alex Haley. Before publishing his genealogical 'faction' of African American history in *Roots* (1976), Haley not only ghosted the autobiography of Malcolm X (who thought that James I had ghostwritten Shakespeare's plays) but increased his own visibility in the process by adding an epilogue about how it came to be written, although it was Murray Fisher's editorial shaping of Haley's manuscript that turned *The Autobiography of Malcolm X* (1965) into a black-power classic.[36] Traditionally, ghostwriting was done for a pittance by hacks like Psalmanazar, who wrote most of that *General History of Printing* which was published in 1732 as the work of the man who commissioned it, Samuel Palmer.[37] However, in Eva Shaw's helpful book on 'how to get into the business', beginners are heartened with the news that ghostwriters produced 'five of the top twenty-five best-sellers of the 1980s'.[38] In revealing various tricks of the trade that enable practitioners to avoid such problems as writer's block ('a hoax perpetuated by unsuccessful writers'), Shaw treats ghostwriting as a potentially lucrative profession.[39] It is certainly not something to anguish over in the way that Taggart does in John Galsworthy's short story, 'Conscience' (1922). For while Taggart knows that 'devilling' – writing things that others receive credit for, which is how he makes his living – is 'quite an art', he comes to have ethical misgivings about it as 'a fraud on the Public'; and so, unswayed by a colleague's argument that even littérateurs do it ('think of old Dumas'), he achieves integrity by resigning from his job.[40]

Ghostwriting becomes a questionable activity whenever those who practise it are suspected of elaborating if not inventing the narratives they claim to have transcribed. The slave-narratives of African Americans are a case in point. Produced before the invention of voice-recording technology, they were mediated to a white readership by white Abolitionists, who acted as amanuenses but felt at liberty to edit and preface the stories they were told in order to maximise their political usefulness as propaganda in the struggle to end slavery in the Confederate States. Yet although such editorial

---

[36] Mills and Mills, '*Roots* and the New Faction', *passim*; Hillel Schwartz, *Culture of the Copy*, 290; Jonathan Bate, *Genius of Shakespeare*, 94.
[37] Foley, *Great Formosan Impostor*, 45–48.
[38] Eva Shaw, *Ghostwriting*, 170.
[39] Ibid., 54.   [40] Galsworthy, *Caravan*, 818, 821, 822.

tampering undermines their credibility as autobiography, and the marketing of them solely for a white readership makes the published versions of such narratives ideologically suspect, white-mediated slave-narratives retain enough documentary detail to be of value to historians.[41] They also exhibit, however, formulaic features and rhetorical manoeuvres that are easily imitated. Fake African American slave-narratives thus came to be published not only by a white man, Richard Hildreth (*The Narrative of Archy Moore*, 1836), and a white woman, Mattie Griffith (*The Autobiography of a Female Slave*, 1857), but also by a free and opportunistic African American called James Williams. Pretending to be 'a driver on a cotton plantation in Alabama', Williams contacted the American Anti-Slavery Society and dictated to John Greenleaf Whittier the story it published in 1836 as *The Narrative of James Williams, An American Slave*. By persuading the Abolitionists to buy him a passage to Liverpool so that he could escape the slave-catchers allegedly on his trail, Williams did not have to front up to his patrons after Southern slaveholders convinced them that they had been conned by a black, who successfully played off one group of whites against another in order to secure by his narrative a place for himself outside racist America.[42] Vocal opponents of literary forgery tend not to mention the ethical conundrum presented by James Williams, who revealed the naivety of white Abolitionists in assuming that 'negroes' would testify as non-duplicitous witnesses, since they were too childlike to be able to lie convincingly.

The practice of publishing a book without 'reference to the legal name of the writer on the title page' was so widespread in Britain during the eighteenth and nineteenth centuries that Robert J. Griffin (mindful of the fact that 'nearly seventy percent' of the novels published between 1670 and 1700 were anonymous) argues that 'some historical understanding of anonymous publication must be integral to our understanding of authorship during the rise of the professional author'.[43] Certainly, many famous books by equally famous authors in fact began their careers in conditions of anonymity. The title-page of the first edition of *Pride and Prejudice* (1813), for instance, attributes the novel not to Jane Austen but to 'the author of *Sense and Sensibility*'. Curious contemporaries who located a copy of

---

[41] Andrews, *To Tell a Free Story*, 35.
[42] Gates, ' "Authenticity" ', 27.
[43] Griffin, 'Anonymity and Authorship', 882, 883, 891.

the earlier novel would have discovered merely another evasion, in so far as the only authorial information offered on the title-page of *Sense and Sensibility* (1811) is that it is 'by a lady'. Several novels which posterity reads as the work of Sir Walter Scott were attributed on their first publication to 'the author of *Waverley*'. That rubric gave away nothing to outsiders, because Scott – who did not want to jeopardise his reputation as a poet – published his first novel, *Waverley* (1814), anonymously in case it was not well received.[44] Game-players sometimes encode clues to their identity in anonyms, as Walpole did when Italianising his name as 'Muralto' in *The Castle of Otranto* (1764). In the first volume of a Shandeian novel entitled *The Doctor*, which Robert Southey published anonymously between 1834 and 1838, the hero's wife slips from English into Garamna when saying to him: 'You, – vema whehaha yohu almad otenba twandri, athancod!' Not until 1994, however, when Michael Shortland noticed that 'Garamna is an anagram of "anagram"', were those words orthogrammatised as 'You, who have written *Thalaba* and *Madoc* and *Kehama*!', i.e. Southey.[45] Those who think that Shakespeare's plays were written by someone else sometimes scan them for similar encryptions. Isaac Hull Platt, who sought *Bacon Cryptograms in Shake-Speare* (1905), found what he was looking for in *Love's Labours Lost* (1595) when he came upon the word 'honorificabilitudinitatibus'. Rearranged as a Latin hexameter, *hi ludi F. Baconis nati tuiti orbi* ('these plays F. Bacon's offspring are preserved for the world'), this sesquipedalian word convinced Sir Edwin Durning-Lawrence that *Bacon Is Shake-Speare* (1910).[46]

In 1925 E.M. Forster defended anonymity on the grounds that, since literary works do not pretend to be information, 'what is not information need not be signed'. Just as Walter Pater claimed that all art aspires to the condition of music, Forster argues that 'all literature tends towards a condition of anonymity'. In so far as the constituent words of a literary text 'are creative, a signature merely distracts us from their true significance'. Indeed, 'literature tries to be unsigned', because unlike the signature (which 'belongs to the surface-personality') 'creation comes from the depths'. Consequently, to read deeply is to 'forget both [the author's] name and our own'.[47] Various

[44] Cooney, 'Scott's Anonymity', 215.
[45] Shortland, 'Southey's *The Doctor*', 61.
[46] Wadsworth, *Poacher from Stratford*, 69; Schoenbaum, *Shakespeare's Lives*, 420.
[47] Forster, *Two Cheers for Democracy*, 91, 92, 94, 96.

ways of concealing authorship are among many 'paratextual' features taxonomised by Gérard Genette. Although we have technical terms to describe both namelessness ('anonymity') and false naming ('pseudonymity'), the unmarked feature in this process, he notes, is the act of naming itself, which he designates (by a backformation) 'onymity'.[48] Further refinements would include 'orthonymity' (the authorial use of one's correct name) and 'antonymity', which involves choosing a name opposite in meaning to one's given name, as when Max Südfeldt ('southern field') renamed himself Max Nordau ('northern meadow') before publishing in 1893 his symptomatology of cultural *Entartung*, which was translated into English as *Degeneration* (1895). 'Homonymity' misled scholars into thinking that the Musaeus who wrote the poem on which Christopher Marlowe's *Hero and Leander* is based was not the Greek poet of AD 500 but the legendary pupil of the legendary Orpheus.[49] 'Mononymity' occurs when several people agree to write under a common name. It happened in the early eighteenth century, when Alexander Pope, John Gay, Jonathan Swift and others decided to publish under the name of 'Martinus Scriblerus'; and it was recommended again as a Situationist strategy at the Festival of Plagiarism in the 1980s, when everybody was invited to start writing under the name of 'Karen Eliot'.[50] As a device for de-individualising authorship, Situationist mononymity was Dadaist in origin. The hero of Wolf Mankowitz's novel, *Exquisite Cadaver* (1990), recalls that the artefacts assembled in the first Dada exhibition were 'all signed LHOOQ to prove they ha[d] no authorship'.[51]

'Allonymity' occurs whenever authors impute their own work to someone else in order to improve their chances of having it noticed. A fourteenth-century treatise on the love of books, *Philobiblon, sive de Amore Librorum*, had considerably more authority as the imputed work of the Bishop of Durham, Richard de Bury, than as the actual work of his Dominican secretary, Robert Holkot.[52] In 1876, when Ralph Waldo Emerson reviewed examples of this phenomenon from Cicero to Carlyle, he concluded that the central issue was authority: each of these writers had 'ascrib[ed] their own sentence to an

[48] Genette, *Paratexts*, 39–42.
[49] Gudeman, 'Literary Frauds among the Greeks', 71.
[50] Home (ed.), *Plagiarism*, 9.
[51] Mankowitz, *Exquisite Cadaver*, 217.
[52] Blumenthal, *False Literary Attributions*, 13.

imaginary person, in order to give it weight'.[53] When Salvian was asked to explain why he had attributed to the Apostle Timothy his own treatise *Ad Ecclesiam*, which was written about AD 440, one of his reasons was that 'he did not wish the obscurity of his own person' to detract from the influence of his otherwise valuable book'.[54] The better-known Church Fathers appear to have been vulnerable to such acts of generosity: Chrysostom, for instance, is credited with about 900 sermons he never composed.[55] As is clear from the cases of more worldly imputees, however, this putatively honorific practice can be a liability for those subjected to it. When it happened to Petrarch, he described such works as 'disfigurements . . . stamped on [his] own face'; but the principal victim of aggravated imputation was John Wilmot, Earl of Rochester, whose notoriety was constructed in part from the attribution to him of obscene and anonymous verses.[56]

The notion that writing can flourish without a concomitant cult of authorship appears implausible in a culture that conceives of it in terms of what Keats (with Wordsworth in mind) calls 'the egotistical sublime'.[57] In such conditions, allonymity will be regarded as an act of suicidal generosity; as Scott remarked in 1804, 'Chatterton would better have consulted his own fame by avowing th[o]se beautiful poems' he attributed to 'Rowley'.[58] Egocentric communities can critique their assumptions about authorship by studying literary practices that are by contrast egofugal. When David the Armenian was trying to determine in the fifth century AD how many of the writings imputed to Aristotle had actually been written by him, he concluded that 'good feeling' had led post-Aristotelian philosophers to attribute their own writings to their master.[59] Neo-Pythagoreans assigned their own treatises to Pythagoras for the same reasons.[60] In the absence of an individualistic cult of authorship, E.K. Chambers remarks, they had thought it their principal duty to develop 'the traditional doctrines of a school'; consequently, 'what was said was of

[53] Emerson, 'Quotation and Originality', 435.
[54] Metzger, 'Literary Forgeries and Pseudepigrapha', 7–8; Constable, 'Forgery and Plagiarism in the Middle Ages', 30.
[55] Metzger, 'Literary Forgeries and Pseudepigrapha', 10.
[56] Max W. Thomas, 'Eschewing Credit', 278; Love (ed.), *Works of John Wilmot*, xxvi.
[57] Keats, *Letters*, ed. Page, 172.
[58] Meyerstein, *Life of Chatterton*, 507.
[59] Chambers, *History and Motives of Literary Forgeries*, 8.
[60] Ibid., 9.

more importance than who said it'.[61] In a now infamous phrase incorporated by Michel Foucault into a genealogy of authorship designed to make us think 'otherwise' about this matter, one of Samuel Beckett's characters asks, 'What matter who's speaking?'[62] It matters a great deal, of course, to those who cannot accept the annihilation of the self as a condition of discipleship in the transmission of a tradition. Yet something of the older altruism – that subordination of the self to *altrui*, 'somebody else' – was still extant in 1785, when John Pinkerton (writing under the pseudonym of 'Robert Heron') suggested in his *Letters of Literature* that 'nothing can be more heroic and generous in literary affairs than a writer's ascribing to antiquity his own production'. Why? Because by doing so he 'sacrific[es] his own fame to give higher satisfaction to the public'.[63] Pinkerton had spent time invisibly mending 'antient' ballads before that kind of work came to be disparaged as textual tampering by the meticulous but irascible Joseph Ritson. Susan Stewart therefore detects 'self-promotion' in Pinkerton's self-effacing remark, since only a year earlier he had been denounced by Ritson as a forger comparable to Macpherson.[64] But if Pinkerton was indeed attempting to redeem his reputation for deviousness by representing his activities as self-sacrificing, he was not alone in resorting to imputationist theory in order to trouble-shoot accusations of literary forgery. 'If a young author wishes to circulate a beautiful poem under the guise of antiquity', Scott was to write in his 1833 edition of *Border Minstrelsy*, 'the public is surely more enriched by the contribution than injured by the deception'.[65] In addition to decoying Ritsonian critics away from his own editorial practices, Scott's response is a generous way of dealing with the probability that he himself had been deceived into accepting forged ballads as genuine. These included 'Auld Maitland', by James Hogg, and 'The Death of Featherstonhaugh', a ballad fabricated by the antiquarian author of *The History of Durham* (1816–40), Robert Surtees.[66]

Literary allonymity has affinities with debates in Reformation theology about the mechanisms for attributing or ascribing something to someone else, especially righteousness or guilt. The Catholic

[61] Ibid.   [62] Foucault, *Language, Counter-Memory, Practice*, 138.
[63] Hustvedt, *Ballad Criticism*, 253.
[64] Stewart, *Crimes of Writing*, 116.
[65] Farrer, *Literary Forgeries*, 254.
[66] Zug, 'Scott and Ballad Forgery', 53, 58–59.

doctrine that the merits of Christ are imparted to us was opposed by
the Lutheran teaching that they are not imparted but imputed. The
orthonymity of authorship is in this respect 'Catholic': writers impart
their merits by their inscriptions, and by doing so produce advertise-
ments for themselves. But in conditions of allonymity, authorship
takes a Lutheran turn. Allonymic writers do not impart their merits
but impute them. And they do so not by *in*scription but by *a*scription:
by ascribing their own writings to someone else, they allocate to that
person credit for what is in fact their own merit. Like writing under a
pseudonym, this procedure enables fledgling authors to sample
public responses to their work vicariously, and avoid adverse criticism of technical incompetence by pretending that it was written in a
less sophisticated era. Any writer 'diffident of his abilities', Macpherson observes in his preface to *Fingal*, could 'ascribe his own
compositions to a person whose remote antiquity . . . might well
answer for faults which would be inexcusable in a writer of this
age'.[67] It was against this Augustan view of the progress of poesy that
Chatterton fabricated the poems of 'Rowley', to show 'that good
poetry might be wrote in the dark days of superstition'.[68] After all,
Alexander Pope rewrote some of John Donne's verse satires, just as
John Dryden had rewritten one of Geoffrey Chaucer's *Canterbury
Tales*, out of a conviction that neither Chaucer nor Donne could
match the prosodic expertise of Dryden and Pope, who had demonstrably perfected the art of poetry. Macpherson hastens to assure us,
however, that the poems which constitute *Fingal* are of such high
quality that if they were really his own work then 'it would be a very
uncommon instance of self-denial' for him 'to disown them'.[69] His
irony raises the possibility that something other than diffidence
motivated allonymity in the 1760s. Perhaps, as someone remarks in
Peter Ackroyd's ingeniously counterfactual novel, *Chatterton* (1987),
the inventor of 'Rowley' and other late-medieval Bristolians was 'so
sure . . . of his own genius that he allowed it to flourish under other
names'.[70]

For centuries people have been writing pseudonymously in order
to off-load responsibilities to which a signature would commit them.
An admirer of Quérard's *Supercheries littéraires dévoilées* (1847), 'Olphar

[67] Folkenflik, 'Macpherson, Chatterton, Blake', 379.
[68] Meyerstein, *Life of Chatterton*, 251.
[69] Folkenflik, 'Macpherson, Chatterton, Blake', 380.
[70] Ackroyd, *Chatterton*, 126.

Hamst' (Ralph Thomas), found 'pseudonym' far too crude a term to describe the varieties of nomenclature by which writers conceal their orthonyms. His *Handbook of Fictitious Names* (1868) accordingly introduces such categorial refinements as 'allonym', 'ananym', 'aristonym', 'cryptonym', 'demonym', 'geonym', 'ironym', 'phraseonym', 'phrenonym', 'polynym', 'prenonym', 'pseudojin', 'scenonym', 'titlonym' and 'translationym' – as well as drawing attention to 'alphabetism', 'asterism', 'initialism', 'pseudandry' and 'telonism'. Speculating about the motives for such practices, James Kennedy and his associates, who compiled an indispensable *Dictionary of Anonymous and Pseudonymous English Literature* (1926), diagnosed 'timidity'.[71] It may be the kind of 'diffidence' displayed by Horace Walpole in not wanting to have his name associated with the first edition of *The Castle of Otranto* (1764) until it had been well received.[72] Or it may be the 'shame' experienced by pornographers like Dominique Aury, who published *The Story of O* (1954) under the pseudonym of 'Pauline Réage'. But it can also be a 'fear of [the] consequences' of publishing something which challenges (or could be construed as doing so) the authority of an authoritarian regime: Jonathan Swift, for instance, first published *Gulliver's Travels* (1726) anonymously in case it was read politically as a seditious libel against the Hanoverian state. Yet timidity does not explain the behaviour of the polyonomous Scharmel Iris who, after Harriet Monroe had refused to print his poems in *Poetry* (she had her reasons: he had used *Poetry* stationery to forge a letter over her name), tricked her into publishing eighteen of them in the early 1930s by submitting them under four different pseudonyms.[73]

Modernist poets like Ezra Pound and T.S. Eliot resorted routinely to such personae as 'Hugh Selwyn Mauberley' and 'J. Alfred Prufrock' instead of writing *in propria persona*. The precursor whose practices they learned from and modified was Robert Browning, who formulated his influential persona-theory in the context of his unwitting encounter with a literary forgery. Browning's divergence from the expressivist aesthetic of an earlier generation of Romantic lyric poets is signalled by his development of the dramatic monologue in *Men and Women* (1855) and *Dramatis Personae* (1864). He designed this generically hybrid form in order to fuse the 'subjective'

[71] James Kennedy, *et al.*, 'Notes on Anonymity and Pseudonymity', xi.
[72] Hazen, 'Literary Forgeries and the Library', 11.
[73] Abbott, 'Case of Scharmel Iris', 20–22.

effects of lyrical intensity with the 'objective' properties of the drama, whose *dramatis personae* enable writers to exhibit a polyvocality much less restrictive than the limited register of what is known in poetry reviewing as 'a personal voice'. Browning first made this tendentious distinction between 'objective' writing like Shakespeare's *Othello* (which 'speaks for itself') and 'subjective' poetry like Shelley's (which speaks for Shelley and is therefore autobiographical) in a substantial essay commissioned by his friend and publisher, Edward Moxon, as an introduction to twenty-five *Letters of Percy Bysshe Shelley* (1852). Twenty-three of these turned out to be forgeries, thus causing the book to be withdrawn.[74] They were the work of a man who called himself Major George Gordon De Luna Byron, partly because he had commanded a regiment of sepoys in the East India service, and partly because he claimed to be the illegitimate son of Lord Byron and a Spanish Countess De Luna.[75] Browning, who preferred not to waste his time writing essays, states that he accepted Moxon's commission only because it would allow him to express long-held opinions about Shelley's poetry. According to Wise, who negotiated a reprint of this essay for the Browning Society in 1888, Browning never saw the originals of the letters that comprise the volume he agreed to introduce, which in any case he barely mentions.[76] Yet although he finds them 'slight', these letters nevertheless evince for Browning 'a profound sensibility and adaptitude for art'.[77] There is no evidence to support his editor's assumption that Browning must have been referring here to one of the genuine letters in the collection.[78] The supposition that authors have a preternatural ability to detect spuriosity in writing is as false as the comparable belief that their literary practices make them unerring as literary critics.

Browning himself never reprinted this essay, which observes *en passant* that the poetry of 'Rowley' exists independently of Chatterton.[79] In fact, the only other essay Browning ever published is on Chatterton: it appeared anonymously in 1842, and masqueraded as a review of R.H. Wilde's book on 'the love, madness and imprisonment' of Torquato Tasso. Here Browning argues that because

---

[74] Robert Metcalf Smith, *Shelley Legend*, 57–58, 61.
[75] Ehrsam, *Major Byron*, 9, 11, 88–100.
[76] Smith, *Shelley Legend*, 57.
[77] Browning, 'Essay on Shelley', 146, 149.
[78] Ibid., 353.   [79] Ibid., 148.

'genius almost invariably begins to develop itself by imitation', Chatterton should not be 'viewed as a kind of Psalmanazar or Macpherson'; furthermore, the 'genuineness of any ten verses of "Rowley"' is so self-evident that the hostility with which those poems were received is 'a real disgrace to the scholarship of the age'.[80] Shelleyans outraged by Major Byron's imposture may have been unaware of the fact that Shelley himself had engaged in literary forgery when not much older than Chatterton was when he either suicided or accidentally overdosed on the arsenic and opium he was taking to treat a venereal disease.[81] In 1810 a certain 'John Fitzvictor' edited the *Posthumous Fragments of Margaret Nicholson*, a woman who was still alive at the time but confined to Bedlam for having attempted in 1786 to kill George III, and whose allegedly *Authentic Memoirs* were published that year as a pot-boiling pamphlet. The 'poems found amongst the papers of that noted female' had been written in fact by Shelley and Thomas Jefferson Hogg, who used Nicholson ventriloquially to express some of their own republican views, and then suppressed the work. When the newly formed Shelley Society was refused permission to reprint it in 1886, Wise took advantage of the fact that *Posthumous Fragments of Margaret Nicholson* had already been typeset, and arranged to have a few copies printed ('privately') as collectors' rarities.[82]

The relationships between personae and authorial personages interest not only biographers in search of unified personalities but also psychiatrists, whose pathologising of the phenomenon was labelled 'multiple personality disorder' in the 1980s before being re-diagnosed a decade later as 'dissociative identity disorder'.[83] Its simplest form is thematised in Romantic literature as 'the double', and its classic embodiments include Fyodor Dostoevsky's 'The Double' (1846) and Robert Louis Stevenson's *The Strange Case of Dr Jekyll and Mr Hyde* (1886). On entering the domain of psychiatry, the 'double' was renamed 'alter' on account of its fissiparousness. For whereas originally 'there was usually only one well-defined alter', writes Ian Hacking, 'today, sixteen alters is the norm'.[84] Popular accounts of what Hacking calls 'multobiography' – a genre instigated by C.H. Thigpen and H. Cleckley's *The Three Faces of Eve* (1957) – are

---

[80] Browning, 'Essay on Chatterton', 165, 166, 167.
[81] Holmes, 'Chatterton: Case Re-Opened', 244.
[82] Collins, *Two Forgers: Forman and Wise*, 76.
[83] Hacking, *Rewriting the Soul*, 17.   [84] Ibid., 21.

now complemented by 'automultobiographical' narratives such as *First Person Plural* (1999), by Cameron West, who claims to host twenty-four alters.[85] 'Writers aren't people exactly', remarks the narrator in Scott Fitzgerald's *The Last Tycoon* (1941): 'if they're any good, they're a whole *lot* of people trying so hard to be one person'.[86] This propensity, of course, is not restricted to writers. The construction and management of alters is a common strategy for negotiating the hazards encountered by a fragile self in transit through everyday life. It is especially useful for surviving professional life, as for example in the phone-sex industry, where workers are obliged to customise fantasy-selves in order to satisfy clients whose sexual proclivities can range across the spectrum of *psychopathia sexualis*.[87] Writers differ from non-writers only by leaving retrievable traces of the various people they are capable of becoming, because imaginative writing offers unique opportunities for naming and exploring alters.

'Persona' is a conservative term for the outcome of such activities, since it conceives of the alter as a 'mask' designed to conceal an unequivocally real self. The neutral word for naming the other is 'heteronym', which the Portuguese poet, Fernando Pessoa, introduced to describe his attempts at conducting different writing careers under different names. This strategy enabled Romain Gary to circumvent the rule that no writer can win the Prix Goncourt twice. Awarded it first in 1958 for *Les Racines du ciel* (published under his own name), he was offered it again in 1975 for *La Vie devant soi*. This is one of four books he published as 'Emile Ajar', an imaginary writer whom a cousin of his agreed to impersonate in public appearances[88] – just as in 1974 Thomas Pynchon persuaded a comedian, Irwin Corey, to masquerade as the novelist and receive the National Book Award for *Gravity's Rainbow* (1973). Prolific authors of popular genre fiction avoid flooding their own markets by means of heteronyms. Frederick Schiller Faust, for instance, whose disciplined work-habits enabled him to write a book a month, published westerns as 'Max Brand' and 'Evan Evans', whodunits as 'Nicholas Silver', spy novels as 'Frederick Frost', historical romances as 'John Frederick' and 'George Challis', Indian stories as 'George Owen

[85] Ibid., 36; Dow, 'Sins of the Mothers', 14.
[86] Fitzgerald, *Bodley Head Scott Fitzgerald*, 325.
[87] Flowers, *Fantasy Factory, passim*.
[88] Gary, *Vie et mort d'Emile Ajar, passim*.

Baxter', and so on.[89] In the European tradition, names are prognos-
ticatory. Since every *nomen* ('name') conceals an omen, renaming is a
way of revealing a hidden truth, which is why Fielding rewrote
Richardson's *Pamela* (1740) as *Shamela* (1741). Pessoa, however, inherited a name which defined him as a man without qualities, since in
Portuguese *pessoa* means 'person', a category of the human as yet
unmarked by those specificities which position it historically as a
gendered subject in a particular social stratum. Pessoa filled this
nominal vacancy with over seventy heteronyms, who write in English
and French as well as Portuguese, and include philosophers and
metaphysicians in addition to poets, short-story writers, translators
and literary critics. The best known are members of a non-existent
coterie of poets. The first to emerge was the serene pastoralist,
'Alberto Caeiro', followed by the pagan formalist, 'Ricardo Reis',
and the somewhat Pessoan 'Alvaro de Campos'.[90] Even their
'author' was treated by Pessoa as a fictional construct, referred to by
the orthonymic initials, 'F.P.' Unlike pseudonyms, heteronyms can
acquire identificatory characteristics, such as having a 'rather dark
complexion' ('Reis'), being 'brought up by an elderly aunt' ('Caeiro')
or sporting a monocle ('de Campos').[91] This enables them to be
fictionalised by other writers such as José Saramago, author of *The
Year of the Death of Ricardo Reis* (1991). 'These individualities', Pessoa
declared in 1928, 'must be considered distinct from that of their
author'; this is how Søren Kierkegaard thought of his own *de facto*
heteronyms, whom he said he had 'not the remotest private relation'
to, and whose writings he would talk about only as another reader of
them.[92] Heteronymity enabled Pessoa and Kierkegaard to explore
the possibilities of otherness within that bundle of selves we call the
self, and to do so without staging those differences agonistically or
dialectically. In this respect, Sreten Bozic's 'B. Wongar' is closer to
Pessoa's conception of the 'heteronym' than to commonsense understandings of the pseudonym. 'Our paths cross', Bozic once replied
when asked about 'Wongar', 'and he's a different personality and a
different writer'.[93] Yet the Romantic institution of authorship is so
powerful in our culture that such diversities are reduced finally to a

89 Richardson, 'Life and Works of Max Brand', *passim.*
90 Lisboa with Taylor (eds.), *Centenary Pessoa*, 51, 64, 78.
91 Green, *Fernando Pessoa*, 14.
92 Ibid., 17; Mark C. Taylor, *Kierkegaard's Pseudonymous Authorship*, 16.
93 Nolan, 'Absent Aborigine', 8.

singularity identifiable with a legal personage. Our only access to
'Alberto Caeiro' and his fellow heteronyms is via the writings copyrighted by Pessoa and published as 'his' work. This ensures that the
Balkanisation of the self into multiple selves will capitulate eventually
to an institutional demand for their reunification.

When Fernando Pessoa and Ezra Pound dissociate themselves as
legal personages from constructs referred to by their orthonymic
initials, 'F.P.' and 'E.P.', they produce their own approximations to
Jorge Luis Borges' fable of endogenetic difference, 'Borges and I'.
While separating the private person called Borges from that identi-
cally named public figure who is a famous writer, it concedes their
interdependence: the private Borges goes on living so that the public
Borges 'may contrive his literature', which in turn 'justifies' the
private Borges.[94] Another articulation of this difference appears in
Roland Barthes' essay on 'The Death of the Author' (1968). Here
Barthes distinguishes the 'author' (that historical person or *auctor*
who has written a particular text) from the *scripteur* (*scriptor* in
Stephen Heath's translation) or author-effect it produces whenever
someone reads it.[95] *Auctores* are legal personages who both pre-exist
and survive the texts they produce; this makes them different from
scriptores, who are wholly coterminous with the texts that engender
them. In these terms, readers of *Down the Road, Worlds Away* should
concern themselves with 'Rahila Khan' as the text's immediate
scriptor rather than with Toby Forward as its anterior *auctor*. Yet such
attempts to break with an expressivist theory of writing meet with
considerable resistance. Virago Press's anger at Forward revealed
nostalgia for the *auctor* as an authenticating presence, and a fear of
the political consequences for women as historically vulnerable
subjects under patriarchy if female subjectivity can be textualised out
of existence so easily. When criticisms of Forward's gender-mimicry
were recycled by The Women's Press as objections to his cultural
transvestism in writing as an Asian, Forward was accused of having
appropriated as a white *auctor* subject-positions that belong to
scriptores of colour. But again, although the identity politics of such
responses are impeccable, they evade problems drawn attention to
by a Barthesian reading of the performativity of Forward's text.

The commonsense association of authorship with ownership is

---

[94] Borges, *Labyrinths*, 282–83.
[95] Barthes, 'Death of the Author', 145.

destabilised whenever a character in a book becomes more famous than its creator. It then risks being either kidnapped by other writers (as Swift's Gulliver was) or legally franchised to them, a process by which admirers of 'James Bond' novels were able to continue reading new ones after the creator of the series, Ian Fleming, died in 1964. Swift had no control over the Gulliveriana generated by *Gulliver's Travels*, which originally was not the isolated text it became through its canonisation as a literary classic, since some four hundred imitations of it appeared in the eighteenth century, half of them before 1730.[96] *Gulliver's Travels* was as deeply enmeshed in the dissemination of Gulliveriana as the novels of Ian Fleming are in the cultural multiformity of the James Bond phenomenon. Fleming franchisees include Kingsley Amis, who published a book on *The Bond Dossier* (1965) before writing (under the pseudonym 'Robert Markham') a James Bond novel called *Colonel Sun* (1968). Screen-writers such as Christopher Wood crafted the gadgetry-plus-stunts narratives for what are always referred to as the James Bond movies.[97] But whereas these various Gullivers and Bonds are connected, however tenuously, to a known author, 'Nancy Drew' the girl detective is the product of a fiction-producing syndicate, whose changing though always anonymous personnel – all writing under the mononym of 'Carolyn Keene' – have produced hundreds of stories about her adventures since the publication of the first one, *The Secret of the Old Clock*, in 1930.[98] In this respect she resembles 'Sexton Blake' (Keating's cockney or 'mockney' for 'fake'), the detective created in 1893 by Harry Blyth ('Hal Meredith') and perpetuated by approximately two hundred authors, who by 1980 had contributed some four thousand titles to the Sexton Blake Library.[99] Fiction has to be 'serious' before its authorship is taken seriously. Since neither spy-novels nor detective stories are thought of as literature with a capital 'L', questions about who wrote them are considered not worth asking.

Franchising becomes a questionable practice only in the case of writers whose books are presumed to have literary merit or at least literary aspirations. Exactly who wrote the novels of Alexandre Dumas *père*, who became one of Hugh Kenner's classic counterfeiters

---

[96] Welcher, 'Gulliver in the Market-place', 129.
[97] Bennett and Woollacott, *Bond and Beyond*, 49.
[98] Dyer and Romolov (eds.), *Rediscovering Nancy Drew*.
[99] Keating, *Fake's Progress*, 78–89; Bates, *Pendex*, 152.

by 'perfect[ing] the art of issuing whole novels without lifting a
pen'?[100] In order to amass hundreds of works he claims in his
Mémoires to have written, Dumas frequently employed people
described in *The Oxford Companion to French Literature* (1959) as
collaborators, who merely 'suppl[ied] plots or historical frameworks
which depended on Dumas himself for life and development'.[101]
Eugène de Mirecourt, however, concluded that many novels 'by'
Dumas are in fact the work of Auguste Maquet. Because no
publisher would pay Maquet at the rates Dumas could command,
the pair struck a deal: Maquet's *Chevalier d'Harmenthal* (1843) would be
published over the name of Dumas, and they would share the profits.
By de Mirecourt's reckoning, other Maquet novels published as the
work of Dumas include both *The Three Musketeers* (1845) and its
sequel, *Twenty Years After* (1845); Maquet was also one of two
contributors to *The Count of Montechristo* (1844–45). An anonymous
reviewer for the *North American Review* of de Mirecourt's *Fabrique de
romans: maison Alexandre Dumas et compagnie* (1854) takes a permissive
view of such practices when concluding that because Dumas had
purchased these books 'in their unpublished state' he was justified in
regarding them as 'perfectly his own', since he had exercised
'perspicacity' in selecting them, and purchased them with his own
money.[102]

Authorship may well be a predominantly masculine anxiety,
engendered in a patriarchal society whose proverbial wisdom –
based on the uncertainties of insemination – is that it takes a wise
father to know his own child, and vice versa. The nightmare of
paternity occupies the very heart of English literature in the controversy about who 'fathered' the plays attributed to William Shakespeare, that 'defaulting tax-payer of Stratford', as Walter Hart
Blumenthal calls him, 'who could not spell his name twice alike'.[103]
Anti-Stratfordians believe, therefore, that the spelling 'Shakespeare'
is prejudicial to their case, since the central question is whether the
Stratford man who twice signed his name 'Shakspere' (but at other
times 'Shakp', 'Shaksper', 'Shakspe' and 'Shakspeare', and then only

---

[100] Kenner, *Counterfeiters*, 74.
[101] Paull, *Literary Ethics*, 186; Harvey and Heseltine (eds.), *Oxford Companion to French Literature*, 235.
[102] Anon., 'Literary Impostures – Alexandre Dumas', 344.
[103] Blumenthal, *False Literary Attributions*, 25, 22; Auchter, 'Did Shakespeare Write Shake-speare?', *passim*.

on legal documents) is the same person as that object of Bardolatry whose name is spelled 'Shakespeare' on the title-page of the 1623 First Folio.[104] J. Warren Keifer's orthographic distinction in *Did William Shakspere Write Shakespeare?* (1904) is thus erased in William Joseph Raddatz's Stratfordian response: *Shakespeare Wrote Shakespeare* (1921). And while the title of William H. Edwards' book, *Shaksper Not Shakespeare* (1900), expresses their common conviction, anti-Stratfordians differ about the identity of the man whose choice of 'Shakespeare' as his pseudonym resulted in 'the great Folio hoax'.[105] As far as Stratfordians are concerned, however, the answer to Horace Deluscar's question, *Was Poet William Shakespere a Cuckoo Impostor?* (1913) had been given already by G.H. Townsend: *Shakespeare Not an Impostor* (1857).

The earliest anti-Stratfordians were the Baconians. They were so called not because they were galvanised by Delia Bacon, the republican author of *The Philosophy of the Plays of Shakspere Unfolded* (1857), but because they developed her original theory that Sir Francis Bacon – and not (in her phrase) 'the Stratford poacher' – was the intelligence behind the plays attributed to Shakespeare.[106] She believed, writes Nina Baym, that as 'a collection of human facts organized to display the laws of a human nature that was ineluctably progressing towards the worldwide institution of republican governments', those plays constitute the praxis of the ideas developed in Bacon's *Novum Organum* (1620).[107] A rival group, the Marlovians, favours a writer once identified (before the odds shifted to George Chapman) as the rival poet mentioned in Shakespeare's sonnets, Christopher Marlowe. But because Shakespeare's plays are regarded as literary classics, and the term 'classic' originates as a marker of social rather than literary distinction, an anti-democratic predisposition has generated an effusion of earls to satisfy the snobbery of those inclined to believe that plays as good as Shakespeare's must have been written not by some plebeian actor from Stratford but by a well-educated aristocrat, whose need to avoid the social stigma of association with vulgar playhouses would have obliged him to remain anonymous. But which earl wrote the plays? Oxfordians who attribute Shakespeare's plays to Edward De Vere, the seventeenth

104 Schoenbaum, *Shakespeare: Records and Images*, 94; Sobran, *Alias Shakespeare*, 10.
105 Wadsworth, *Poacher from Stratford*, 121.
106 Hope and Holston, *Shakespeare Controversy*, 1–21; Wadsworth, *Poacher from Stratford*, 27–29.
107 Baym, 'Delia Bacon', 237.

Earl of Oxford, are at odds with Derbyites, who are persuaded by
Abel Lefranc's argument in *Sous le Masque de Shakespeare* (1919) that
'W.S.' is William Stanley, the sixth Earl of Derby. Oxfordians are
equally unimpressed by Rutlanders, whose candidate is Roger
Manners, the fifth Earl of Rutland. At the top end of this market,
George Elliott Sweet attributes Shakespeare's plays to Queen Elizabeth I in *Shake-Speare: The Mystery* (1956). None of these manoeuvres
impresses R.C. Churchill in his survey of *Shakespeare and His Betters*
(1958).[108] The generic term most commonly used by Stratfordians of
nominees for the authorship of Shakespeare's plays (and which
testifies to the interest taken in this matter by members of the legal
profession) is 'claimant': H.N. Gibson, for instance, surveys the
shortcomings of Baconians, Oxfordians, Derbyites and Marlovians
in *The Shakespeare Claimants* (1962). This word has connotations of
bogusness, however, through its association since 1866 with the
Tichborne Claimant, Thomas Castro (né Arthur Orton), an English
butcher resident in Australia who fancied a baronetcy and was
eventually jailed for claiming to be the shipwrecked heir to the
Tichborne estates in Hampshire.[109]

Fiction has often been the medium in which to venture counter-
Stratfordian speculations. The hero of William Douglass O'Connor's
novel, *Harrington* (1860), is a Baconian whose creator thought it more
profitable when thinking about the authorship question 'to be
insane' with Delia Bacon 'than sane with Dr. Johnson'.[110] The
Marlovian hypothesis was put in the form of a novel by Wilbur
Gleason Zeigler entitled *It Was Marlowe* (1895) before Calvin
Hoffman presented the case in *The Murder of the Man Who Was
'Shakespeare'* (1955) and D. Maure Wilbert reiterated it in *Silent
Shakespeare and Marlowe Revivified* (1998).[111] And the question, 'Who is
Shakspeare?', was asked in Benjamin Disraeli's *Venetia* (1837) – a
novel mined by Major Byron for his forgeries of Byron and Shelley –
before 'Who Wrote Shakespeare?' became the title of an article
contributed by Robert W. Jameson to *Chambers's Edinburgh Journal* in
1852.[112] By then, Shakespeare studies had been institutionalised as a
co-operative venture for only a decade or so with the establishment

[108] Hope and Holston, *Shakespeare Controversy*, 195, 197.
[109] Andreas Schroeder, *Cheats, Charlatans, and Chicanery*, 178–205.
[110] Wadsworth, *Poacher from Stratford*, 37.
[111] Hope and Holston, *Shakespeare Controversy*, 83–84; Gibson, *Shakespeare Claimants*, 27–28.
[112] Ehrsam, *Major Byron*, 165; Hope and Holston, *Shakespeare Controversy*, 151, 153.

in 1841 of the very first Shakespeare Society. Its inaugural director was the literary forger, John Payne Collier, a target of Andrew Edmund Brae's *Literary Cookery* (1855).[113] A possible answer to Jameson's query appeared when William Henry Smith asked, *Was Lord Bacon the Author of Shakespeare's Plays?* (1856).[114] In the subtitle of his generally derided book on *The Great Cryptogram* (1888), a cipher-seeking Baconian, Ignatius Donnelly, referred audaciously to 'the so-called Shakespeare plays'. Bardoclastic speculations encouraged reprisals. 'Did Shakespeare write Bacon's works?', James Freeman Clarke asked readers of the *North American Review* in February 1881; but by 1901, when Leslie Stephen reiterated the question in the *National Review*, the hypothesis that Bacon paid Shakespeare to write *The Advancement of Learning* was devised as an anti-Baconian joke.[115] The notion that Bacon wrote Shakespeare's plays developed concurrently with the publication of James Spedding's great edition of Bacon's writings (1857–74). Spedding, who met Delia Bacon at the Carlyles in 1853, and sat 'in speechless astonishment' while she expounded her theory over afternoon tea there, never came upon any text that implicated Bacon in Shakespeare's plays.[116] Much has to be made, therefore, of Bacon's more enigmatic remarks, as when he associates himself with 'concealed poets'.[117] Bacon scholars ignore 'Baconian' speculations, confident that the allegations which contributed to 'the troubled life of Francis Bacon' included corruption and sodomy but not the authorship of Shakespeare's plays, which the historian of his 'character assassination', Nieves Mathews, treats as one of the 'vicissitudes of Bacon's legend'.[118] But Baconians are not inhibited by such historicising manoeuvres. For James Phinney Baxter, 'the authorship of the Shakespeare works' remains *The Greatest of Literary Problems* (1915), the solution to which will dispel forever what Edward D. Johnson calls *The Shakspere Illusion* (1947).[119]

Professional Stratfordians do not share Michael D. Bristol's view that 'the real Shakespeare doesn't actually exist at all, except as the imaginary projection of an important tradition of social desire'.[120]

113 Ganzel, *Fortune and Men's Eyes*, 71, 200.
114 Schoenbaum, *Shakespeare's Lives*, 401.
115 Hope and Holston, *Shakespeare Controversy*, 159, 166.
116 Schoenbaum, *Shakespeare's Lives*, 387; Wadsworth, *Poacher from Stratford*, 36–37.
117 Auchter, 'Did Shakespeare Write Shakespeare?', 65.
118 Jardine and Stewart, *Hostage to Fortune*, 459, 108–09; Mathews, *Francis Bacon*, 321, 384–93.
119 Hope and Holston, *Shakespeare Controversy*, 174, 188.
120 Bristol, 'Shakespeare the Myth', 490.

They therefore tend either to ignore all those 'fat, bad, sad books' by anti-Stratfordians or to treat them as amusing interludes in the serious business of establishing the texts of Shakespeare's plays, reconstructing the cultural conditions in which they were first produced and understood, and tracing their afterlife in societies which have appropriated them for various purposes.[121] Most Stratfordians regard the authorship controversy as a pseudo-problem invented by the lunatic fringe of Shakespeare studies. Although the *Shakespeare Quarterly* began publishing its annual bibliography of Shakespeare studies in 1950, not until 1995 did the 'authorship controversy' appear there as a separate category. 'Without possibility of question', James G. McManaway declared in 1992, 'the actor at the Globe and the gentleman from Stratford were the same man'.[122] Such attempts at foreclosure merely strengthen the resolve of anti-Stratfordians, who point out that the absence of incontrovertible evidence that their preferred candidate wrote the plays of Shakespeare does not compensate for the absence of incontrovertible evidence that Shakspere did. A prominent Oxfordian, Charlton Ogburn, accuses Stratfordians of maintaining a 'policy of total denunciation of dissent and dissenters', because to admit even 'the tiniest doubt' would catalyse a process that would 'speedily consume the whole'.[123] Stratfordians, on the other hand, are not surprised to learn that by the time Delia Bacon published her book in 1857, she herself had become so 'violently insane' as to be incarcerated in a mental hospital, where she died in 1859.[124] Onomantic asides by Stratfordians reveal their delight that the first Oxfordian and author of *Shakespeare Identified* (1920) was called J. Thomas Looney (a Manx name disappointingly pronounced, however, 'Low-ney'); and they had another windfall when anti-Stratfordians were joined by an American genealogist called George Battey.[125] These jocularities have been strategically important in shoring up the ideology of authorship on which Stratfordian Bardolatry rests. By first homogenising the various Shakespeare claimants as equally implausible, and then treating the most bizarre cases as typical, Stratfordians

---

[121] Jonathan Bate, *Genius of Shakespeare*, 98.
[122] McManaway, *Authorship of Shakespeare*, 19.
[123] Ogburn, *Mysterious William Shakespeare*, 153.
[124] Wadsworth, *Poacher from Stratford*, 35.
[125] Garber, *Shakespeare's Ghost Writers*, 3; Jonathan Bate, *Genius of Shakespeare*, 95; Schoenbaum, *Shakespeare's Lives*, 450.

have succeeded in discrediting (as the work of amateurs obsessed to the point of insanity) any proposition that the plays attributed to Shakespeare may have been written by someone else. As a result, while commentaries on Shakespeare's plays have proliferated beyond anybody's capacity to read more than a fraction of them, there has been a moratorium on questions about their authorship. That decision is no doubt welcomed by the lucrative Stratford-upon-Avon tourism industry, whose 'curio vendors' are in Louis B. Wright's opinion the only people with a vested interest in Shakespeare-as-author. Even if it could be proved that Bacon had written Shakespeare's plays, Wright continues, 'Britons and Americans' (who 'appreciate a skillful hoax') would continue to visit the Birthplace in order 'to do reverence to one of the shrewdest operators in history'.[126]

The most interesting aspect of this authorship controversy is not who wrote Shakespeare's plays but why the resulting polemic is symptomatic of insecurities at the heart of English studies. As Marjorie Garber argues, this is what makes it 'an exemplary literary event even in its own right'.[127] One of the difficulties evaded by the exclusionist behaviour of professional Stratfordians is that some eminent American writers have been anti-Stratfordians. Honest doubters include Walt Whitman, who on the authorship question stood 'firm against Shakspere . . . the Avon man, the actor'.[128] Emerson, who gave Delia Bacon a letter of introduction to Carlyle, declared in 1850 that it was 'no longer possible' to name the author of Shakespeare's plays. Nathaniel Hawthorne wrote the preface to Delia Bacon's book; and Mark Twain, in *Is Shakespeare Dead?* (1909), declares that 'Shakespeare of Stratford-on-Avon never wrote a play in his life'.[129] The most significant recusant in this company is Henry James, who in 1903 confided to 'immodest' Violet Hunt his 'conviction that the divine William is the biggest and most successful fraud ever practised on a patient world'.[130] That was the year in which James published a story called 'The Birthplace', whose implicit referent is that 'Mecca of the English-speaking race', the Shakespeare

126 Louis B. Wright, 'Anti-Shakespeare Industry', 294.
127 Garber, *Shakespeare's Ghost Writers*, 3.
128 Allen, *Talks with Elizabethans*, 26.
129 Hope and Holston, *Shakespeare Controversy*, 153, 156; Schoenbaum, *Shakespeare's Lives*, 387; Twain, *Is Shakespeare Dead?*, 35.
130 Schoenbaum, *Shakespeare's Lives*, 409.

Birthplace in Stratford-upon-Avon, alias 'Blackport-on-Dwindle'. The explicit themes of James' story are the factitiousness of that place and the duplicity expected of people employed there, who have to avoid 'giv[ing] the Show away' by making up stories about it for the benefit of gullible visitors.[131] The situation fictionalised by James had been experienced by the Northumberland poet, Joseph Skipsey, who in 1891 relinquished his position as custodian of the Bard's birthplace because 'not a single one of the many so-called relics on exhibition could be proved to be Shakespeare's', and even 'the Birthplace itself is a matter of grave doubt'.[132]

If the Stratford man was not Shakespeare, the corpus of his plays becomes a body in the library, deposited there as the result of a crime of writing which transforms the authorship question into 'the ultimate who-dun-it', to quote the subtitle of Ron Allen's *Who Were Shake-Speare?* (1998). This prospect enables Louis B. Wright to disparage the writings of anti-Stratfordians as popular fiction, no doubt 'entertaining for people with a taste for "whodunits" or science fiction', but generically inferior to the serious fiction of Shakespeare studies.[133] Yet every time a Stratfordian puts down a defender of one of the Shakespeare claimants on the grounds that there is insufficient evidence to sustain a case for non-Stratfordian authorship, the question again arises of why so little is known about the man who, according to his contemporary, Ben Jonson, was the greatest writer of 'all time'. Responses to what Helen W. Cyr calls *The Shakespeare Identity Crisis* (1986) render visible the operations of the uncanny in that unstable cultural institution, literary authorship.

[131] Hope and Holston, *Shakespeare Controversy*, 57–65, 168–69.
[132] Ousby, *Englishman's England*, 55.
[133] Louis B. Wright, 'Anti-Shakespeare Industry', 290.

CHAPTER 5

Fantasies of originality

In what was to become for historians of literary forgery the decade of Macpherson and Chatterton, the category of 'original genius' was invented and displayed in the titles of a couple of books published in 1767: William Duff's *Essay on Original Genius* and Robert Wood's *Essay on the Original Genius of Homer*. This formula was a conjunction of two key-terms, one foregrounded in the title of William Sharpe's *Dissertation upon Genius* (1755) and the other in Edward Young's *Conjectures on Original Composition* (1759). As a contribution to literary genetics, original genius (*ingenium*) was used as a way of distinguishing Homer, who allegedly exemplified it, from Virgil, who did not, but had made do instead with art (*ars*). That binary structure could be used homologously to discriminate the polished *ars* of Pope from the raw *ingenium* of Shakespeare, which Elizabeth Montagu celebrated in her anti-Voltairean *Essay on the Writings and Genius of Shakespeare* (1769). For mid-century writers such as Macpherson and Wilkie, therefore, more prestige accrued to the 'Homeric' Macphossian than to *The Epigoniad*, whose studied classicism made it correspondingly Virgilian.

In the proto-Romantic aesthetics which informs Young's *Conjectures on Original Composition*, 'original' is a talismanic word. It remains so. The first publicity brochure for a recent series of facsimiles of medieval manuscript books describes them as 'quasi-originals'. Their 'parchment-like paper' is said to have 'the same touch, thickness and smell as the original', thus adding to the visual and tactile pleasures of direct contact with illuminated vellum pages an as yet untheorised aromatics of reading. Eventually, and with the connivance of scholars, they will become virtual originals, as has happened in the case of the early fifteenth-century *Très Riches Heures du Duc de Berry*, requests to examine which were refused once an expensive facsimile of it had been published.[1] 'Original' is here an unequivocal criterion of value, self-evident to anybody who, acknowledging that 'copies surpass not their originals', concurs with the anti-imitative spirit of Young's rousing question: 'Born originals, how comes it to pass that we die copies?'[2] Yet if, as geneticists have demonstrated, 'our bodies take shape from the transcription of protein templates', how are we to avoid Hillel Schwartz's conclusion that 'copying makes us what we are', or question Edward Said's dictum that both 'nature and language are orders of duplication'?[3]

Even in the eighteenth century, however, Young was not – as he encourages us to believe – the first to valorise a term which he prudently refrains from defining. For as Patricia Phillips has shown, it was already conspicuous in the titles of such books as Henry Baker's *Original Poems: Serious and Humourous* (1725), Tipping Silvester's *Original Poems and Translations* (1733), Thomas Newcomb's *Miscellaneous Collection of Original Poems* (1740) and Francis Hawling's *Miscellany of Original Poems on Various Subjects* (1752).[4] Young's conjectures are not an original but a polemical presentation of a century of misgivings about assessing modern writing in terms of its success in imitating the ancients. Their central contradiction, Joel Weinsheimer points out, is to claim that 'originality must be imitated in order to be originative', and yet at the same time 'be inimitable in order to be unique'.[5] One indication of the pressure exerted by the prestige of originality in this period is the extraordinary behaviour of the Warton brothers, Joseph and Thomas *fils*, who infiltrated ten of their own poems into their father's posthumously published *Poems on Several Occasions* (1748). By doing so they created the illusion that although Thomas Warton the Elder was an exact contemporary of Alexander Pope, and equally Augustan in his themes and style, he nevertheless managed to create – a generation before anybody else – a poetry that celebrates the pleasurable melancholy of solitude in rustic settings, and which his son Joseph was to be instrumental in making a period style of the mid-eighteenth century. Their deception was to disturb the periodisation of English literature by causing unsuspected problems for trend-spotting historians of that proto-

---

[1] Camille, 'The *Très Riches Heures*', 72–73.
[2] Young, *Conjectures on Original Composition*, 332.
[3] Schwartz, *Culture of the Copy*, 211; Said, *World, Text and Critic*, 138.
[4] Phillips, *Adventurous Muse*, 149–56.
[5] Weinsheimer, 'Conjectures on Unoriginal Composition', 66.

Romanticism first named in the title of Paul Van Tieghem's *Le Préromantisme* (1924) and subsequently anglicised as 'Pre-Romanticism'.[6] Yet despite its status as a key component in the Romantic ideology of authorship, 'originality' was not an article of faith to every writer commonly classified as Romantic. 'As to originality', wrote Byron after mistakenly assuming he had been accused of plagiarism by John Galt ('almost the last person on whom any one would commit literary larceny'), 'all pretensions [to it] are ludicrous', because ' "there is nothing new under the sun" '.[7]

To defend 'originality' as the matrix of imagination and the supreme criterion of literary excellence involved developing it as a counter-discourse to imitation, and ignoring the antiquity and durability of *imitatio* as a pedagogical practice for enabling literary apprentices to acquire mastery of their craft. *Imitatio* was institutionalised as a creative application of the textual know-how taught under the rubric of 'rhetoric', which involved identifying and systematising the complete repertoire of stylistic devices used by acknowledged masters of the art of writing. The incorporation of rhetoric into the schooling system therefore perpetuated *imitatio*, the rationale being that a student required to imitate canonical writers would not only appreciate their artistry but learn how to emulate or even surpass them. Quintilian thought it crucial to begin with an 'intention to excel', because even if your *imitatio* fails to do so 'it may at least reach the quality of the example'.[8] Cinthio likewise advised students in 1554 not to be satisfied with having 'equalled' their literary models, but to strive instead 'to surpass [them] . . . as Virgil did with Homer' – or, indeed, as Cinthio himself attempted to do with Boccaccio, when he modelled on *The Decameron* (1348–58) the 'hundred tales' that constitute his own *Hecatommithi* (1565), some of which were translated in William Painter's *Palace of Pleasure* (1566–75) before being creatively imitated in 1604 by Shakespeare in *Othello* and *Measure for Measure*.[9] The potentially debilitating effects of unrelieved servility in the presence of acknowledged masterpieces were thus avoided by figuring the relationship between apprentice and master as agonistic. Successful attempts to out-Cicero Cicero were not

---

[6] Fairer, 'Poems of Thomas Warton the Elder', 400; Scouten, 'Warton Forgeries and the Concept of Preromanticism', 440–41.

[7] Byron, *Letters and Journals*, ed. Prothero, vol. II, 373.

[8] Lausberg, *Handbook of Literary Rhetoric*, 499, quoting Quintilian, *Institutio Oratoria*, x.ii.10.

[9] White, *Plagiarism and Imitation during the English Renaissance*, 22.

disparaged as derivativeness. Such latitude is not enjoyed by recent advocates of 'patchwriting' as a way of encouraging beginners. Rebecca Moore Howard explains that this 'involves "copying from a source text and then deleting some words, altering grammatical structures, or plugging in one-for-one synonym substitutes"'.[10] Whereas patchwriting threatens to domesticate plagiarism in institutions challenged by websites that make it easier for cyber-savvy cheats, *imitatio* nourished the production of texts which blur the distinction between emulation and forgery. Carlo Sigonio was so expert at writing in the manner of Cicero that two centuries elapsed before Tiraboschi discovered the letter which proved that Sigonio had not merely edited the lost text in which Cicero attempts to console himself for the death of his daughter (published in 1583 as *De Consolatio*) but completed it seamlessly from surviving fragments.[11]

The practice of *imitatio* is situated precariously between sameness and difference. Each *imitatio* has to bear at least a family resemblance to that classic text which is the pretext for its own existence, while at the same time improving on it by doing something different. This is achieved more easily when the model is written in some other language than your own, for then instead of aiming to write better Latin than Cicero you can fashion 'Ciceronian' English, as Richard Hooker did when defending the Church of England in his treatise on *The Laws of Ecclesiastical Politie* (1594–97). Whereas translation involves subordinating self to other, neo-classical *imitatio* is an act of insubordination. By treating his classical model as a guide rather than a commander, Johnson transcended the otherwise restrictive conditions of secondariness by imitating Juvenal's tenth satire creatively in 'The Vanity of Human Wishes' (1749). The rhetoric of imitation facilitated literary comparisons by encouraging readers to answer not only the generic question ('what kind of text is this?') but also the evaluative question ('does this text surpass its model?'). The epistemological rationale for imitation was that because 'there is nothing new under the sun' (Ecclesiastes, 1.9), whatever can be said has been said already: *tout est dit*. An eighteenth-century legacy of that Renaissance *querelle des anciens et des modernes*, whose purpose was to determine whether or not the moderns were superior to the ancients, was a battle of the books which inadvertently reminded the

---

[10] Howard, 'Plagiarisms, Authorships, and the Academic Death Penalty', 788.
[11] Chambers, *History and Motives of Literary Forgeries*, 20–21; Grafton, *Forgers and Critics*, 45; Farrer, *Literary Forgeries*, 8.

moderns of their belatedness in cultural history. That conviction generates and sustains cultural pessimism about the possibility of writing anything original. By placing on authors what Walter Jackson Bate calls *The Burden of the Past* (1970), it creates in them a condition psychoanalysed by Harold Bloom as *The Anxiety of Influence* (1973), one of whose symptoms was diagnosed by John Barth as 'The Literature of Exhaustion' (1967).

Post-Romantic critiques of originality, which include both the modernist revival of literary allusiveness and the postmodernist practice of textual appropriation, have created conditions highly favourable to literary forgery. A significantly modernist moment in that history is Flaubert's decision to eliminate quotation marks from the text of *Bouvard et Pécuchet* (1881), a radical move that enables the development of 'a literature of the intertextual' by 'deliberately blurr[ing] the hierarchy between the original text and the secondary text'.[12] Bookish people innocent of the textual politics of this manoeuvre see it instead as one those sophistications that add to the pleasures of reading. Quotation marks, E.E. Kellett observes, direct '*too much* attention to the quotations', and thus grossly intrude on the sensibilities of belletrists, who delight in an unmarked quotation because it stimulates 'a *slight* titillation of the memory'. Contrary to what Kellett thinks, however, there is no 'line dividing quotation from plagiarism', since the identical practice can be classified as either a literary felony or the ultimate in literary sophistication.[13]

In postmodern conditions, fiction emancipates itself from that 'pre-plagiaristic' fantasy disparaged by Raymond Federman as the 'lie of originality'. It does so by accepting 'the fact that literature merely plagiarizes itself', and that since there can be 'no original enunciation', then *to write* is 'first of all *to quote*'.[14] Postmodernism breaks with the ideology of originality by privileging repetition, parody and pastiche. 'In the pastiche-effect of parodic practices', Judith Butler observes, 'the original, the authentic and the real' are de-reified and 'constituted as effects' of discursive processes.[15] Post-modernist fiction signals its distance from fantasies of originality by thematising plagiarism and substituting repetition for singularity. As a result, *Great Expectations* is now the title of novels by both Kathy

[12] Sartiliot, *Citation and Modernity*, 13.
[13] Kellett, *Literary Quotation and Allusion*, 11, 12.
[14] Federman, *Critifiction*, 57, 58, 62.
[15] Butler, *Gender Trouble*, 146.

Acker (1982) and Charles Dickens (1861). The opening chapter of Acker's novel (entitled 'Plagiarism') replicates the first three sentences of Dickens', but does so imperfectly – partly by omitting one word ('father's'), and partly by substituting another ('Peter' for 'Pip') – because evolution in literature as in life depends on errors in the copying process. The Dickens passage reappears (with the substitution intact but the omission corrected) in *My Death, My Life* (1983), a novel attributed by Acker to Pier Paolo Pasolini.[16] Plagiarism can no longer remain the guilty secret of literary production when it is paraded so shamelessly as the appropriatory component in a dynamics of textual dissemination. It becomes pointless to accuse Acker of plagiarism when one of her novels – *In Memoriam to Identity* (1990), the first section of which is entitled 'Rimbaud' and the last 'The Wild Palms' – ends by pointing out that 'all the preceding has been taken from the poems of Arthur Rimbaud, the novels of William Faulkner, and biographical texts on Arthur Rimbaud and William Faulkner'.[17] If the function of this disclaimer is not to mask other and undeclared plagiarisms, then it testifies ironically to Acker's originality, since not everything in this novel is plagiarised from the books she mentions.

The substitution of 'iterability' and 'seriality' for 'originality' is figured with lapidary economy in the numerical title of Joseph Heller's novel, *Catch-22* (1961), which bypasses 'one' (the firstness of origin) in favour of both 'two' (repetition) and 'two-two' (seriality). For as Heller explains in a phrase that itself exemplifies both iteration and seriality, 'everything that happens has happened once before', the corollary of which is that narratives become intelligible only as twice-told tales.[18] What Aristotle calls *anagnoresis* – the 'shock of recognition', in Melville's phrase – can be achieved only by matching what we encounter with what we expect. Recognition, in other words, is less dependent on first encounters with singularities than on the secondariness of those repetitions that constitute replications, since 'the finding of an object is always a *refinding* of it'.[19] This perception is not only thematised brilliantly in William Gaddis' novel about art forgery, *The Recognitions* (1955), but instantiated also in its reception, in so far as its 'originality' was not widely appreciated

---

[16] Acker, *Blood and Guts in High School*, 171, 339.
[17] Acker, *In Memoriam to Identity*, 265.
[18] Nagel, 'Early Composition History of *Catch-22*', 267.
[19] Whitney Davis, *Replications*, 3.

until twenty years later, when Gaddis repeated the demonstration of his literary talents by publishing his second novel, *JR* (1975). In the discipline of cultural studies, which emerged concurrently with such developments, the question of whether cultural artefacts are original attracts less attention than the uses to which they are put by the powerless, whose 'textual poaching' of them for creative purposes signals a rejection of passive consumerism.[20] 'Originality' lost its kudos with a far more traditional constituency when middle-brow readers – whose literary tastes, as expressed in their likes and dislikes, are broadly Romantic – encountered what they took to be 'original rubbish' in a modernism programmatically opposed to Romantic and Victorian tastes.

Since nothing human is created *ex nihilo*, everything is made of something else, and is in that respect a *bricolage*. Somewhat perversely, therefore, the concept of originality in literary studies rests on the hypothesis that there is a single and ascertainable origin for everything, which it is the business of scholarship to discover. Lexicography exemplifies the benefits of this practice, in so far as the *OED* attempts to record not only the original etymon of every word in the English language but also the earliest recorded dates of those different usages that constitute the trajectory of its semantic changes. To valorise the investigation of origins by identifying and dating what seem to be their first recorded appearances is to comply with the diachronic imperative of an 'originological' type of thinking. It is manifest in codicology, which seeks to establish the provenance of manuscripts, and constructs stemmata to trace their descent from a putative or 'lost' original. Such activities identify lacunae that scholars *manqués* are tempted to fill. This happened when a couple of students, 'Mlle Akakia-Viala' [Marie-Antoinette Emilie Allevy] and Nicolas Bataille, wrote a much sought 'missing' poem by Rimbaud ('La Chasse Spirituelle') which they misled *Le Mercure de France* into publishing in 1949.[21] Similar gap-filling opportunities are afforded by bibliography, where the originological impulse fosters a fascination with the 'first' editions of books. As a physical object in print culture, every book has an origin which the Copyright Act of 1710 was designed to recognise legally. The commodification of such objects as collectables by dealers in the rare books trade provided

[20] Jenkins, *Textual Poachers*, 62–3.
[21] Morrissette, *Great Rimbaud Forgery*, iii, 45–87.

Wise with opportunities to feed insatiable desires for an infinitely regressing origin by fabricating for gullible collectors pre-first editions of texts by well-known writers, thus prompting Edmund Gosse to observe that when Wise met God on Judgement Day he would tell Him that 'Genesis is not the true first edition'.[22] But as George Bernard Shaw pointed out when meditating on the origin of the specious, Wise was an original forger: he 'did not forge first editions' but instead 'invented imaginary ones', whose effect was to demote actual originals to a condition of secondariness.[23] However, as soon as we stop thinking of books as objects whose physical properties can be ascertained by positivistic modes of enquiry, and focus instead on what they contain and transmit, then to speak of their 'origins' becomes problematic.

Originological activities undertaken in the name of literary studies include those elaborate forms of textual editing which segue back into famous literary works all those passages that discriminating editors like Maxwell Perkins (who cut thirty per cent of the words from the manuscript of Thomas Wolfe's 1935 novel, *Of Time and the River*) flenched out of them before they were first published.[24] Although such 'restorations' usually retain the titles everybody is familiar with, they were never read by those critics whose enthusiastic appraisals of the 'cut' versions made them famous in the first place. In misrepresenting a utopian reconstruction of an already published text as its suppressed original, such editions are profoundly ahistorical, since a respect for historicity in a print culture is much better served by cheap facsimile reprints of first editions. Yet for Jean-Yves Tadié, who edited the Pléiade edition of Proust, even those sketches and drafts rejected by Proust himself need to be reintegrated into a comprehensive edition of *A la Recherche du temps perdu*. Tadié laboured to reimmerse Proust's novel in those compositional processes from which it pulled clear before being published. As Roger Shattuck was to recall in his hostile response to Tadié's Proust, in 1968 Edmund Wilson similarly criticised 'boondoggling' editors of the MLA's scholarly editions of American authors for cluttering up the texts of famous books with 'rejected garbage'. Such acts of restoration, Shattuck argues, 'unmake a work of literature'.[25] They

[22] Partington, *Wise in the Original Cloth*, 94.
[23] Ibid., 319; Leith Davis, ' "Origins of the Specious" ', 132.
[24] Skipp, '*Of Time and the River*: Final Editing', 313.
[25] Shattuck, 'Threat to Proust', 12, 11.

do so in my opinion by substituting for the first edition – the version of a text that enters the historical record through the public act of publication – a simulacrum made up of the text they think we ought to have had instead. A bizarre instance of the damage done by originological ambitions is the modernised edition of Chatterton published in 1871 by Walter W. Skeat. Convinced (as Malone was) that Chatterton composed in modern English and then antiqued the words, Skeat advocated de-distressing the 'Rowley' poems as a way of uncovering their Chattertonian originals – an aim largely achievable, he thought, by 'substituting Chatterton's words in his *footnotes* for his words in the *text*'.[26]

The dubious idealism of such practices is acknowledged unapologetically by a well-known advocate of architectural restoration. 'To restore a building', Viollet-le-Duc wrote in 1863, 'is to reinstate it in a condition of completeness which could never have existed at any given time'.[27] But whereas anybody who wants to unmake Tadié's edition can do so by returning to the still extant first editions of Proust's writings, in the visual arts repristination is irreversible, which is why debates about it are correspondingly more heated. Passionate sightseers who believe that Renaissance paintings are enhanced by the grime of centuries consider the cleaning of the Sistine Chapel ceiling painted by Michelangelo to be a restoration tragedy, and relish James Beck's polemic against 'the culture, the business and the scandal' of *Art Restoration* (1993). In the rare books trade, on the other hand, restoration engenders different anxieties, since a bibliographical forgery may result from the skilful repair of a defective book by such practices as *remboîtage* (putting it into covers that did not belong to it originally) and 'grangerism' (adding pages cut from other books, a practice first observed in *A Biographical History of England* [1769], by the eponymous James Granger). Craftsmen employed as book-restorers by Robert Riviere, John Collins reports, were so good at their job that a book 'perfected' in their workshops – its missing pages restored in type-facsimile, its worm-holes filled in, and its torn and grubby pages repaired and washed uniformly white – could easily pass as an original and be sold as such.[28]

Attributionists, who seek an origin in a person rather than a text, exemplify the residual power in literary studies of the Romantic

---

26 Skeat, 'Essay on the Rowley Poems', xxxix; Malone, *Cursory Observations on Rowley*, 41.
27 Hillel Schwartz, *Culture of the Copy*, 273.
28 Collins, *Two Forgers: Forman and Wise*, 278–79.

ideology of authorial originality. When G.E. Bentley reported the existence of 'about one hundred anonymous pieces' among the surviving Jacobean and Caroline plays, his finding was treated not as evidence that several theatre companies in seventeenth-century England saw no commercial value in naming their scriptwriters, but rather as a problem for attributionists to solve.[29] Attribution studies are now assisted by stylometrics, a forensic linguistics that uses computer-generated data on the distribution of sub-stylistic features in order to identify authorial 'fingerprints' invisible to literary critics, who are limited to impressionistic observations of surface-effects describable by such adjectives as 'Byronic' or 'Audenesque'. Since technophobic littérateurs are not enticed by the prospect of number-crunching stylistically unspectacular words, stylometric research must generate literary insights comparable to those displayed in J.F. Burrows' book on Jane Austen's novels, *Computation into Criticism* (1987), before it attracts much attention. In addition to naming the actual authors of anonymous or pseudonymous works, and determining who wrote what in collaborative exercises, attributionists also concern themselves with 'works not written by their supposed authors, or doubtfully ascribed', to quote the subtitle of Walter Hart Blumenthal's *False Literary Attributions* (1965). This may result in 'de-attribution', a scholarly practice already sanctioned in the third century BC, when Aristarchus was busy removing pseudo-Homeric accretions from the Homeric canon. A recent example of the phenomenon is *Defoe De-Attributions* (1994), a book in which P.N. Furbank and W.R. Owens winnow some forty-five per cent of the 570 works attributed to Daniel Defoe.[30] Their purificatory act has not generated the hysteria that follows a comparable scrupulousness in the fine arts, where a zealous pursuit of the authentically original has induced cultural anorexia by removing eighty per cent of the corpus of paintings formerly attributed to Rembrandt.

Another major originological endeavour in literary studies is known in the Germanic philological tradition as *Quellenforschung*, which aims to help readers gauge the originality of any literary work by juxtaposing it with its antecedents. Anglophone scholars who regarded it as an arid way of presenting speculations about the genesis of literary texts transformed it into 'influence studies', which

---

[29] Bentley, 'Authenticity and Attribution in Jacobean and Caroline Tragedy', 101.
[30] Furbank and Owens, 'The Defoe That Never Was', 276, 284.

operates with a dual agenda. One is to register traces of the source-text in the work of later writers in order to demonstrate its generative powers as a seminal event in the history of literature, thereby confirming its status as a literary classic; the other, by shifting attention from texts to authors, embeds paired works in narratives of dependency, and does so with the aim of showing just how 'indebted' a later writer is to an earlier one. In their heyday, such procedures were supported by a belief in the autonomy of literature as a symbolic system, which made books appear far more dependent on one another than on what is called life. That perception, which is the guiding principle in Northrop Frye's synoptic *Anatomy of Criticism* (1957), underpinned the diachronic study of literary influences long before structuralism refashioned the object of such enquiries as synchronic 'intertextuality'. In *tout est dit* conditions, when every word is chosen in the knowledge that it has been used countless times already in writings one has never even read, it is heartening – especially if one hopes 'to deculpabilize plagiarism' – to encounter the conclusion Julia Kristeva reached in 1967 after thinking about the implications of Mikhail Bakhtin's dialogic theory of language: namely, that since 'every text is constructed as a mosaic of quotations', and thus 'absorbs and transforms other texts', all writing takes place in conditions of 'intertextuality'.[31] 'Texts are therefore not structures of presence', John Frow argues, 'but traces and tracings of otherness'.[32] To theorise that perception would have been difficult without the revolutionary linguistics of Ferdinand de Saussure. By privileging synchronic relations over diachronic origins in order to break with those originological assumptions which underpin the philological model of language study, Saussure developed a new kind of structural linguistics, based on the rival assumption that how things relate to one another synchronically is more important than where each of them has come from diachronically. In studies of literary influence, literary works are conceived of as singularities with diachronic 'taproots' that scholarly spadework can uncover. Inter-textualists, by contrast, imagine the literary work to be merely a node in a synchronic network of other texts (some literary, most not), whose interrelationships can be figured more accurately – if the organicist analogy is to be retained – by the labyrinthine fibrousness

---

[31] Redfern, *Clichés and Coinages*, 91.
[32] Frow, 'Intertextuality and Ontology', 45.

of a 'rhizome', on which Deleuze and Guattari modelled in 1976 their 'rhizomatic' way of thinking about cultural processes.[33] Borges' intriguing story about a nineteenth-century Frenchman, Pierre Menard, who decides to acculturate himself into early seventeenth-century Spain so thoroughly as to be able to write Cervantes' *Don Quixote*, is concerned much more with 'the power' and 'the limits of intertextual reading', Linda Hutcheon observes, than with 'the influences or sources available to a writer or rewriter'.[34]

Misgivings about the origin as an epistemological concept circulate concurrently with the aesthetic cult of originality as a criterion of value. In 1876 Emerson observed that the 'origin' is merely the name given to derivations we are unaware of: even 'the originals', he remarks, 'are not original'.[35] Freud searched for the 'primal scene' (*Urszene*) of childhood neurosis, only to discover 'a multiplicity of origins', and in each case 'another origin in the origin'.[36] Since what the 'origin' marks is not the beginning of something but the horizon beyond which our understanding of its genesis can go no further, hermeneutically it is always irretrievable. A desire for 'the' origin is symptomatic of a monism that seeks to subordinate diversities to a prior singularity from which they are deemed to have derived. A famous example is that Indo-European *Ursprache* which nineteenth-century philologists tried to reconstruct in response to Sir William Jones' conjecture in 1786 that Sanskrit, Greek and Latin had evolved from a no longer existent common source. What questers find when they reach the limits of their enquiries, however, is never a singularity. Instead, it is one of those hybridities or creolisations that lead Jean-Loup Amselle to argue in his *Mestizo Logics* (1990) 'that mixture is originary', as Daniel Defoe had revealed when exposing the 'Roman–Saxon–Danish–Norman' pedigree of *The True-Born Englishman* (1701).[37] Other theorists who critique the problem of the 'origin' from widely different perspectives are equally sceptical. What is to Derrida a logocentric construct in need of deconstruction is to Edward Said the product of a 'theological' state of mind, and therefore much less useful in cultural analysis than the correspondingly 'secular' concept of a

---

[33] Deleuze and Guattari, *A Thousand Plateaus*, 3–25.
[34] Hutcheon, 'Literary Borrowing . . . Stealing', 233.
[35] Emerson, 'Quotation and Originality', 428.
[36] Carroll, 'Freud and the Myth of Origin', 523.
[37] Amselle, *Mestizo Logics*, x; David Nichol Smith (ed.), *Oxford Book of Eighteenth Century Verse*, 7.

constructed 'beginning'.[38] Consequently, when declaring that something is original we do not put an end to further enquiries but
merely foreclose them. Like 'genius', the 'origin' turns out to be
one of those pseudo-explanatory words that explain nothing, and
the 'original' a mere mystification of something presumed to
antecede the materialities of residual objects. Distinctions between
literature and literary forgery, therefore, need to be based on
something more substantial than a belief that the former is original
whereas the latter is not.

Literary forgers have been given *Lebensraum* because neither the
literary world nor the profession of English studies has managed to
develop workable distinctions between 'quotation' (the scrupulous
acknowledgement of someone else's words), 'allusion' (that subtlety
of textual recall which offers the pleasures of recognition to well-read
people) and 'plagiarism' (which is commonly treated as theft). The
relationship between the phrase 'lucid intervall' in Dryden's 'Mac
Flecknoe' (1682) and the title of James Carkesse's *Lucida Intervalla*
(1679) could be explained equally well as a sophisticated 'allusion' or
a blatant 'plagiarism'.[39] Such terms fail to establish the differences
they claim to distinguish because they are constructs generated by
aspect-seeing. This makes them vulnerable to destabilisation by a
number of variables: speculations about authorial intentions, pre-
suppositions about the literary value of the work in which traces of
texts by other people are discernible, and class distinctions (gentlemen 'allude'; Grub Street hacks 'plagiarise').[40] In conditions of high
literacy, to be well-read is a virtue, and to be seen to be so in one's
own writings poses no problems, provided certain protocols are
observed. 'A great man quotes bravely', Emerson declares, 'and will
not draw on his invention when his memory serves him with a word
as good'.[41] Characteristically, 'genius borrows nobly' by means of its
'assimilating power', which is why Shakespeare – and here Emerson
bravely quotes Walter Savage Landor – came to be 'more original
than his originals'.[42] But if writers deemed neither great nor noble
attempt this sort of thing, it is classified as a fault, because then
'quotation confesses inferiority'.[43]

---

[38] Derrida, *Of Grammatology*, 92; Said, *Beginnings*, 372–73.
[39] Nichol, 'Rewriting Plagiarism', 16.
[40] Rogers, *Grub Street*, 359.
[41] Emerson, 'Quotation and Originality', 429.
[42] Ibid., 433.   [43] Ibid., 432.

Emerson's pseudo-distinction typifies the failure of literary critics who venture into that interstitial space where quotation, allusion and plagiarism coexist to explain why it is deemed all right for some, but not for others, to engage in the same recombinant practices. A frequently misquoted aphorism in T.S. Eliot's essay on Philip Massinger (1920) declares that 'immature poets imitate; mature poets steal'. The corollary of this, Eliot goes on to say, is that 'bad poets deface what they take', whereas 'good poets make it into something better'.[44] It was probably in the spirit of this high-brow and hierarchical version of the *così fan tutte* defence of plagiarism that W.A. Edwards subtitled his 1933 book on the subject 'an essay on good and bad borrowing'. And Eliot's distinction was to surface again in Harold Bloom's argument that plagiarism is sometimes admirable and sometimes not. To plagiarise 'great writers' is a 'pious activity' which signals 'reverence' if not 'idolatry' on the part of the plagiarist, whose work serves the 'critical function' of reminding us of just how great the great really are. To plagiarise second-rate authors, on the other hand, is not only an 'immoral' act (because 'bad currency drives out the good') but an unequivocal sign of a second-rate talent.[45] Shakespeare's verbatim incorporation into *Antony and Cleopatra* (1606–07) of phrases from Thomas North's translation of Plutarch's *Lives* (1579) is not regarded as plagiarism by a hard-pressed scriptwriter for a Jacobean theatre company, but mystified instead as the transmutation of a literary source by a verbal alchemist. Far from being concealed, the parallel passages are paraded as offering a rare glimpse of Shakespeare at work. There seems to be one law for canonical writers and another for the rest. Who would have thought Coleridge capable of surviving Norman Fruman's attack on him in 1971 as an 'archangel' who 'damaged' his reputation by being a compulsive plagiariser? Fruman made it more difficult for editors enthralled by the Romantic ideology of originality to extract traces of authentic Coleridge from the plagio-textuality it is embedded in.[46] Yet Coleridge was defended by Coleridgeans who engaged in damage control on behalf of their archangel by attacking Fruman's book.[47] By revealing one of the internal contradictions of literary

---

[44] Eliot, *Selected Prose*, ed. Kermode, 153.
[45] Bloom *et al.*, 'Plagiarism', 413.
[46] Fruman, *Coleridge, the Damaged Archangel, passim.*
[47] Peter Shaw, 'Plagiary', 333–36.

studies, such episodes question the commonly encountered assumption that literature is allusive whereas literary forgery is plagiaristic.

Dissatisfaction with attempts to make originality the *sine qua non* of first-rate writing is signalled by a widespread ambivalence about its alleged antithesis, plagiarism. The disturbing recognition that plagiarism is not a corruption of literature but systemic to it is epitomised in H.M. Paull's observation that 'the history of plagiarism is indeed the history of literature'.[48] If 'literary plagiarism' is taken to be a solecism like 'free liberty', the plagiarising of plagiarists becomes fair game. Scandalously, Shakespeare himself first attracted attention in London as a plagiarist, when Robert Greene – who describes Shakespeare in his *Groatsworth of Wit* (1592) as an 'upstart Crow, beautified with our feathers' – renamed him 'Shake-scene', which was Elizabethan argot for 'scene-stealer'.[49] Even writers whose work is praised for its originality confess to plagiarism. Mark Twain, who plagiarised Max Adeler's short story, 'The Fortunate Island' (1882), in *A Connecticut Yankee at the Court of King Arthur* (1889), told Helen Keller that there is not 'much of anything in any human utterance, oral or written, *except* plagiarism!'.[50] Spotting plagiarisms was a favourite pastime of Poe, who intended to write (but never did) a 'Chapter on American Cribbage' designed to reveal 'the minute trickeries' used by literary kleptomaniacs 'to disguise their stolen wares', and whose own works are what his more generous critics call 'indebted' to various writers, including E.T.A. Hoffmann, Byron and Milton.[51] From 1835 until 1837 he contributed to the *Southern Literary Messenger* a feature called 'Pinakidia', which anthologises a large number of literary plagiarisms from biblical to modern times. His learned notes on them mix genuine with bogus erudition for ironic effect. Typical of Poe's double-take on his subject-matter is the item in which he quotes five lines from Tasso's *Gerusalemme Liberata* (1581) before denouncing them as 'a curious specimen of literary robbery' from the Roman poet Lucan's *Pharsalia* and one of Sulpicius' letters to Cicero. Poe achieves this erudition-effect by concealing his own literary robbery of both the example and its sources from the second dialogue in Dominique Bouhours' *La Manière de bien penser* (1687).[52]

---

[48] Paull, *Literary Ethics*, 103.
[49] Berek, 'The "Upstart Crow" and Shakespeare as Reviser', 205.
[50] Kruse, 'Literary Old Offenders', 10; Swan, 'Helen Keller, Plagiarism, Authorship', 68.
[51] Adkins, 'Poe and Plagiarism', 169.
[52] Poe, *Brevities*, ed. Pollin, 68–69.

Psychoanalytic critics offer predictable diagnoses of writers who protest too much about plagiarism. 'The man who is always compulsively searching for plagiarisms of others', observes Edmund Bergler, 'is *a priori* to be suspected of wanting to plagiarize himself'.[53] But such banalities are unlikely to net self-conscious tricksters like Poe who, disguised as 'Walter G. Bowen', wrote in 1846 a piece called 'A Reviewer Reviewed', in which he complains that Poe the plagiary-catcher has himself committed 'wilful and deliberate literary theft'.[54] More recent investigators of plagiarism have focused on its hidden gender politics, an iconic case being the dispute between Zelda Sayre and Scott Fitzgerald as to who plagiarised whom. Convinced that Fitzgerald had illicitly made use of her diary and letters when writing *The Beautiful and Damned* (1922), Sayre concluded that her husband 'seem[ed] to believe that plagiarism begins at home'. Fitzgerald, on the other hand, later claimed that a whole section of Sayre's *Save Me the Waltz* (1932) imitated both the rhythm and content of his own novel-in-progress, *Tender Is the Night* (1934). Reciprocities which sustain a partnership that works become the source of recriminations in one that does not, and so critics need to be wary of taking sides in domestic spats such as this one, which concerns rival fictional transformations of the same marriage.[55]

Plagiarism continues to thrive as a political (and specifically anti-capitalist) act directed against ownership, property and the law which sustains them. Pierre Prudhon's revolutionary paradox that 'all property is theft' – reiterated in 1987 at the International Festival of Plagiarism – thus recirculates in the world of cultural capital when Bertolt Brecht describes 'theft' as 'the first-law of creativity'.[56] Recognising that in the cultural conditions of late capitalism the Aladdin's Cave of literature has been incorporated into a global supermarket at which 'all the artists of history . . . offer their wares', William S. Burroughs has no qualms about advising young writers to 'steal anything in sight': by doing so they will disemburden themselves of 'the fetish of originality', that mystification of 'the idea of words as *property* – one's "very own words"'.[57] Burroughs' own coming-out as *un voleur honteux* ('a closet thief') was encouraged by

53 Silverman, *Edgar A. Poe*, 491.
54 Ibid., 318–19.
55 Dale Spender, *The Writing or the Sex?*, 175–92.
56 Cosgrove, 'In Praise of Plagiarism', 38.
57 Burroughs, 'Les Voleurs', 21, 19, 20.

Brion Gysin, whose literary practice condones 'overt and *traceable* plagiarism', justified on the grounds that by judiciously selecting precursors to steal from you actually 'honor' them with the 'benediction of [your] theft'.[58] By figuring the relationship between writers and their predecessors in terms of consumer choice, Gysin demystifies that earlier and astrological conception of the literary tradition as a firmament inhabited by 'stars' whose charismatic works 'influence' subsequent generations of writers. Burroughs, on the other hand, here favours the kind of plagiarism which is untraceable because it dispenses with verbal similarities. Since its presence is never even suspected, it escapes the attentions of whistle-blowers on the lookout for evidence of literary malpractice. For if Burroughs himself had not drawn attention to the fact, who would have guessed that 'the interview between Carl Peterson and Doctor Benway' in *Naked Lunch* (1959) 'is modelled on the interview between Razumov and Councillor Mikulin in Conrad's *Under Western Eyes* [1911]'? What Burroughs stole was neither the characters nor the content of their dialogue but certain formal and stylistic properties of Conrad's text, such as 'Mikulin's trick of unfinished sentences, his elliptical approach, and the conclusion of the interview'.[59] Poe thought this 'the most barbarous class of literary robbery', because in bypassing 'the words of the wronged author' it 'purloin[s]' his 'most intangible, and therefore his least defensible and least reclaimable property'.[60]

Some people think that the status of plagiarism can be determined by looking up the word in the *OED*, unaware of the fact that the business of such dictionaries is to show how words have been used rather than to pronounce authoritatively on what they mean. A commonly accepted etymology uncovers the metaphor hidden in the word 'plagiarism' by sourcing it to the Latin *plagiarius* ('a stealer of slaves'), thus confirming its origin as an offence against property. That dead metaphor was both reactivated and literalised when the African American novelist, Barbara Chase-Riboud, claimed that her best-selling *Echo of Lions* (1989) – which describes a revolt by slaves being transported from Africa to Cuba on the Spanish ship, 'L'Amistad' – had been plagiarised in the film by Steven Spielberg called *Amistad* (1997), only to be told that it was based on William O. Owens' *Black Mutiny* (1953), which Chase-Riboud was then accused

---

[58] Ibid., 21, 20.   [59] Ibid., 20.
[60] Adkins, 'Poe and Plagiarism', 195.

of having plagiarised.[61] Alternative etymologies assembled by lexicographers support different reactions to the presence in any text of
traces of earlier ones. The etymon of your choice will enable you to
figure the *plagiarius* as a 'child-seducer', 'slave-thief', 'enslaver of the
free', or 'game-hunter' whose *plaga* is both the 'territory' he roams
and the 'nets' he sets there. These incompatible senses establish
'plagiarism' as the site of an endogenous difference, a word burdened
with the impossible task of overcoming the contradictory associations
of both 'freedom and constraint' and 'enslavement and release' in
texts that are somehow both private property protected by law and
common property available for appropriation.[62]

Creative etymologisers introduce further complications. In 1887,
when Oscar Wilde had already acquired a reputation for plagiarism
as a poet but was yet to achieve fame as a dramatist, he shifted the
emphasis from etymon to homophone by apparently quoting Mark
Twain and defining 'plagiarist' as 'a writer of plays'.[63] This pun is
embedded in the subtitle of the book in which that champion of
consumer-rights, Gerard Langbaine, exposed the malpractices of
'crafty Bookseller's' who 'vent old Plays with new Titles': *Momus
Triumphans; or, the Plagiaries of the English Stage* (1688).[64] Whereas
orthography stabilises the spelling as 'plagiarism', heterographies
register reconceptualisations and therefore revaluations of the
activity thus labelled. Raymond Federman, who defines 'imagination' as 'plagiarism' (because it involves 'bringing together pieces of
other discourses'), prefers the spelling 'pla[y]giarism', because it
draws attention to those ludic elements that turn writing into 'a
game, a performance'.[65] When the imagination is conceived of as an
antinomian activity, the plagiarism that serves it is rendered visible
by a Joycean neologism in *Finnegans Wake* (1939), 'pelagiaris[m]'. Like
the spelling 'plagianisme' in Sir Thomas Browne's *Pseudodoxia Epidem-
ica* (1650), it evokes the name of that early fifth-century heresiarch,
Pelagius, whose arguments against Christian doctrine on sin and
grace came to be denounced as Pelagian heresies.[66] Another spelling
that seeks to erase from the word its history of negativity is the

[61] Huck, 'A Fraction too Much Fiction', 30, 32.
[62] Hayes, 'Plagiarism and Legitimation in Eighteenth-Century France', 116–17.
[63] Guy, 'Self-Plagiarism, Creativity and Craftsmanship in Wilde', 9.
[64] McGrail, 'From Plagiaries to Sources', 170–71; Kewes, 'Langbaine's "View of Plagiaries" ',
4.
[65] Federman, *Critifiction*, 49, 51.
[66] Grace, 'Respecting Plagiarism', 461, 478; Kewes, 'Langbaine's "View of Plagiaries" ', 9.

calculatedly opaque 'plagerism'. John Berndt introduced it in 1986 when advocating the importance of transcending 'the capitalist values of "originality" and "creativity"' in post-industrial societies. These are so burdened with 'information overload', he argues, that the business of 'choosing what material to plagerize' becomes 'as much a "creative" act as the construction of the images, ideas and texts in the first place'.[67] To defend plagiarism in these terms is to reject the capitalistic basis of a cultural institution that legitimates authorship as ownership.

As the case of Martin Luther King was to show, such licence is not tolerated in institutions whose mission statements recognise cultural diversity but whose practices reify cultural uniformity. The son of a Baptist preacher, King grew up in a culture of African American pulpit oratory whose conventions include the phenomenon of 'voice-merging'. Developed in communities accustomed to treat words as 'shared assets, not personal belongings', writes Keith D. Miller, it involves 'creating a voice by melding it with those of previous speakers'.[68] Those cultural conditions did not prevail in Boston University's School of Theology, which awarded him the degree of Ph.D, although the 'text-merging' he had used when writing his thesis was not detected by the examiners who passed it. Unsourced polyvocality may well be permitted in pulpits or on political platforms, but in the academy it is treated as plagiarism, and was denounced as such in 1990 when the *Wall Street Journal* reported that King's doctoral dissertation contains unacknowledged quotations from other writers. Evidently, the defence of 'plagiarism' in terms of cultural difference is more successful in diachronic than synchronic instances. For whereas Giles Constable argues persuasively that 'plagiarism' is an unsuitable term to use of appropriatory practices by medieval writers ('since it expresses a concept of literary individualism and property that is distinctively modern'), no university nowadays would accept the argument that King's behaviour as a postgraduate student should be judged in terms of the black culture he came out of rather than the white culture he went into.[69] The protocols of the academy King sought accreditation from could not be waived on the grounds that they represent un-African American conceptions of literary property.

---

[67] Home, *Plagiarism*, 8.
[68] Keith D. Miller, 'Composing Martin Luther King, Jr.', 78–79.
[69] Constable, 'Forgery and Plagiarism in the Middle Ages', 39.

Traditionalists convinced that there is nothing new under the sun expect to discover their every move anticipated by some precursor. In extra-literary conceptions of plagiarism, however, intertextual relationships are criminalised as a cross-generational phenomenon, in which the younger are always the accused. This is inevitable when time is understood to be unidirectional, since only posterity can enjoy the privileges of plagiarism. But if the structure of time is imagined instead to be palindromic – that is, capable of being read 'backwards' as well as forwards, like the word 'level' – it becomes possible (as it was for the Oulipo group) to describe as an 'anticipatory plagiary' any author who has previously published what you yourself have just written.[70] This strategy enables authors prone to the anxiety of influence to avoid the paranoia displayed by an imaginary Portuguese writer in a short story by Joyce Carol Oates, who was convinced that 'an army of young men' was 'plagiarizing [his] works . . . before they were written'.[71]

We should not be surprised to discover, therefore, considerable resistance to the idea that literary 'plagiarism' is not the deplorable practice it is generally made out to be. After all, since writers tend to be readers, what they have read is likely to show up in what they write. Tolerance of plagiarism is aided by the fact that the law takes no interest in self-plagiarism, which is the use of bits of one's earlier writings as unmarked components of a 'new' text. Some readers object if they happen to notice it, as Poe did when he caught Longfellow in the act; but as a recent biographer observes, Poe himself 'frequently. . . shift[ed] sentences or whole paragraphs from one of his hundreds of reviews and notices to another'.[72] Self-plagiarism was likewise second-nature to Oscar Wilde, who treated his epigrams and aphorisms as reusables. But then Wilde – the conversationalist accused by Whistler in 1888 of dining with his friends so that he could 'pick from [their] platters the plums for the pudding he peddle[d] in the provinces' – had no qualms about inserting into an unpublished lecture he gave in 1886 on Chatterton *objets trouvés* from both Daniel Wilson's biographical study of *Chatterton* (1869) and David Masson's *Chatterton: The Story of the Year 1770* (1874).[73]

---

[70] Home, *Plagiarism*, 6.
[71] 'Fernandes de Briao', 'Plagiarized Material', 177.
[72] Silverman, *Edgar A. Poe*, 256.
[73] Whistler, *Gentle Art of Making Enemies*, 164; Guy, 'Self-Plagiarism, Creativity and Craftsmanship in Wilde', 7, 21.

Wilde's admirers tend not to dwell upon this aspect of his work, and those who do prefer to treat it as symptomatic of the anti-Romantic artifice he cultivated in order to dandify his style, rather than as evidence of either the laziness encouraged by a decadent cult of lassitude or the corner-cutting measures prompted by a need to meet deadlines. Similarly, autoplagiarism is treated as merely part of the repertoire of postmodernist fiction when Peter Ackroyd is observed recycling in *Chatterton* (1987) an observation made in his earlier novel, *The Last Testament of Oscar Wilde* (1983).[74] Johnson's habit of quoting from his own writings in order to illustrate the definitions in his *Dictionary* (1755) – over half of the 'anonymous' quotations in which are also from texts by Johnson – is regarded merely as an eccentricity comparable to Laurence Sterne's economical reissue for his mistress of some of the love-letters he had formerly addressed to his wife.[75] But when such goings-on were uncovered in the prolific *oeuvre* of a best-selling writer, 'Jack Higgins' (Harry Patterson, the author of *The Eagle Has Landed* [1975]), the media, which habitually segregates pulp-fiction from 'literature', represented his self-plagiarism as a literary scandal.[76]

Experienced readers, on the other hand, tend to be more tolerant of such practices. When John Dryden describes Ben Jonson as 'a learned plagiary' of the ancients, whom an equally learned reader could 'track ... everywhere in their snow', he does so out of admiration.[77] The literary economy in which both writers worked obliged them to return with interest whatever they had borrowed. This can be seen in Jonson's much anthologised lyric, 'Drink to me only with thine eyes', where half-a-dozen images and phrases translated without acknowledgement from the *Epistles* of Philostratus have been skilfully fashioned into a simulacrum of effortless spontaneity.[78] Literariness encourages such obliquities, the outcomes of which can be complicated. About three-quarters of the way through Sir Philip Sidney's sonnet sequence, *Astrophil and Stella* (1582), the poetaster who is its hero declares himself to be 'no pick-purse of another's wit'. This affirmation of originality is embedded in a

---

[74] Finney, 'Ackroyd, Postmodernist Play and *Chatterton*', 253–54.
[75] Wimsatt and Wimsatt, 'Self-Quotations in Johnson's Dictionary', 62; Mallon, *Stolen Words*, 21.
[76] Steinhauer, 'Jack Higgins', 52.
[77] Dryden, 'Essay of Dramatic Poesy', ed. Jones, 137.
[78] Kenner (ed.), *Seventeeth Century Poetry*, xxv–xxvi.

sonnet in which Astrophil explains that he writes without the
privileges accorded ancient Greek poets, whose enviable access to
inspirational locations is legendary. Unlike them, Astrophil remarks,
he himself 'never dranke of Aganippe well' (which was sacred to the
Muses) nor ever sat 'in shade of Tempe', the valley in which the god
of poetry, Apollo, pursued Daphne until she metamorphosed into a
laurel bush. Although Astrophil's apology for his poetry reads
nowadays like a refreshingly personal testimony in poems whose
artifice is misrecognised by Romantic readers as artificiality, it was
already a commonplace in Renaissance poetry. Sidney picked it out
of the purses of French Pléiade poets such as Pierre de Ronsard and
Joachim du Bellay; they in turn had filched it from the Roman poet,
Persius, who prefaces his *Satires* by remarking that he has neither
drunk from the fountain of Hippocrene on Mt Helicon nor dreamt
on the twin-peaks of Parnassus.[79] Like the modesty *topos* used by
Shakespeare in *Julius Caesar* to introduce a superbly oratorical
performance by Mark Antony ('I am no orator'), the deprivation
topos deployed by Astrophil mobilises the rhetorical device of *dubitatio*
('feigned oratorical helplessness') in order to elicit a sympathetic
response from a potentially hostile audience. Sidney here plagiarises
his predecessors in order to compose Astrophil's declaration of
originality. Such deviousness is known in literary studies as 'sophistication', since it effects an ironic distance between the author of a
work and the characters within it. In the case of *Astrophil and Stella*,
however, that distance appears to contract if not disappear altogether, in so far as the fictional person who loves Stella ('star') is
given a name based on that of the author of the work in which he
appears. Because the 'phil' in Philip is Greek for 'lover', and the 'sid'
in Sidney suggests the Latin *sidus* ('star'), the star-loving character
called 'Philisides' in Sidney's *Arcadia* is renamed in the sonnet
sequence 'Astrophil' (from Greek *aster*, 'star'). Inexperienced readers
who think that first-person statements in literary works have the
veridical status of an authorial affidavit or statutory declaration are
unlikely to welcome the irony here of a plagiarised declaration of
originality by a fictional character who in some ways is and in other
ways is not identical with the author who invented him.

Moments like this are especially piquant to readers with a taste for
the literariness of literature, and who appreciate jocular evasions like

---

[79] Sidney, *The Poems*, ed. Ringler, 203–04, 480.

Chaucer's acknowledgement of an imaginary 'auctor called Lollyus' (rather than Boccaccio's *Filostrato*) for information about the Trojan war he used when writing *Troylus and Criseyde* (1372–86).[80] Such people make ideal readers of Book 5 of *Tristram Shandy* (1762), where Sterne denounces plagiarism in words plagiarised from the 1652 edition he owned of Robert Burton's *Anatomy of Melancholy* (which is itself a vast cento), but then adds that 'showing the *relicks of learning*' is excusable provided you work some 'miracle with them'.[81] The most famous example of a plagiarised claim to originality, however, occurs in Jonathan Swift's transformation of the mock-obituary into a mock-auto-obituary called 'Verses on the Death of Dr Swift' (1739). Respecting the generic convention that to elegise is to eulogise (*de mortuis nil nisi bonum*), Swift describes himself as an author who 'to steal a Hint was never known', since 'what he writ was all his own'. The irony of this remark not only escaped such well-read contemporaries of Swift as Alexander Pope but remained unrecorded until 1905, when the editor of Samuel Johnson's *Lives of the Poets* (1779–81), George Birbeck Hill, sourced it to a couplet in Sir John Denham's elegy on the death of Abraham Cowley (1667): 'To him no author was unknown / Yet what he wrote was all his own'.[82]

Swift's unrivalled reputation as an ironist encourages us to assume that his plagiarism of Denham was both intentional and designed as a double-take. But in many other cases, authorial intent is less easy to determine. This problem is bypassed in conditions of intertextuality, however, where textual convergences are likely to occur irrespectively of authorial intentions, as Coleridge indicated when objecting to source-sleuths who assume that 'every rill they behold flowing' derives from 'a perforation made in some other man's tank'.[83] In a shared lexicon whose semantic and rhythmical components are continuously in use and always undergoing transformation, words and phrases interact with one another promiscuously, and in ways beyond the control of someone who happens to put them together at a particular moment and with particular purposes and readers in mind. A pertinent example of the slippage between a controlled allusion like Swift's and the uncontrollable associations woven into the web of intertextuality is the evocative title of a book described in

[80] Pask, *Emergence of the English Author*, 10; Nelson, 'From Fraud to Fiction', 30.
[81] Jackson, 'Sterne, Burton and Ferriar', 460, 468, 461.
[82] Slepian, 'Ironic Intention of Swift's Verses on His Own Death', 255.
[83] Ruthven, *Critical Assumptions*, 121.

a note by its author, 'Helen Demidenko', as 'a work of fiction', a generic marker wilfully ignored by people who denounced it as anti-Semitic propaganda masquerading as revisionist history. *The Hand That Signed the Paper* (1994) conjures up through its epigraph a poem by Dylan Thomas first published in 1935, when the Nuremburg Laws formally denied political rights to German Jews by depriving them of Reich citizenship. Reprinted in 1971 as one of Frederic Prokosch's bogus 'Butterfly' pamphlets, it was backdated to 1939, when the hand that had signed the Munich agreement felled Czechoslovakia. The rhythmical structure of Thomas' opening line, 'The hand that signed the paper felled a city', appears to recall ironically the pseudo-proverbial statement in a poem published by William Stewart Ross in 1894: 'the hand that rocks the cradle . . . rules the world'. The spectral paradigm for such formulations is discernible also in one of the lines in Jonathan Swift's 1720 verses on the death of a usurer called Demar: 'The hand that signed the mortgage paid the shot'. And who knows what text was being rewritten here, deliberately or inadvertently, by the man who, in his poem 'On Poetry' (1733), mocked those who 'quote quotation on quotation'?[84] As a writer who appears allusive to some readers but plagiaristic to others, 'Demidenko' is unlikely to find all of these intertexts equally useful. In conditions of intertextuality, however, her preferences have no exclusionary power over the range of resonances generated by the title of her novel.

What we call 'plagiarism' and 'originality' are merely reifications of different vectors in the composite and interactive processes that sustain an economy of literary production in which the same author can be both agent and patient in transactions with other writers. After Defoe had plagiarised a 1695 edition of William Camden's *Britannia* (1586) in *A Tour through Great Britain* (1724–27), his own *Political History of the Devil* (1726) was plagiarised by Mary Hamilton in her novel, *Munster Village* (1778).[85] Seeing that plagiarism in the domain of literature does not create the problems caused by comparable practices in the sciences or even in literary studies, I see no harm in trying to think more positively about so ubiquitous a practice. As Neal Bowers admitted, being plagiarised was the most notable event in the first twenty-five years of his career as a poet, not

---

[84] Redfern, *Clichés and Coinages*, 77.
[85] Rogers, 'Defoe as Plagiarist', 772; Johns, 'Mary Hamilton, Daniel Defoe, and Plagiarism', 25.

least because the press-release for the book he wrote about his pursuit of the felon, *Words for the Taking* (1997), was syndicated as a news item around the world.[86] Being plagiarised by Alex Haley in *Roots* (1976) enabled Harold Courlander to settle out of court in 1978 for half-a-million dollars and consequently publish a new edition of his out-of-print novel in question, *The African* (1967). And both agent and patient attracted extensive media attention when Stephen Spender, 'arguing that he had the "moral right" to control the presentation of his own life', threatened to sue the publisher of David Leavitt's novel, *While England Sleeps* (1993), which rewrites explicitly a homosexual episode in Spender's autobiographical *World within World* (1951). Leavitt's novel – already in American bookshops when his publisher decided to avoid a lawsuit by withdrawing it – became 'a valuable collector's item'; and Spender's autobiography, which had been out of print for a dozen years, was reissued in 1994.[87] In fact, Leavitt's plagiarism aroused so much interest in a writer who is thought of as a 1930s poet that Spender was able to celebrate his eighty-fifth birthday by publishing his first book of poems in nearly a decade, *Dolphins* (1994), which is dedicated to Christopher Isherwood and the other three members of that composite beast of yesteryear, 'MacSpaunday'. But there was no Spenderian nostalgia in Leavitt's goodbye to all that. Between the first and second paperback versions of *While England Sleeps* he published a novella about a 'term paper artist' called David Leavitt, who is 'in trouble' because he has been sued by 'an English poet (now dead)', and who helps college boys fulfil their course requirements by writing essays for them in exchange for sexual favours.[88] The consequences of such episodes indicate that the cultural phenomenon they represent cannot be accounted for merely by replicating the understandable anger expressed by writers who have been plagiarised. Other forces are in operation, and other values are at stake.

---

[86] Bowers, *Words for the Taking*, 128.
[87] Leeming, *Stephen Spender*, 255–56.
[88] Leavitt, *Arkansas*, 3.

CHAPTER 6

Rhetorics of authenticity

The continuing success of literary forgeries will not surprise anybody familiar with the scandal of literature itself, which results from its ancient alliance with rhetoric (the art of persuasion) rather than with logic (the science of reasoning) or ethics (the principles of moral conduct). In order to uncover that rhetorical pedigree it is necessary to peel off the moralistic overlay imposed not only on literature by liberal humanist literary studies but also on rhetoric by ethics.

In the final book of his treatise on how to educate an orator, *Institutio Oratoria* (XII.i.1), Quintilian borrows from the Elder Cato his definition of the orator as *vir bonus dicendi peritus* ('a good man, skilled in speaking'). This formulation was to prove strategically useful in humanistic theories of education, where *dicendi peritus* means speaking well in a morally responsible manner, and the study of rhetoric is legitimated by being made subordinate to ethics. Yet this conception of rhetoric is much more the work of a moral philosopher than a rhetorician, whose skills are described more accurately in the definition of rhetoric given in the second book of Quintilian's treatise (II.xvii.37): *ars bene dicendi* ('the art of speaking well'). For although ethics may resort to rhetoric in order to persuade us to lead morally responsible lives, rhetoric has no need whatsoever of ethics. As an autonomous, comprehensive and structured ensemble of linguistic devices designed to induce specific effects, rhetoric equips those who master it with the know-how to say well whatever needs to be said in any situation, whatever their personal opinions might be. 'He is a poor author', Chatterton declared, 'who cannot write on both sides' in a debate.[1] Rhetoric enables this flexibility by tabulating the connections between particular arrangements of words and the responses they are likely to induce in people who hear them. As a

---

[1] McGann, 'Infatuated Worlds of Chatterton', 235.

146

verbal technology designed for suasive rather than confessional purposes, it erodes belief in the sincerity of heart-felt utterances (and similar delusions fostered by a naively expressivist theory of language) by revealing both the discursive procedures for feigning sincerity and the art of creating the illusion of artlessness. The point of studying the art of rhetoric is to become *dicendi peritus*, whether or not you happen to be a *vir bonus*; if you are not, rhetoric will not make you into one, although it will teach you how to masquerade as one. In this respect, rhetoric is both an impersonal and amoral form of verbal expertise, which is why moralists seek to control it: for if a *vir* is not *bonus*, his rhetorical skills will become 'dangerous' when put to equally effective use in what are agreed to be socially undesirable practices, such as demagoguery and propaganda.

Literature's long-standing alliance with rhetoric as a suasive rather than a probative mode of discourse compromises its intermittent claims to be a veridical medium. Rhetoric catalogues and explains the uses of such figures of deception as hyperbole and litotes, irony and metaphor. Its repertoire of devices includes *apophasis* ('pretending to deny what is really affirmed'), *apoplanesis* ('evading the issue by digressing') and *occultatio* ('emphasizing something by pointedly seeming to pass over it').[2] Ever since Aristotle observed that plausible fictions served the needs of ancient Greek tragedy much better than implausible facts, creators of literature have been advised that verifiable truths are less important to their craft than a simulacrum called *vraisemblance*. A penchant for indeterminacy has led creative writers to prefer ambiguities to the disambiguation procedures of philosophy. Their willingness to be enchanted by words – to surrender to the seductions of the signifier – allows them liberties forbidden in Wittgenstein's conception of philosophy as 'a battle against the bewitchment of our intelligence by means of language'.[3] Like a Papuan phallocarp, poetry (in Francis Bacon's formulation) 'submit[s] the shows of things' – the way things are – 'to the desires of the mind'.[4] In the realm of fiction, whose native inhabitants are unreliable narrators, truth is complicated rather than clarified by the custom of a relativising 'point of view', which enables William Faulkner to show in *As I Lay Dying* (1930) how the 'same' story filtered through different narrators comes out differently. By privileging

---

[2] Lanham, *Handlist of Rhetorical Terms*, 191, 194.
[3] Wittgenstein, *Philosophical Investigations*, 47.
[4] Bacon, 'Nature of Poetry', ed. Jones, 106.

'showing' (*deixis*) over 'telling', writers signal their preference for ironical indirectness. Anxious to avoid the explicit moralisation denounced by Baudelaire as *l'hérésie de l'enseignement*, they cultivate the implicit by valorising obliquity, especially if they heed Emily Dickinson's advice that in order to 'tell all the Truth' you need to 'tell it slant'.[5] The collective effect of such practices is to weaken any claim that literature itself is so free of duplicitousness as to constitute the polar opposite of literary forgery.

As readers of imaginative writing we therefore experience many unresolved contradictions. Acting on Coleridge's advice, and submitting to authorial deceptions by exercising a 'willing suspension of disbelief', we find ourselves derided for our gullibility if the work in question turns out to be a literary forgery.[6] A desirable aptitude for being 'illuded' by fiction becomes indistinguishable from that susceptibility to the overtures of confidence tricksters which is memorialised in the proverb, *mundus vult decepi* ('the world wants to be deceived'). Not surprisingly, the most successful defences of literature have been conducted in terms of non-assertion theories of truth, like the one used by Sidney when arguing in 1580 that since 'the poet . . . nothing affirmeth' he 'therefore never lieth'.[7] When Sidney made that remark, the most common word for describing the imaginative processes which result in a poem was the same as the one used for telling lies: 'feigning'. Imaginative writers claim the right both to lie and to do so with impunity by means of a protective fiction called 'poetic licence', which is as important to the constituency of authorship as 'benefit of clergy' was to the separation of ecclesiastical from secular jurisdiction. Poetic licence gives poets the right (in Chatterton's phrase) to 'soare 'bove trouthe of hystorie'.[8] Such permissiveness condones the suspension of verification procedures so that 'untruths' can be told in the interests of 'art'. That 'not entirely rational means of discourse', fiction, is necessarily 'a false document', E.L. Doctorow argues, because 'compositions of words are not life'.[9] Some writers worry about this, as Charles Lamb evidently did when choosing as his pseudonym in *The Essays of Elia* (1820–33) a name

[5] Baudelaire, *Baudelaire as Literary Critic*, 135; Dickinson, *Poems*, ed. Johnson, poem no. 1129.
[6] Ruthven, *Critical Assumptions*, 178–80.
[7] Sidney, 'Apology for Poetry', 31.
[8] Meyerstein, *Life of Chatterton*, 192.
[9] Doctorow, 'False Documents', 215, 221.

almost homophonous with 'a liar' and glossed as 'e-*lie*-a'.[10] But few have responded as drastically as Laura Riding, who eventually gave up publishing poetry on account of its 'inveterate unveraciousness'.[11]

Vraisemblance is not the only rhetorical legacy to compromise literature's attempt to dissociate itself from literary forgery. Equally damaging is the rhetoric of 'authenticity-effects', the discursive reproduction of which enables any text that contains them to be read as authentic, irrespective of its provenance. Their efficacy makes it difficult to defend 'authenticity' as an originary state from which the authentic emanates and the inauthentic deviates. On the contrary, the concept of 'authenticity' appears to be extrapolated from the inauthenticities of everyday life as an imaginary and ideal alternative to them, just as the idea of paradise succeeds an awareness of paradise lost. 'Inauthenticity', Kimberly Dovey concludes, 'emerges out of the very attempt to retain or regain' an authenticity which is always felt to be elsewhere – geographically exotic, historically remote, or both.[12] Authenticity-effects can be created by various devices, many of which were used by Daniel Defoe, who incorporates into *Robinson Crusoe* (1719) and *Moll Flanders* (1722) stylistic features commonly associated with factual reportage. These include 'inconsequential' episodes that would be edited out of a text by any self-consciously literary author who had internalised that functionalist and ultimately Aristotelian economy of writing which promotes the importance of carefully concatenated episodes in the cumulative development of a plot. Another authenticatory device is Defoe's use of vivid but 'irrelevant' details – 'authentication by density', as Taylor calls this technique apropos Chatterton – which are frowned upon in a functionalist aesthetic committed to eliminating superfluities. Yet as George Dawson was to observe, 'there is nothing, if you wish to deceive, like being accurate', that is, specific.[13] In October 1726 Mary Toft did not claim merely to have given birth to a rabbit in the way Agnes Bowker gave birth to a cat in 1569, or the ex-convict woman in Tom Gilling's novel *Sooterkin* (1999) gives birth to a seal; instead, she gave birth to *seventeen* rabbits. This combination of exactitude and implausibility categorises Toft's unnatural parturition as one of those events which prove that 'truth is stranger than

---

[10] Woodring, 'Lamb's Hoaxes and the Lamb Canon', 40.
[11] Seymour-Smith, 'Riding's "Rejection of Poetry"', 11.
[12] Dovey, 'Quest for Authenticity and the Replication of Environmental Meaning', 36.
[13] Dawson, 'Literary Forgeries and Impostures', 145.

fiction' – the motto adopted by *Wide World*, a London magazine which in 1898–99 serialised the Robinsonnade by 'Louis de Rougemont' (Henri Louis Grin) of his alleged adventures among Australian Aborigines.[14] Carefully designed not to look like 'literature', and published anonymously, Defoe's *A True Relation of the Apparition of one Mrs. Veal, the Next Day after Her Death, to One Mrs. Bargrave at Canterbury, the 8th of September, 1705* (1706) is offered as the edited text of Bargrave's seemingly factual account of an incident she herself may have invented. Either way, it became 'the best and best-selling ghost-story of the century'.[15]

The authenticatory device which readers find most disturbing, however, is the presentation of a fictional text as autobiographical. By simulating both the immediacy and authority of personal testimony, such writings encourage us to believe that the link between author and first-person narrator is what Peircean semiologists call 'indexical', because – 'like Friday's footprint in the sand in *Robinson Crusoe*' – it presumes the existence of 'a phenomenal or existential connection between the sign and what it signifies'.[16] Indexically speaking, the hand that signed the paper is assumed to belong to the body that had the experiences represented in the book. Signs are read as referents in autobiography, which some people value more highly than 'mere' fiction precisely because it refers to an extratextual reality, however much it is skewed by the prejudices of a narrator who is also the author. The drawback of indexicality as a truth-telling device is the ease with which it can be reproduced as a *vraisemblance* that readers will find equally compelling. This is evident in Lorenzo Carcaterra's *Sleepers* (1995), a first-person narrative about being systematically beaten and raped as a thirteen-year-old boy in a juvenile detention centre: 'I sat across the table', it begins, 'from the man who had battered and tortured and brutalized me nearly thirty years ago'.[17] While *Sleepers* was enjoying best-seller status as non-fiction, investigators who could find no evidence to support its claims argued that it should be reclassified as fiction. Yet although the consequent redesignation of its opening sentence as pseudo-indexical converts the referents into signifiers, such a move in no way weakens its rhetorical effectiveness.

---

14 Todd, *Imagining Monsters*, 1; Burton, *Impostors*, 6.
15 Baine, *Defoe and the Supernatural*, 76.
16 Scholes, *Semiotics and Interpretation*, 144.
17 Carcaterra, *Sleepers*, 5.

Other authenticatory devices include the presentation of the text as an edited version of a 'discovered' document, as Nathaniel Hawthorne does in *The Scarlet Letter* (1850), a novel set in seventeenth-century Boston. Such information is usually transmitted paratextually. Sometimes the text is 'authenticated' by being described as based on an original written in some other language. This was the case when Elizabeth Barrett decided to conceal her love poems to her husband, Robert Browning, under the title of *Sonnets from the Portuguese* (1850). The imaginary discovery of the 'lost originals' of those poems – in a 'flimsy booklet' (published in Lisbon in 1843) containing 'Algunas sonetas' – was amusingly reported in 1988 by Eric Korn, who rough-hewed a Portuguese mock-up of Barrett's most famous line: 'Como eu amo-ti? Vamos comptar as maneras' ('How do I love thee? Let me count the ways').[18] Here if anywhere it might be said – as Borges remarks of the English version of William Beckford's *Vathek* (1786) – that 'the original is unfaithful to the translation'.[19] Such literary delights become possible whenever the layers of mediation between us and the 'origin' of a text are increased, thus enabling authors to exploit the fictiveness of fiction and allure their readers by playing games with them. *The City of Light* (1997), for instance, purports to be translated by David Selbourne from a previously unknown Italian manuscript (still 'in private hands', and therefore unavailable for inspection) by a certain 'Jacob D'Ancona', a Jewish merchant who is said to have visited China in 1271, just a few years ahead of Marco Polo – if, indeed, Polo himself ever got there: Frances Wood thinks it unlikely, and that Polo's travelogue is fiction.[20] Selbourne's consummately executed manoeuvres along the border between plausibility and implausibility trapped reviewers unfamiliar with the intricacies of fiction into solemnly declaring it bogus, much to the amusement of its author as well as devotees of such spectator-sport.[21]

The tables can be turned, however, when critics who have identified a hoax pretend to have been deceived by it, and write spoof reviews in the expectation of hoaxing the hoaxer. Käte Hamburger thinks that this happened in 1981 when Johannes

---

[18] Korn, 'Remainders', 357.
[19] Redfern, *Clichés and Coinages*, 92.
[20] Wood, *Did Marco Polo Go to China?, passim.*
[21] Wasserstein and Wasserstein, 'Jacopo Spurioso', 15–16; 'Jacob D'Ancona', *City of Light*, trans. and ed. Selbourne.

Kleinstück reviewed Wolfgang Hildesheimer's *Marbot* (1981) for *Die Welt*. Like Steven Millhauser's first novel, *Edwin Mullhouse: The Life and Death of an American Writer, 1943–1954, by Jeffrey Cartwright* (1972), *Marbot* is a mock-biography. Documented by bogus quotations from extant memoirs and letters, it narrates the life of an imaginary connoisseur and aesthetician called Sir Andrew Marbot, who hobnobbed with well-known writers in the early nineteenth century.[22] In 1982 the *London Review of Books* published a spoof-review of *Marbot* by the British Germanist, J.P. Stern. This tit for tat exhibition of generic *trompe-l'oeil* elicited a letter from Hildesheimer, who (overlooking Stern's sly remarks about the 'flawless German' of a 'ghostly' Marbot, whose biographer has 'a penchant for complex and ambitious literary jokes'), pointed out that 'it speaks for the book that the reviewer has taken Marbot's existence for granted'. Stern's editor replied that 'it speaks for the reviewer that the author of the book should take for granted an assumption, on the reviewer's part, of Marbot's existence'.[23] Far from being as scandalous as they are usually made out to be, such 'fraudulent' activities stimulate debates that sharpen our understanding of how texts perform as literature and get read as such. An even more provocative response to a provocative deception was Thomas De Quincey's engagement with G.W.H. Haering, who published a couple of Scott items in 1824: under his pseudonym, 'Willibald Alexis', a translation of *The Lay of the Last Minstrel* (1815), and under his own name a 'translation' of a nonexistent three-volume novel by Scott entitled *Walladmor*. After reviewing this pseudo-Waverley in the *London Magazine* as 'the boldest hoax of our times', De Quincey decided to translate it, 'build[ing] upon this German hoax a second and equally complete English hoax'.[24] Reduced to two volumes by having the 'rubbish' removed from it, De Quincey's *Walladmor* (1825) is dedicated to Haering ('a German of ultra-dulness') with an invitation to translate it into German, so that his next sow's ear can be turned by De Quincey into the 'hyperlustrous' silk purse of 'the final *Walladmor*'.[25] Haering responded, however, by 'translating' another novel Scott never wrote, *Schloss Avalon* (1827). Scott himself was more amused than

22 Adams, 'Mock-Biography of Edwin Mullhouse', 205; Hamburger, 'Authenticity as Mask: Hildesheimer's Marbot', 97.
23 Stern, 'Sweet Sin', 5, 6; Dorrit Cohn, *Distinction of Fiction*, 79–80.
24 De Quincey, '*Walladmor*: A Pseudo-Waverley Novel', 136, 138.
25 Ibid., 137, 132–33, 141.

distressed by this perverse evidence of his popularity as a novelist. In his preface to *Tales of the Crusaders* (1825), he associates the author of *Walladmor* with the German *diablerie* exhibited by Dirk Hatteraick in *Guy Mannering* (1815) and above all by Hermann Dousterswivel in *The Antiquary* (1816), that 'juggling mountebank' whose real-life exemplar was Raspe, the chronicler of Baron Munchausen's fabulous exploits.[26]

The most respected authenticatory device in written communications is the signature, which is why techniques for detecting forgeries of it are explained in manuals like Wilson K. Harrison's *Suspect Documents* (1966). In the somatics of textual production, signatures are graphemic traces which evoke metonymically the bodies of those who have produced them, and strikingly so in the case of a thirteenth-century glossator identified solely by his chirographic infirmity, and known to medievalists as The Tremulous Hand of Worcester.[27] Authorial input into a work is usually figured as the presence of a 'hand' in it, a typical example being recorded in the title of A.W. Pollard's collection of essays on *Shakespeare's Hand in the Play of Sir Thomas More* (1923). As handwriting, each signature evokes someone's hand, writing: hence its talismanic appeal to collectors as the auratic residue of an authorial presence (the autograph as 'authorgraph').[28] And if, like most people's signatures, it is difficult to decipher, it is said to be written in an illegible 'hand', although signatorial distinctiveness does not depend upon legibility. Considering the irregularities of its history, the problems it poses for critical theorists, and the uncertainties of its future in that 'datasphere' which Douglas Rushkoff calls *Cyberia* (1995), it is surprising that the signature continues to be valorised as the authenticating sign of origin in the production of literary texts.

In studio practice the signature has functioned sometimes as a hallmark of quality rather than an acknowledgement of who produced the work it is attached to. François Boucher required his students to copy his drawings, and those who did so to his satisfaction had their excellence rewarded by the addition of his signature to their work. Although Boucher's signature was authentic, what it authenticated was not the origins of those drawings but their quality in exhibiting the mastery that his students sought to learn from

---

[26] Coleman O. Parsons, *Witchcraft and Demonology in Scott's Fiction*, 92–93.
[27] Franzen, *Tremulous Hand of Worcester, passim.*
[28] Gilbert and Gubar, 'Ceremonies of the Alphabet', 21.

him.[29] Modern art-dealers and collectors, on the other hand, view such matters differently. Their disturbing propensity to value the signature on a work more highly than the work itself led Salvador Dalí to decide that instead of scrupulously overseeing the production of prints bearing his name he might just as well sign and sell otherwise blank pieces of paper on which printmakers could execute Dalís of their own. Similarly, once the second-hand books trade succumbed to what William Roberts denounced in 1894 as the 'first edition mania', the commodity exchanged was no longer books but the dates on their title-pages. This enabled Wise, a commodity dealer by profession, to market his spurious first editions of texts by collectable authors.[30] Dalí's boldly minimalist move – equivalent to the disappearance of all but the signature smile of the Cheshire Cat in *Alice in Wonderland* – was mercenary in ways expected of the man whose name was anagrammatised by a fellow surrealist, André Breton, as 'Avída Dollars'.[31] But it was also a well-directed assault on the commodification of art as a market in which investors purchase signatures rather than works.[32] It is worth remembering that the acclaimed author of *The Golden Notebook* (1962) had a novel turned down by her own publisher when, wanting 'to be reviewed on merit, as a new writer, without the benefit of a "name"', she submitted *The Diary of a Good Neighbour* (1983) under the name of 'Jane Somers' instead of Doris Lessing.[33] This is not an isolated case. In 1975, when Chuck Ross typed out the first twenty-one pages of Jerzy Kosinski's National Book Award-winning *Steps* (1969) and submitted them under a pseudonym to the original publisher they were rejected; and in 1991, when Pete Silverton sent to various publishers under the name of 'R. Perkins' the opening chapter of P.H. Newby's Booker Prize-winning novel, *Something to Answer For* (1968), the original publisher warned him that his 'chances of publication' were 'probably quite small'.[34]

Those who think that manual signatures will continue to be used for legal purposes in the electronic age, despite their worrisome variations and susceptibility to forgery, have developed signature-

---

[29] Tietze, *Genuine and False*, 13.

[30] Collins, *Two Forgers: Forman and Wise*, 167.

[31] Catterall, *Great Dalí Art Fraud*, 35.

[32] Ibid., 43–44, 61.

[33] Lessing, *Diaries of Jane Somers*, [5]; Goodman, 'Doris Lessing Hoax', 213.

[34] Silverton, 'Publish and Be Shammed', 30, 31.

verification software capable of discerning such invisible characteristics of a signature as the dynamics of its timing and rhythm.
Although such technology will flush out amateur forgers, it is unlikely
to worry professionals like Eric Hebborn. When copying someone
else's signature, he advises, you should treat it not as 'a series of
letters but rather as an abstract line or series of lines', which, with
practice, you will learn to replicate 'at the same speed as the original
writer, thus producing the same natural flow of lines'.[35] But now that
increasing amounts of business are conducted with computers rather
than with people, that traditional instrument of the written signature,
the pen, is being replaced by the PIN. By dispensing with the
alphabet, and thus eliminating the chirographic vagaries of its
inscription, the 'personal identification number' constitutes an electronic 'signature' at once unambiguous and machine-readable.
Digital signatures function as the guarantors of identity in cyberspace. Yet if current developments in biometrics result in commercially affordable products, the body may soon reaffirm its
identitarian superiority over the numerical abstractions of the PIN. It
will do so, however, not by restoring the hand that signed the paper
in the old manuscript culture, but by recording the epidermal
patterns on its finger-tips. Alternatively, the next generation of
automatic teller machines may be equipped with biometric identification software that enables them to recognise our 'eye-dentity' by
scanning our irises, which contain a greater number of unique and
immutable features than our fingerprints. Such developments
promise to re-somatise the signature in a post-grammatological
form.

Chirographic idiosyncrasies confer uniqueness on signatures but
cause problems for those whose business is to authenticate them.
Shakespeare is known to have signed his name only half-a-dozen
times, yet on each occasion he not only spelled it differently but
wrote it differently. The only thing that authenticates these signatures
as Shakespeare's is their 'documentary location', writes Jonathan
Goldberg.[36] The individualising irregularities of a signature were at
risk during the Renaissance from the formalism taught in schools
and promulgated in manuals of handwriting, whose idealised con-
catenations of well-formed letters eventually came to be called

---

[35] Hebborn, *Art Forger's Handbook*, 64.
[36] Goldberg, *Writing Matter*, 241.

'copper-plate', a form of writing homogenised and thus depersona-
lised into a print-like regularity that made it fit to be engraved on a
polished copper plate and reproduced mechanically. Because differences between the 'secretary' and 'italic' styles of handwriting could
be construed as class differences, the nobility signed their names in
italic.[37] The signature of a nobleman thus achieved authenticity not
by escaping copy-book italic but by complying with it.[38] Although
eventually the authenticating signature became individualised, it
originated as a substitute for non-individualised modes of 'authentication previously conveyed by seals and witnesses'.[39] In early
modern England, therefore, the signature mimicked the immutabi-
lity of a seal, not the mutability of a signatory. And since it could do
so only by means of what Goldberg calls 'self-forgery' – that is, by
reiterating and replicating previous instances of itself – the need to
achieve authenticity in the production of such signatures opened up
'the possibility of unauthorised forgery'. Since the powerful found it
tedious to sign innumerable documents with the requisite care, an
ability 'to forge their master's hands' became a valued competency
in secretaries employed by royalty.[40] Henry VIII's chronic reluctance
to sign documents resulted in the invention of a 'dry stamp' of his
signature, which, when pressed on to paper, left indentations that a
clerk could follow with pen and ink. But as soon as 'the signature of
the king became a form of mechanical reproduction', Goldberg
observes, 'authorized forgery passed into the hands of the secretarial
corps', which was then obliged to invent procedures for preventing
*un*authorised forgery. Goldberg relishes the paradoxes generated by
the ensuing contortions of authentication, and describes with
bravura how 'the authorizing hand in the hand of others required
countersignatures to countersign the authentic counterfeit'.[41]

Ever since the sixteenth-century invention of the perspective
machine or pantograph, which enabled drawings to be copied
simultaneously, various prototypes have been trialled in the hope of
developing a device that would mechanise the iteration of a signature
and thereby reduce the work-loads of people required to sign their
approval before anything gets done.[42] By 1803 Thomas Jefferson had
invented a machine called the polygraph, 'which, in response to the
movement of a master-pen in the hand of the writer, would start a

[37] Ibid., 234.   [38] Ibid., 236.
[39] Ibid., 244.   [40] Ibid., 248.   [41] Ibid., 261, 262.
[42] Hillel Schwartz, *Culture of the Copy*, 222–23.

whole row of pens and simultaneously sign a dozen or more documents'.[43] This relatively simple device profoundly changed a couple of inherited notions about the relationship between an original and its copies: namely, that an original always instantiates a singularity, and always precedes a copy. Jefferson's polygraph, by contrast, produced copies simultaneously with the original, and every original that emerged from it did so in a condition of multiplicity. Unless you had actually seen which of the multiple sheets had been signed by the master-pen held by Jefferson, how could you identify – on the evidence of the sheets alone – his original and authentic signature? Jefferson's polygraph rendered spectral the corporeal presence of a presidential hand in a presidential signature. By the time that John F. Kennedy was occupying the White House, writes Charles Hamilton, the presidential signature had been robotised by an 'Autopen' capable of producing 'as many as 3,000 signatures in a single eight-hour day from a "master" signature on a matrix, each an exact reproduction of the original'.[44] This time-saving device also obviated a problem posed by Kennedy's actual signatures, which differed from one another so greatly ('from day to day, even from hour to hour') as to risk looking inauthentic.[45] Those produced by the Autopen from six matrices of Kennedy's signatures were much more plausible, even though one of them was 'probably from a Kennedy imitation furnished by an aide'.[46] The Autopen, in other words, produced signature-effects authenticated not by their origin in an author but by their reception in a community of readers willing to participate in the bureaucratic fiction that simulacra of presidential signatures were genuine.

Always vulnerable to forgery, signatures lost whatever credibility they might once have had as markers of authenticity when the development of facsimile technology enabled them to be reproduced perfectly. This point was made by the editor of the *Southern Literary Messenger*, Edgar Allan Poe, when he contributed anonymously to that journal between 1835 and 1837 thirty-eight fictitious letters, each followed by a facsimile of the signature of an actual public figure.[47] Poe's ironic title for this assemblage was 'Autography'. For literary theorists the signature is a problematic entity because it is always an abstraction, and never the unambiguous and material imprint of a

[43] Hamilton, *Robot That Helped to Make a President*, 2.
[44] Ibid., 6.   [45] Ibid., 52.   [46] Ibid., 2.
[47] Silverman, *Edgar A. Poe*, 108; De Graef, 'Dead Herrings', 240.

human singularity that we would like it to be. Since we never sign our names in exactly the same way, 'the' signature is an insubstantial ideal, something extrapolated from what are treated as resemblances between different versions of it. This makes the signature, in Peggy Kamuf's phrase, 'always detachable from the singular instance it supposedly designates'.[48] Every time this putative sameness leaves its graphic trace on the page, it has already instantiated a difference, however slight. Theoretically, therefore, we have no means of knowing whether its origin is autographic or allographic. Since 'there is no telling after you signed whether it was indeed you who signed', Kamuf argues, each signature displays an 'unsettling otherness within an economy of the same'.[49]

Among those undisturbed by such arguments are not only graphologists, who believe that the way people write is the key to their personalities, but readers who think that books are consubstantial with their authors, and therefore value authorial signatures as confirmations of that supposition. The autographing of books by writers at literary festivals and other 'appearances' staged for commercial benefits by publishers and booksellers sustains the fiction that a signature is the corporeal trace of an otherwise absent author, something which adds to the book both the immediate pleasure of a personal association and the deferred pleasure of its increased resale value as an autographed copy. Yet as Derrida points out, far from being the trace of a presence, a written signature 'implies the actual or empirical non-presence of the signer'. Furthermore, our desire to treat the 'signature-event' as a singularity is frustrated by the fact that unless a signature has 'a repeatable, iterable, imitative form' it will be unreadable. In this respect, therefore, the 'condition of possibility' of a signature is 'simultaneously . . . the condition of [its] impossibility'.[50]

Authenticity is institutionalised by being accorded a foundational status in the construction of knowledge in the humanities. All its noetic domains produce their own versions of the distinction made in 1950 by Richard M. Dorson between genuine 'folklore' (as William Thom first called it in 1846) and that synthetic and commercialised 'fake lore' Dorson subsequently labelled 'fakelore', much of which is

---

[48] Kamuf, *Signature Pieces*, ix.   [49] Ibid., ix, x.
[50] Derrida, 'Signature Event Context', 194.

generated by urban nostalgia for the cultures of pre-industrialised societies.[51] Dorson argues that although some fakelore originates in folklore, it undergoes the kind of literary elaboration displayed in Richard Chase's *The Jack Tales* (1943); the rest – popular stories about Paul Bunyan, for instance – have never been anything other than modern fabrications. Dorson's dissociation of traditional 'folklore collected directly in the field' from fakelore produced by 'parlor folklorists' was a significant moment in the credentialising of an emergent academic discipline. Anxious to distance itself from the hobby-folklorism of amateurs, it sought to professionalise its activities by contributing 'folkloristics' to the social sciences. It shared with modernist literary studies in the 1950s a high-brow contempt for that 'booming new enterprise . . . known as popular culture', which Dorson treats as an ersatz and commercialised commodity produced by and for modern 'people', who are disappointingly different from the primitive and passionate *Volk* ('folk') of Romantic fantasy.[52] Yet in 1893 Joseph Jacobs was already arguing that the problem with folklorists is that they know a lot about 'lore' but next to nothing about 'folk', a concept he denounces accordingly as 'a fraud, a delusion, a myth'.[53]

The post-war America in which Dorson developed his binary model of the subject had not yet been transformed by those ideologies of cultural pluralism and ethnic identitarianism that would politicise cultural specificity and aggravate a disciplinary crisis for folklore studies. One effect of this was to reposition fakelore (alias 'poplore', 'fakelure' or *Folklorismus*) inside rather than outside the field of study, thus enabling it to escape its former classification as second-rate because second-hand, and become instead part of the phenomena investigated by folklorists. 'The dichotomy between genuine and spurious folk materials would crumble', writes Regina Bendix, 'as the static, text-oriented approach yielded to a process- and performance-oriented folkloristics'.[54] But that transformation may have been effected as much by social as epistemological factors according to Dave Harker, who dismantles a similar distinction in his book on 'the manufacture of British "folksong"', *Fakesong* (1985). Middle-class tampering with the songs of working-class people, he argues, resulted in a simulacrum called 'folksong' that was bogus

[51] Dorson, 'Folklore and Fake Lore', 335.   [52] Ibid., 5, 122.
[53] Boyes, *Imagined Village*, 15.
[54] Bendix, *In Search of Authenticity*, 194.

from the very beginning, and certainly long before the identification of something even more bogus ('fakesong') conferred retroactively the aura of authenticity on folksong. In such redefinitions of the enquiry, there is no anterior and authentic folklore and folksong against which fakelore and fakesong can be judged secondary and inauthentic. Even the commonsense distinction between genuine music and meretricious 'muzak' (a portmanteau term coined in the 1930s by George Owen Squier from 'music' and 'Kodak') becomes difficult to sustain when the former is recycled as the latter to telephone users whose calls have been placed on hold.[55] Once again, a tendentious discrimination turns out to be a distinction without a difference.

The institutional function of authentication in English studies is to establish disciplinary credibility for an academic subject often derided (in the phallocratic cliché) as a 'soft' option. To install authenticity as a foundational value is to legitimise 'authentication' as a disciplinary practice, particularly as it relates to questions of authorial attribution and the establishment of 'correct' texts, and thereby to demonstrate that literary studies have developed veridical procedures as stringent as those used in the correspondingly 'hard' sciences. Both authorship and textual authority are predominantly although not exclusively print-specific concerns: Margreta de Grazia, for instance, argues that the authenticity of Shakespeare's plays was not systematised as a problem until 1790, when Edmond Malone edited them.[56] Because printing was the first technology for reproducing a work of art mechanically, it is regarded by Walter Benjamin as one of those agents which jeopardised the authenticity of a text by eliminating its 'aura' as a unique object – a quality unrecognisable, incidentally, until copies of it have appeared.[57]

It seems to me, however, that instead of being lost irrecoverably in the shift from a manuscript to a print culture, 'aura' was reinvented and continues to be reaffirmed by publishers who distinguish the trade edition of a book from a private or limited edition of the same text. Some of the latter can be individualised by rarefying both the paper they are printed on and the materials chosen for their binding, by hand-numbering the copies, and by getting the author to sign them. Another conduit of auratic resonance in print-culture is a

[55] Lanza, *Elevator Music*, 22–30.
[56] De Grazia, *Shakespeare Verbatim, passim*.
[57] Benjamin, *Illuminations*, 223.

bibliographical category invented for commercial purposes by book-sellers, namely the 'association copy'. This term is used to describe printed books that exhibit written traces of ownership, usually by associates of the author who are themselves historically significant. To hold in one's hands the very copy of Sir Joshua Reynolds' *Discourses* (1798) in whose margins William Blake once scribbled his dissenting opinions would be an auratic experience for people who believe in contagious magic, and are thrilled by the apostolic experience of touching materials touched by famous people; hence the incentive to produce bogus association copies, like *Théâtre à l'usage des jeunes personnes* (1780), inscribed 'Horatio Nelson from his affectionate Emma Hamilton'.[58] Another commercially motivated attempt to reintroduce aura into a printed text is the so-called 'trial book', a term coined by Wise in 1896 to describe a bibliographical category represented by certain proof copies of Tennyson's *Idylls of the King* (1859). Trial books, as described by Roger C. Lewis, are usually 'genuine proofsheets, often corrected by the author, [and] bound up into a volume with a pre-first edition date stamped on the spine'. They are then 'marketed as a rare, privately printed first edition designated by the author to serve as printers' copy for the "next" edition which is in fact the true first edition'.[59] Although Lewis adds that 'trial books are not often forgeries', they certainly encourage confusion between actual, putative and fake first editions, and show how the kudos of authenticity in literary studies en-courages the production of inauthenticities.

Literature avoids confronting the spectre of its own inauthenticity by displacing the problem on to some other medium and thematising it as fiction. The nominal subject of Sophie Masson's novel, *The Hoax* (1997), is a possible case of music fraud, namely the 'discovery' by someone called Pym of a hitherto unknown sonata by Ravel; metafictionally, however, her novel explores the literary ramifications of authenticity through its engagement with Poe's *The Narrative of A. Gordon Pym* (1838). The favoured analogue when fictionalising literary forgery is painting, the cultural category which most clearly supports Toni del Renzio's argument that 'authenticity' is neither 'an intrinsic nor a necessary quality of art, but only a guarantee of its exchange value' in the market.[60] The association between literature and the

58 McDonald, 'Forgeries in the Library', 625.
59 Lewis, *Wise and the Trial Book Fallacy*, xii.
60 Del Renzio, 'Multiple Authenticity', 25.

visual arts is fostered by an ancient tradition – epitomised in the Horatian maxim, *ut pictura poesis* – that painting and poetry are what John Dryden called 'sister arts'.[61] Wyndham Lewis' remarks on 'false bottoms' in part six of *The Revenge for Love* (1937) refer as much to the fiction he's writing as to the art forgery described in his novel. The analogous duplicities of art restoration are as central to J.L. Carr's novel, *A Month in the Country* (1980), as they are to *What's Bred in the Bone* (1985), by Robertson Davies. Rembrandt's famous painting of 'Aristotle Contemplating the Bust of Homer' is the catalyst for Joseph Heller's anatomy of spuriosity in *Picture This* (1988), partly because the bust is 'an authentic Hellenistic imitation of a Hellenic reproduction of a statue for which there had never been an authentic original subject', partly because 'the man [depicted] is not Aristotle', and partly because 'the Rembrandt painting . . . may not be by Rembrandt'.[62] But the most profound of these novelistic meditations on how a yearning for authenticity is connected to ' "that romantic disease, originality" ' is William Gaddis' *The Recognitions* (1955).[63] Novels about literary forgery are correspondingly rare, perhaps because their subject matter is too close for comfort. Ian Kennedy Williams avoids that problem in *Malarky Dry* (1990) – a counterfactual recension of the 'Ern Malley' case, based on the hypothesis that there was a real Ern Malley whose poems were written by Henry Fitzhubert-Ireland – by focusing on the characters rather than the literary politics that produced the poems. And William H. Hallahan's *The Ross Forgery* (1977), which chronicles an attempt to deceive 'the world's leading collector' of Wiseana by manufacturing 'an authentic Wise forgery' – a counterfeit counterfeit – capable of passing all the tests devised by Carter and Pollard, is more interested in the technical minutiae of material forgery than in the cultural significance of spuriosity.[64] Literary forgeries themselves avoid such evasions and displacements by the deictic strategy of 'presenting' inauthenticity as a *Darstellung*, instead of merely 'representing' it obliquely as a problem in some other medium.[65]

In literary studies, authentication aspires to the condition of science, which continues to develop techniques for performing more

---

[61] Hagstrum, *The Sister Arts, passim*.
[62] Heller, *Picture This*, 14, 351.
[63] Gaddis, *Recognitions*, 89.
[64] Hallahan, *Ross Forgery*, 18, 31.
[65] Iser, 'Representation: A Performative Act', 236.

precisely the calculations connoisseurs make by guesswork based on experience. Since the aim of such techniques is to ascertain the constituent properties of material objects, they have been especially helpful in the detection of forgeries in the fine arts. The actual age of a pot whose surface has been distressed to make it look ancient can now be calculated by means of thermoluminescence; radiocarbon dating provides a similar service for any artefact that contains carbon; and electron spin resonance complements the chemical analysis of paint to determine how old its pigment and binder are. In each case the evidence adduced is totally beyond the reach of unaided sense perceptions. Consequently, the price paid for such remote and abstract forms of authentication is sometimes deemed too high, especially in the case of artefacts that people have come to love. If, for example, the principal thing wrong with those beautiful Etruscan warriors formerly on display in the Metropolitan Museum of Art is that a spectrograph has revealed the presence of manganese dioxide in their black glaze, then anybody who used to visit the Museum for the pleasure of looking at them might feel justly aggrieved at their removal on the grounds that they are fakes.[66] The privileging of authenticity in such cases downgrades the category of the aesthetic. Publicity given to the removal from museums and galleries of 'inauthentic' objects strengthens the illusion that the remaining artefacts are authentic, although some argue that every one of them is already inauthentic as a result of having been 'wrenched out of its originally intended context' for display purposes.[67]

Although fewer scientific techniques can be brought to bear on the material form of a literary forgery, their findings can be equally significant. Because literary texts are not made out of wood, they exhibit no tree-rings for dendrochronologists to analyse; but both the paper they are written on and the ink used to inscribe the text are susceptible to scientific investigation. Nevertheless, the supposition that scientific data eliminate the need for informed judgement in the detection of forgeries is not supported by those who work on such problems. In this respect they occupy the same middle ground as sceptical connoisseurs like Kenneth Clark, who believed that although 'hunches' are far more reliable than scientific data in the

[66] Banfield, 'Art versus Collectibles', 32.
[67] Lowenthal, 'Counterfeit Art: Authentic Fakes', 85.

detection of a fake, 'they are by no means infallible'.[68] If you are trying to determine whether corrections in the manuscripts of poems by Gerard Manley Hopkins should be attributed to Hopkins himself or to his friend and redactionist, Robert Bridges, then the kind of infra-red image converter described in Wilson Harrison's *Suspect Documents* (1966) and used by Scotland Yard to gather forensic evidence of forgery will come in handy. For in cases where 'something written in one ink has been obliterated after it has dried with ink of a different chemical formula', the converter will enable you 'to read through the overlay'; and with the aid of a video spectral comparator you can 'judge whether a word was deleted or mended while the ink was still wet'.[69] But you will still need to be as good a Hopkins scholar as Norman H. MacKenzie to know what to make of the data.

The same is true of the use of scientific evidence when investigating the literary forgeries attributed in the mid-nineteenth century to John Payne Collier, and specifically the question of whether he or Frederic Madden wrote the pseudo-seventeenth-century marginalia found in a 1632 copy of Shakespeare's plays called the Perkins Folio. In the course of ten years spent searching unsuccessfully for what he calls 'the J.P. Collier ink syndrome', David C. Jenkins pushed ahead of his predecessor in this field, Neville Maskelyne (whose ink-testing techniques included tasting it), by using 'proton beam analysis . . . and electron microprobe to search for a "fingerprint" of the ink that might typify the forgeries of which Collier has been accused'.[70] Even if Jenkins had succeeded, however, Dewey Ganzel would still have been able to argue that the annotations in the Perkins Folio are the work of Madden, who allegedly framed Collier by not only forging Collier's handwriting but also using the same kind of ink as he did.[71] Another problem for would-be authenticators is that different scientific techniques produce different results, and whenever they do so the suspect artefact gets shunted in or out of the sidings of the spurious, that transvalued world in which the genuine is imaginable only as a 'counterfeit counterfeit'.[72] Such has been the fate of the Vinland Map. Discovered in 1957, it appears to be a mid-fifteenth-

[68] Clark, 'Forgeries', 725.
[69] Hopkins, *Poetical Works*, ed. MacKenzie, xl, xli.
[70] Jenkins, 'Search for the Collier Ink Syndrome', 96.
[71] Ganzel, *Fortune and Men's Eyes*, 349–54.
[72] Schüller, *Forgers, Dealers, Experts*, 178.

century and therefore pre-Columban map of the Atlantic coast of Canada, the region referred to in a couple of Old Icelandic sagas (one about the Greenlanders, the other about Erik the Red) as *Vinland* ('Wine-land'). In 1972, chemical analysis of the ink used to produce the Vinland Map revealed the presence of anastase, a precipitate of titanium dioxide that was 'not commercially available as a pigment before 1920'; as a result, in 1974 the Yale University Library announced that its 'famous Vinland Map may be a forgery'.[73] A decade later, however, the new technique of proton-induced x-ray analysis uncovered only a small and naturally occurring trace of titanium dioxide, whereupon the Vinland Map became 'genuine' again, although still sufficiently suspect to be worth including in the British Museum's 1990 exhibition of fakes and the art of deception.[74] It may be bogus, however, for reasons other than the composition of the ink used to produce it, such as Kirsten A. Seaver's argument that 'the medieval Norse did not use cartographical representations to convey their sailing lore'.[75]

The authenticatory saga of the Vinland Map illustrates the importance of treating scientific evidence as an adjunct to other methods used in fake-detection rather than as a substitute for them. Nevertheless, since any literary forgery written or printed on paper is a material object susceptible to scientific investigation, the evidence generated by such methods can be a powerful component in the establishment of its spuriousness, as Carter and Pollard first showed when specifying Wise's bibliographical malpractices in their *Enquiry into the Nature of Certain Nineteenth Century Pamphlets* (1934). Chemical analyses of Wise's forgeries of pre-first editions of texts by various nineteenth-century authors revealed that the paper they had been printed on contained ingredients not in use at the alleged date of publication: esparto grass, for instance, was first introduced into the paper-making process about 1861, and printing paper was not made out of chemical wood pulp until after 1874.[76] An analysis of the type-founts used by Wise's printer yielded further evidence of the spuriousness of those pamphlets. This included typographic anachronisms, such as the letter 'f' designed without a kern, which is the technical term for that top bit of the letter which encroaches into the

---

[73] Painter, 'Introduction to the New Edition', *Vinland Map*, ed. Skelton *et al.*, ix.

[74] Mark Jones (ed.), *Fake?*, 297–98.

[75] Seaver, *Frozen Echo*, 164.

[76] Carter and Pollard, *Enquiry into Nineteenth Century Pamphlets*, 48–49.

space reserved for any letter that follows it. Printers did not use the kernless 'f' until 1877, and then in response to the damage done to the kerned form of it by the new typesetting machines.[77]

In order to spell out Wise's bibliographical malpractices, Carter and Pollard pioneered new techniques of detection that made it correspondingly harder for literary forgers of material texts to succeed. One man willing to face the challenge was Mark Hoffman, who in 1985 attempted to fill a gap in the historical record by forging the lost printed text of an early – perhaps the earliest – American published document: 'The Oath of a Freeman' (1639), which is known to have existed but has survived only in manuscript. Hoffman did this by photographing a facsimile of the 1640 *Bay Psalm Book*, enlarging the photos, cutting out the letters and then using them to compose 'The Oath'. After reducing his text to the correct size, he made a process line block, and then machine-drilled the letters one by one so that they would produce irregular impressions on the seventeenth-century paper he had acquired, some of which he burnt and mixed with beeswax and linseed oil to produce 'seventeenth-century' ink.[78] Although Hoffman's forgery of 'The Oath' survived scrutiny by the Library of Congress, it failed to deceive the British Library's Nicolas Barker, who noticed among other things that the initial drop-capital of 'The Oath' was out of alignment. Hoffman understood what was needed in order to produce a document that would have to survive various scientific tests before being accepted as genuine. He therefore acquired the right kind of materials, developed the requisite skills, and was willing to put in the time to do the job properly. These characteristics identify him as a professional in comparison with Konrad Kujau, who forged Hitler's handwriting plausibly, but did so in diaries made of paper whitened by a chemical agent not used until the 1950s – even though paper and ink from the Nazi period were still readily available, which is why the forgers of Mussolini's diaries had been able to use historically authentic paper. There is no point, however, in going to the trouble of procuring the right kind of paper if, like the unknown forger of love letters between Abraham Lincoln and Ann Rutledge, you get just about everything else wrong.[79] Skilfulness and carelessness often cohabit the same

[77] Ibid., 58–59; Collins, *Two Forgers: Forman and Wise*, 245.
[78] Barker, 'Forgery of Printed Documents', 118–23.
[79] Angle, 'Minor Collection', 524.

literary forgery. Mariano Alberti, who in the mid-nineteenth century forged manuscript annotations by Torquato Tasso in sixteenth-century books acquired specifically for this purpose, managed to invent an ink 'of that peculiar reddish color that black ink attains after a few centuries'; but then, instead of using a quill, he made the mistake of writing with 'a metal pen . . . not in use before 1803'.[80]

Such stories invite fictional treatments of the ingenuity needed in order to overcome material obstacles to the successful forgery of a literary artefact. As scientific techniques for detecting literary forgery become more sophisticated, fiction based allegedly on 'lost' manuscripts – such as Byron's memoirs, destroyed after his death, but published from a fictional first draft in Christopher Nicole's novel, *The Secret Memoirs of Lord Byron* (1978) – manifests an increasing self-consciousness. 'When and if the notebooks appear', writes Frederic Prokosch in the foreword (signed 'T.H. Applebee') to his novel, *The Missolonghi Manuscript* (1968), 'we can leave it to the experts to determine, by an analysis of the ink, paper, glue, calligraphy, etc., whether they are indeed in Lord Byron's own handwriting'.[81] Prokosch was to progress immediately from the fictional treatment of an imaginary manuscript to the production of Wise-style bibliographical forgeries in the form of his so-called 'Butterfly' books, which comprise seventy-nine pamphlets allegedly published between 1932 and 1940 but actually printed between 1968 and 1972.[82] A more interesting example of the genre is Joe Haldeman's novel, *The Hemingway Hoax* (1990). Its hero, John Baird, is a Hemingway scholar who decides to forge the typescripts of short stories lost by Ernest Hemingway in December 1922 when the suitcase containing them was stolen.[83] Since they were never recovered, Baird's project begins as an 'amiable academic hoax', namely to embed the printed texts of his pseudo-Hemingway stories in a book containing his own commentary on them; but he also considers 'market[ing] the forgery for real'. It is not difficult to imitate Hemingwayese; if it were, there would have been no competitors in the first International Imitation Hemingway Contest, and Digby Diehl would have found it correspondingly harder to compile his follow-up publication, *The Best of Bad Hemingway* (1989). It is equally easy to imitate Hemingway's

[80] Altrocchi, *Sleuthing in the Stacks*, 5, 21.
[81] Prokosch, *Missolonghi Manuscript*, 3.
[82] Barker, *Butterfly Books*, 175, 24.
[83] Meyers, *Hemingway*, 68.

practice of typing spaces before and after full-stops and commas. Baird's biggest problem is first to locate and purchase a 1921 Corona portable typewriter, and then to tamper with it in such a way that it will reproduce perfectly the idiosyncrasies of typescripts from Hemingway's own machine.[84]

Clearly, it is extraordinarily difficult to replicate the materiality of yesteryear's texts to the satisfaction of experts assisted by scientific equipment capable of discerning textual properties undetectable by the unaided reader. Like those who practise the hermeneutics of suspicion – and operate on the assumption that, since no interpretation can ever be innocent, our task is to discover what it is guilty of – the authenticators of literary texts are obliged to treat every document as suspect until it is proven otherwise, which in practice means until they have exhausted the currently available ways of detecting its spuriousness. Given what they are up against, it is hardly surprising that most literary forgers opt for less time-consuming forms of duplicity. Yet the obsolescence of material forgery by scientific methods of detection has made life even harder for literary investigators by encouraging immaterial forgery. Confronted with modern printed texts which may or may not be spurious, and which not even the latest scientific hardware can provide assistance with, fakebusters allay their anxieties by fantasising humorously about imaginary machines like the one that Hemingway said every good writer needs: 'a built-in, shock-proof, shit detector'.[85] Post-Hemingwayan speculative instruments include the 'bogometer', devised by computer-nerds for calibrating the degree to which something is bogus. P.T. Barnum – the impresario of 'humbugs, delusions, quackeries, deceits and deceivers generally' (to quote the subtitle of his 1866 book on *The Humbugs of the World*) – observed that it would be 'a wonderful thing for mankind if some philosophic Yankee would contrive some kind of "ometer" that would measure the infusion of humbug in anything'.[86] A prototype of Barnum's 'humbugometer' was built shortly afterwards, although by a European rather than a Yankee, and offered as a spoof rather than a working spuriometer. It was called a *microscope phakomètre*, or 'fakometer'.[87]

---

[84] Haldeman, *Hemingway Hoax*, 38, 18, 33, 50.
[85] Meyers, *Hemingway*, 139.
[86] Barnum, *Humbugs of the World*, 159.
[87] Mark Jones (ed.), *Fake?*, 91.

The reification of authenticity results in an ontological fiction called the 'real thing'. Marketed as the 'genuine article', it is credited with redemptive powers to repair the damage we do to ourselves by being addicted to the inauthentic. The heritage and tourism industries are frequently criticised for inferiorising the real by habituating us to simulacra, thus heightening our sense of disappointment with some shabby actuality first drawn to our attention by a glossy reproduction of it: a ubiquitous inauthenticity, we are told, has now superseded the unproblematically authentic. This assumption is questionable in two respects. First, like the condescending supposition that people who watch tacky television shows always do so passively, it underestimates a camp taste for inauthenticity that involves enjoying the bogus *because* it is bogus, and which constitutes the phenomenon described by Maxine Feifer as 'post-tourism'.[88] Second, it overlooks the fact that, far from being unproblematic, the 'authentic' is already compromised by being identified as such. 'To be experienced as authentic it must be marked as authentic', Jonathan Culler observes of anything subjected to the tourist's gaze; 'but when it is marked as authentic it is mediated', thus becoming 'a sign of itself, and hence lack[ing] the authenticity of what is truly unspoiled, untouched by mediating cultural codes'.[89] The human incarnation of the real thing is an equally elusive 'real McCoy', whose historical identity, it turns out, is contested by several claimants, including a runaway slave who improved the efficiency of railway engines, a runaway sailor who bootlegged in Prohibition America, a Glaswegian exporter of Scotch whisky ('the real McKay') and a boxer whose professional name was Kid McCoy.[90] Our search for those phantom singularities, the real thing and the real McCoy, continues to be frustrated by evasions, deferrals and diffusions. But who needs 'The Real Thing', to quote the title of a much anthologised short story by Henry James, syndicated originally to eight newspapers, which published it simultaneously in April 1892?[91] Certainly not writers, James gives us to understand. The artist in his story, who makes a living by illustrating magazine fiction about the upper classes, finds his working-class models far more satisfactory than a high-society couple (the real thing) down on their luck. He

---

[88] Feifer, *Going Places*, 259–68.
[89] Culler, *Framing the Sign*, 164.
[90] Hillel Schwartz, *Culture of the Copy*, 11–12.
[91] Nordloh, 'First Appearances of James's "The Real Thing"', 69–70.

needs the provocation of their inauthenticity in order to create that distinctive illusion of the real which makes art what it is. Like James' own fiction, his drawings establish their alterity as art by unapologetically preferring verisimilitude to the truth, and by valuing effects more highly than origins.

CHAPTER 7

Fake literature as critique

As the repressed text of literary studies, literary forgery constitutes an indispensable critique of those cultural practices that foster the so-called genuine article, and for reasons specified by social anthropologists. For like 'pollution' in Mary Douglas' analysis of it in *Purity and Danger* (1966), or 'rubbish' in Michael Thompson's *Rubbish Theory* (1979), 'spuriosity' is a constitutive category in what Thompson calls in his subtitle 'the creation and destruction of value'. This is why cultural theorists cannot afford to ignore it. Douglas expresses her key insight axiomatically: 'where there is dirt there is system'. Since nothing is intrinsically dirty, 'dirt' is best understood as 'matter out of place', in the way that 'weeds' are vegetation out of place. In so far as 'dirt is the by-product of a systematic ordering and classification of matter', what a society treats as dirt reveals implicitly what it values.[1] Whether designed as an 'archaeology of garbage', like William Rathje and Cullen Murphy's *Rubbish!* (1994), or a 'social history of trash', like Susan Strasser's *Waste and Want* (1999), a comprehensive history of literary forgery would calibrate shifts in what corresponds to pollution behaviour and garbage guilt in the literary world. By doing so it would also reveal the fragility of both literature and 'litter-ature' as cultural categories.

Literary forgery is criticism by other means. Like Wise's bibliographical forgeries, which exposed the ineptitudes of dealers in rare books, it is directed not at readers in general but at critics in particular, whose 'expertise' it seeks to expose as illusory. 'You cannot rely on expert authentication', Philip Knightley told the editors of the *Sunday Times*, which had purchased forged Mussolini diaries in 1968, and in 1983 was about to serialise forged diaries by Hitler. After all, the 'Mussolini' diaries had survived scrutiny by 'the

---

[1] Douglas, *Purity and Danger*, 35.

author of the standard work on Mussolini, the world's greatest authority on paper, a famous handwriting expert, an internationally known palaeographer and an academic who authenticated the Casement diaries'.[2] The only oddity in this list is the choice of an expert on Roger Casement, which betrays a common misapprehension that expertise acquired in one noetic domain is a floating asset that can be drawn upon to solve problems in another. Yet this is not necessarily the case. An unrivalled knowledge of Rembrandt's paintings did not prevent Abraham Bredius from regarding one of Han van Meegeren's forgeries of Vermeer as genuine.[3] Testimony by experts may not be expert testimony, especially when the media pressures them into pontificating before they have had time to examine thoroughly the work in question. Even a demonstrated competence in one's own field of knowledge will not eliminate the possibility of deception. Being the author of *The Last Days of Hitler* (1947) gave Hugh Trevor-Roper the confidence but not the authority to declare the 'Hitler' diaries authentic.

Expert authority rests not only on the amount of knowledge laid claim to (which can be formidable) but also on what John Locke describes in his *Essay Concerning Human Understanding* (1690) as our 'respect' (*verecundia*) for the authority of presumed experts. This encourages us – wrongly, in the view of lawyers who discredited the *argumentum ad verecundiam* by relabelling it 'the *ad verecundiam* fallacy' – to capitulate prematurely to 'expert' opinions.[4] Popular audiences uninhibited by *verecundia* simply ignore expert criticism of art they take pleasure in. Consequently, historians who drew attention in the media to factual errors and political bias in Peter Weir's anti-British film, *Gallipoli* (1981), had no adverse effect on box-office takings from all those Australians who flocked into cinemas to see a persuasive enactment of the Anzac legend that innocent Australia was betrayed at Gallipoli by perfidious Albion. Popular suspicion of experts is justifiably prudent behaviour, given the history of inexpert judgements made by 'experts' fluent in the rhetoric of authority. By mystifying their practices as connoisseurship, literary experts like to represent the judgements they deliver as the products of a natural inwardness rather than of predispositions fostered by processes of acculturation. Connoisseurs characteristically claim to know what

[2] Robert Harris, *Selling Hitler*, 289.
[3] Bredius, 'New Vermeer', 10; Radnóti, *The Fake*, 22–23.
[4] Walton, *Appeal to Expert Opinion*, 58, 260.

they know without being able to explain how they know it, and therefore resent being asked to justify their taste-based literary judgements, especially to tasteless literary theorists. In the realm of connoisseurship, 'taste' stands in the same relation to the consumption of literature as 'genius' does to its production. Only a lifetime spent reading great literature, it is assumed, will prepare you to experience in the writings of your contemporaries that shock of recognition which enables you to know immediately and unerringly that you are in the presence of a masterpiece. Those outside the charmed circle of connoisseurship, however, expect to be given reasons why something is or is not the 'real thing', and are unimpressed by a critical discourse whose constitutive terms include 'genius' and 'taste'. For these are the kind of words described by Peter Medawar as 'analgesic pills', because far from explaining anything they merely 'dull the aches of incomprehension'.[5]

Eric Hebborn, who placed himself in that elite group of artists 'whose virtuosity makes experts phony', describes in *Drawn to Trouble* (1991) both why it is necessary to con the 'con-you-sir' and how to be as successful at it as he himself was.[6] Never imitate what you personally think are characteristic features of an old master's work, he advises. Instead, produce something that complies with what is currently being said about it by experts, who will then mistake your forgery for the genuine article. The name of the game is 'delightful duality', which Hebborn thinks is not worth playing unless you 'choose worthy opponents', since 'the greater the expert, the greater the satisfaction of deceiving him'.[7] Practitioners of forgery in the arts occasionally deposit in their spurious artefacts what Tom Keating calls 'a clue for the experts'. He himself would 'sometimes wr[i]te a swear word' on his forgery of an old master, just as another art forger inscribed the word *merde* on the shawl of one of the women depicted in a painting regarded by Anthony Blunt as a genuine Georges de La Tour.[8] In addition to such profanities, Keating would also write '"ever been had" or "this is a fake" directly on the canvas before starting work', and use white lead paint for this purpose because it would 'show up under a picture if it [were] X-rayed'.[9] Psychologisers of such practices find evidence here of a suicidal desire to be found

[5] Medawar, *Art of the Soluble*, 97.
[6] Hebborn, *Drawn to Trouble*, 124.   [7] Ibid., 218.
[8] Keating, *Fake's Progress*, 82, 85; Christopher Wright, *Art of the Forger*, 67.
[9] Keating, *Fake's Progress*, 85.

out, prompted by guilt at committing such wilful acts of deception. My own view is that clue-planting intensifies the vertigo of deception – Caillois' *ilinx* – by increasing the chances of discovery. As in other forms of gambling, you raise the stakes in the knowledge that the winner takes all. For if your clue-encrypted deception is not detected, you will have demonstrated that so-called experts are not only as gullible as everybody else but so inept that they cannot recognise the bogus even when it's drawn to their attention. After examining Prokosch's 'Butterfly' books, Nicholas Barker likewise decided that their shoddiness must have been deliberate, the rationale being that 'the poorer the likeness, the greater (to the forger) the ineptitudes of the experts who are deceived'.[10]

Some perpetrators of successful literary hoaxes similarly claim that their works contain 'clues' that any competent critics would spot immediately: Psalmanazar, for instance, pointed out in 1747 that any 'judicious Reader' of his *Description of Formosa* (1704) would have seen that it is 'stuffed' with 'many Absurdities'.[11] Busy reviewers with deadlines to meet cannot be expected, however, to treat every book that lands on their desks as a potential forgery in breach of that fiduciary contract between author and reader which justifies our assumption that what we are reading is genuine. Although authorial lapses are condoned in the charitable dictum that even Homer nods, no such sympathy is ever accorded literary critics caught catnapping. Yet not even the most distinguished critic is spoof-proof. The great Renaissance scholar, Joseph Scaliger, who laid the foundations of modern historical scholarship by developing philological methods for sifting the genuine from the spurious in the corpus of texts preserved from antiquity, was deceived into publishing in his edition of Varro some fragmentary verses he attributed to an ancient dramatist called Trabeas, but which in fact had been forged by Marc-Antoine Muret.[12] It is therefore surprising that a focal point in most accounts of a successful literary deception is the gullibility of the experts who were fooled rather than the literary skills of the author who fooled them. This habitual bias in the narrative construction of literary forgery ignores Hebborn's observation that 'if the fake is good enough, no expert need blame himself for having

---

[10] Barker, *Butterfly Books*, 183.
[11] Foley, *Great Formosan Impostor*, 55.
[12] Anon, 'Literary Impostures – Alexandre Dumas', 312.

been deceived'.[13] Narratives that shift attention away from the artfulness of literary forgeries reveal a profound compulsion in our culture to dissociate spuriosity from creativity. As a result, first-rate literary forgers are rarely accorded the respectful admiration that comparably successful authors of 'genuine' literature receive.

How can we be expected to recognise as a 'clue' something we are not even looking for in a text not yet under suspicion? If I were to argue that a diary first published in 1920 as *The Story of Opal*, and said to have been written by a seven-year-old, is far too *faux-naif* to be the work of a girl that age brought up in Oregon lumber camps, part of my evidence would be that Opal Whiteley named her pet wood-rat 'Thomas Chatterton Jupiter Zeus'.[14] This looks like the kind of knowingness that characterises metafiction such as Charles Palliser's novel, *Betrayals* (1994), in which a would-be novelist called William-Henry Ireland writes about another would-be novelist called Thomas Chatterton. The name of Opal Whiteley's wood-rat is likely to be construed by any literary critic familiar with literary history as a 'clue' to the spuriosity of her diary, although to true believers it may simply evince the remarkable imagination of a precocious little girl, who bridged the gap between her American environment and the European worthies she heard or read about by naming the local rooster 'Napoleon' and a couple of oak trees 'Wordsworth' and 'Keats'.[15] Literary 'clues', however, are rarely so conspicuous. Readers of Ian McEwan's *Enduring Love* (1997) are encouraged to believe that this novel fictionalises a case study of erotomania, which its discoverer named after himself in 1921 as de Clérambault's syndrome. It was reported in an article by Robert Wenn and Antonio Camia, first published in the *British Review of Psychiatry*, which was reprinted as an appendix to *Enduring Love*.[16] If you happen to know that there is a *British Journal of Psychiatry* but no *British Review of Psychiatry* you may suspect that 'Wenn' and 'Camia' are made-up names, and if deciphering cryptonyms is your forte you may recognise them as an anagram for 'Ian McEwan'. On confessing to his 'shocking attempted fraud', McEwan revealed that in 1997 he had 'submitted the paper to the *British Journal of Psychiatry* in the name of . . . Dr Wenn', and had been 'both disappointed and

---

13 Hebborn, *Drawn to Trouble*, 348.
14 Whiteley, *Singing Creek Where the Willows Grow*, ed. Hoff, 79.
15 Ibid., 78, 79, 77.
16 McEwan, *Enduring Love*, 249–60.

relieved' when it was 'respectfully turned down'.[17] How could fiction reviewers be expected to know these things? Even the psychiatrist who reviewed McEwan's novel in the January 1999 issue of the *Psychiatric Bulletin* of the *British Journal of Psychiatry* described it as being 'based on a published case report'.

Literary clues are often embedded in paratextual materials concerning provenance. 'Ern Malley', for instance, was said by his creators, McAuley and Stewart, to have died of 'Graves' disease'. Critics ought to have known that exophthalmic goitre isn't fatal, Stewart explained forty-five years later, and therefore should have been 'alerted' to the hoax by this misinformation.[18] If that were the case, then Victorian critics who happened to know that people don't die from 'spontaneous human combustion' might well have concluded from the evidence of what happens to Dickens' Mr Krook that *Bleak House* (1853) was not what it purported to be. The important question here is not whether medical errors turn up in literary texts by accident or design, nor how much medical knowledge literary critics need to acquire in order to be proficient at their art, but how anyone who read the paratextual material about Ern Malley (*before* he became 'Ern Malley') could have suspected the poems of being a literary forgery after seeing 'Graves' disease' linked to the death of the author. For in matters of interpretation, no 'fact' pre-exists the hypothesis that constructs it as such, and no 'clue' precedes a suspicion. You need either to know or at least suspect that 'Ern Malley' never existed before you can recover 'evidence' of that fact from the texts of his poems. Only then will they appear to bristle with clues put there deliberately by McAuley and Stewart to advertise their deception. 'Our serious frolic' will suddenly seem as revelatory a phrase as Ireland's 'solemn mock'ry', and what looked like a mere Dylan Thomas-ism ('this No-Man's-language') will be read as a blindingly obvious clue when linked to the statement elsewhere in these poems 'that a poet may not exist'. Not until you know that *two* people fabricated them will you experience 'confirmation' of that fact in the phrase, 'we are as the double almond concealed in one shell'.[19] But the matter does not end there. For in the course of searching for 'clues' planted deliberately by the authors

[17] McEwan, 'Shocking Attempted Fraud', 508.
[18] Heyward, *Ern Malley Affair*, 107.
[19] Ibid., 244, 262, 247, 259.

of these poems you may notice others they must have been unconscious of. These in turn will have been rendered visible only by another hypothesis, namely, that neither of those two antimodernists could have known, when they invented (as 'a transposed version / Of [their] too rigid state') a modernist poet called 'Ern Malley', that the poems they attributed to him would become more influential in Australian literary culture than anything they themselves would ever publish under their own names. Consequently, they could not have recognised the proleptic potential of the words they chose in making 'Ern Malley' refer to himself as a 'permanent revenant' – an uncanny phrase relished by later readers as one of the unconscious ironies of their text.[20]

In spite of the ubiquity of literary forgeries, there has been no interest in identifying criteria for evaluating spurious texts, even though it is widely acknowledged that some are better than others. Before discovering that the New York Public Library had already implemented his proposal, Mark Holstein argued that there ought to be a 'five-foot shelf of literary forgeries', equivalent to the one that Charles W. Eliot thought would accommodate the Harvard Classics.[21] Since occupancy of the Holstein shelf would transform the meretricious into the meritorious, candidates are frequently proposed for this honour: Chatterton as poet, Wise as bibliographer, Ireland as dramatist (although not in the opinion of anti-Stratfordians like Ogburn, who would substitute for *Vortigern* the plays of Shakespeare, 'the most amazing literary hoax of all time').[22]

Forgery-specific selection criteria might include the scale of an enterprise, as witnessed by the 2,995 ancient epigrapha created in sixteenth-century Naples by Pirro Ligorio, the 800 pages of Mary Chestnut's bogus diary of the American Civil War, the 20,000 emendations in the Perkins Folio, and the 27,320 letters (from such notables as Cleopatra and Mary Magdalen) forged in the 1860s by Denis Vrain-Lucas.[23] These belie the commonsense opinion that forgers avoid unnecessary risks by not writing at length, a view sometimes encountered among those who think that the Roger Casement diaries must be genuine because Special Branch would

---

[20] Ibid., 251, 247.
[21] Holstein, 'Five-Foot Shelf of Literary Forgeries', 567.
[22] Wadsworth, *Poacher from Stratford*, 127.
[23] Abbott, 'Some Spurious Inscriptions and Their Authors', 27; Ganzel, *Fortune and Men's Eyes*, 147, on the Perkins Folio; Chestnut, *Diary from Dixie*; Farrer, *Literary Forgeries*, 203.

never have risked forging more than one of them.[24] Farrer's view
that ballads are the easiest kind of literature to fake suggests that
another criterion in the evaluation of literary forgery should be the
degree of difficulty involved, which is linked to the argument about
whether or not some works of art are so complex as to be inimitable
and thereby unfakable.[25] As a *difficulté vaincue*, the invention of a
whole culture and language by Psalmanazar, and the description of it
in ways that would have made him (in Rodney Needham's opinion)
'a marvellous genuine ethnographer', secure a place on Holstein's
shelf for *A Description of Formosa* (1704).[26] Although linguists like
Daniel G. Brinton think it 'no great labor . . . to manufacture a new
language', monoglots remain unconvinced, especially on encountering textual traces of the glossolalic medium Elise Müller, who
began speaking 'Martian' in 1894.[27] A more down-to-earth case is
the Amerindian 'Taensa', which was invented by two young semi-
narists, Jean Parisot and A. Dejoy, after encountering the word
'Tansa' in Chateaubriand's *Voyage en Amérique* (1827). The eleven
poems they wrote in that language (published in 1883 as *Cancionero
Americano*) were regarded as authentic until Brinton demonstrated
their 'humbuggery' in 1885.[28] Closer to home is the fifteenth-century
'Rowleyan' English in which the polyglot Chatterton became fluent;
denounced by Skeat as a 'farrago' of philological errors, it failed to
impress Walpole, who ranked Psalmanazar above Chatterton on
account of his ability to 'create a language'.[29]

If audacity were to become a criterion of value in literary forgery,
then the exemplary author would be Clifford Irving, who was
contracted to ghost but actually wrote the 'autobiography' of
Howard Hughes. But if the key criterion were to be literary
influence, then undoubtedly the benchmark would be Macphossian,
which achieved cult status among European readers for whom
authenticity (in the Ritsonian sense) was no more an issue than it
would be for a subsequent readership in the 1840s, when Elias
Lönnrot, deciding to do for Karelo-Finnish folksongs what Macpherson had done for the Gaelic equivalent, pieced together fifty

---

[24] Nicholl, 'Into the Dark Heart', 32.
[25] Farrer, *Literary Forgeries*, 260; Aargaard-Mogensen, 'Unfakables', 97.
[26] Needham, *Exemplars*, 115.
[27] Brinton, 'Curious Hoax of the Taensa Language', 452; Cifali, 'Making of Martian', 269–70.
[28] Brinton, 'Curious Hoax of the Taensa Language', 458.
[29] Skeat, 'Essay on the Rowley Poems', x-xi; Foley, *Great Formosan Impostor*, 70.

poems (comparatively untampered with) in order to fabricate in 1849 a homogeneous *Kalevala*.[30] Euro-Macphossian could not be contained within the terms that governed debates about it by English critics, who had no way of dealing with this textual *doppelgänger* that masqueraded as ancient and succeeded as modern. In the years when Macphossian was becoming 'the greatest literary sensation of the eighteenth century', provenance-driven investigations into its authenticity were as irrelevant to an understanding of that phenomenon as comparable enquiries would be into the 'genuineness' of the Irish dancing in globally successful entertainments like *Riverdance*.[31] Thomas Twining, for instance, who enjoyed reading Thomas Tyrwhitt's edition of Chatterton's *Poems* (1777), expressed surprise at the 'fuss people make [about] whether Rowley or Chatterton' had written them.[32] By revealing that poems of dubious provenance could nevertheless make readers as '*extasié* with their infinite beauty' as Gray was on his first encounter with *Fragments of Ancient Poetry*, the Macphossian effect contributed significantly to a developing sense of the 'aesthetic' – first theorised in Alexander Gottlieb Baumgarten's *Aesthetica* (1750–58) – as the locus of desirable experiences unaffected by questions of who their authors 'really' are.[33] The immediate beneficiary of that revolutionary move and the debate it provoked was the Romantic generation of writers, whose assumptions still inform popular notions of the imagination as a place of freedom outside history.

How people react to evidence of a successful literary deception depends on whether or not they approve of what they take to be its outcome. For instance, in Irene L. Szyliowicz's account of how *Les Désenchantées* (1906), a novel by 'Pierre Loti' (Julian Viaud), originated in an elaborate subterfuge organised by three European women, gender-based interpretations of this episode differ markedly from assessments of it that focus on ethnicity. Critical of Loti's sexist exploitation of women in his serial performances as an 'Orientalist' writer, Marie Léra (a Frenchwoman who wrote under the andronym of 'Marc Hélys') persuaded a couple of friends she visited in Constantinople to join her in masquerading as veiled Turkish women when meeting the novelist. Aiming to make Loti understand

---

30 Lönnrot, *Kalevala*, trans. Magoun, 354.
31 Gaskill, ' "Ossian" Macpherson', 113.
32 Meyerstein, *Life of Chatterton*, 462.
33 Levinson, *Romantic Fragment Poem*, 36, 43, 47–48; Gray, *Correspondence*, vol. III, 680.

just how oppressive life was for women in Turkish society, they persuaded him to write a novel which, while proselytising to French readers on behalf of Turkish women, would bring him credit as a pro-feminist male. As 'Marc Hélys' revealed in *L'Envers d'un roman* (1923), her book on the secret history of the genesis of *Les Désenchantées*, the conspirators regarded their deception as a triumph, since it side-tracked a notorious womaniser from pandering yet again to European male fantasies that stereotype Turkish women as passive but sensual odalisques. But from a post-colonial perspective, this episode remains disturbingly Eurocentric in its assumption that Turkish women are mere pawns in a power-struggle between the New Woman and philandering Frenchmen. By not checking the accuracy of what his pseudo-native informants told him, Loti perpetuated Western misunderstandings by overlooking the efforts that Turkish women were making at that time to broaden their horizons through gaining access to more than a religious education. The cultural spuriousness of *Les Désenchantées* was abundantly clear to a Turkish critic of Loti's novel, Lutfi Fikri Bey, who concluded in 1907 that its female characters were 'three Frenchwomen disguised as Turkish women'.[34]

This unusual episode draws attention to the fact that although literary forgery is not gender-exclusive, it has certainly been perceived as a predominantly masculine domain. That would not surprise Chatterton's psychobiographer, Louise J. Kaplan, who regards imposture as a pubertal disorder that is 'prototypically masculine'; 'with few exceptions', she adds, it is 'nonexistent among females', whose corresponding problem is anorexia nervosa.[35] Nevertheless, a few females are featured in Bram Stoker's *Famous Impostors* (1910), including Olive Wilmot (Mrs Serres), who masqueraded as 'Princess Olive', and several others are mentioned in Sarah Burton's *Impostors* (2000). In the seventeenth century there was Mary Carleton (née Moders), the female rogue to whom Defoe's Roxana compares herself, the woman who pretended to be 'the German Princess' and subsequently acted the part of herself in the play of that name seen by Samuel Pepys at the Duke's Theatre on 15 April 1664.[36] In 1817 the daughter of a Devonshire cobbler, Mary Wilcox, achieved her upwardly mobile ambitions for ten weeks by

---

[34] Szyliowicz, *Pierre Loti and the Oriental Woman*, 114, 151.
[35] Kaplan, *Family Romance of Chatterton*, 6–7.
[36] Todd and Spearing, *Counterfeit Ladies*, xxvii, xxix–xxx.

exoticising herself Psalmanazar-like as 'the Princess Caraboo'; and afterwards, she too hoped to act the part of herself in a dramatisation of her story.[37] But very few women are known to have combined literary imposture with social imposture as Darville did briefly when she became 'Demidenko'. Indeed, one indication of a residually negative attitude towards literary forgery is the absence, after three decades of second-wave feminist scholarship, of an alternative to 'malestream' accounts of the phenomenon. For a while, the anomalous fact that three canonical women writers of the Victorian period – Charlotte Brontë ('Currer Bell'), Emily Brontë ('Ellis Bell') and Mary Ann Evans ('George Eliot') – all published under male pseudonyms supported a feminist conviction that nineteenth-century women writers were obliged to 'forge' their identities in this way in order to avoid being either patronised or dismissed by male critics. Yet in this period, Catherine A. Judd reports, men wrote pseudonymously as often as women, and in fact 'were more likely' when doing so 'to use a cross-gendered pseudonym'.[38] Unprecedented archival searches since the 1960s to retrieve the texts of a 'lost' (that is, patriarchally suppressed) women's literature have not resulted in a revisionist history of literary forgery, comparable to feminist rewritings of the history of literary modernism. Why not? One answer is that, because such investigations were part of a consciousness-raising programme designed to identify positive role-models for women, a laudable desire to show that women can write at least as well as men was not accompanied by a corresponding urgency to reveal that they can behave just as badly.

Such oversights are now being addressed. As Elizabeth Brunazzi observes, by comparison with the public humiliation of *les collabos horizontales* there has been a curious silence about French women who wrote for the Nazi-controlled press during the Occupation of Paris.[39] Yet because the quest for evidence of female innovativeness has not resulted in Lady Wardlow being celebrated as the first forger of a Scottish ballad, there has been no interest in reinvestigating the 'great likelihood' (as Robert Chambers put it in 1859) that she wrote all the best-known ballads.[40] As is evident from feminist works of reference that lack entries on literary forgery, literary historians have

---

37 Russett, 'The "Caraboo" Hoax', 41.
38 Judd, 'Male Pseudonyms and Female Authority', 252, 250.
39 Brunazzi, 'Question of Colette and Collaboration', 282–83.
40 David Masson, *Edinburgh Sketches*, 121.

been as reluctant to concede that women do this sort of thing as Queen Victoria apparently was to believe that some of them have sex with one another.[41] Yet if the scholars best qualified to demonstrate that some women writers have been as duplicitous as their male counterparts refuse to do so because they feel it would be politically inappropriate, then literary history will continue to be skewed by the occlusion of textual improprieties by women.

That this situation could be remedied by anybody with the will to do so is shown by recent developments in the study of confidence tricksters. In the century following the publication of Herman Melville's novel, *The Confidence Man* (1857), the 'con man' was treated (like that other self-fashioning performance artist, the dandy) as an exclusively male phenomenon, despite the fact that women as well as men figure in the earliest English writings on the subject, namely Robert Greene's 'conny-catching' pamphlets of 1591–92. 'In literature', John G. Blair remarks, 'the con man is associated as easily with the artist as with the criminal', because he 'generates fictions for his victims while himself inhabiting a fiction generated by the writer for his readers'.[42] If con man is to victim as author is to reader, then to include a confidence trickster in a novel is to create ample opportunities for self-reflexive writers to explore at one remove the duplicities of fiction as a medium, and particularly by means of those first-person 'con-fessions' that concern Thomas Mann in *The Confessions of Felix Krull, Confidence Man* (1911). Recently, however, this eminent domain has been challenged by both Kathleen De Grave's book on the confidence woman in nineteenth-century America (1995) and Lori Landay's on the female trickster in American culture (1998).[43] And in the same period Jean E. Kennard has linked that masterpiece of cross-dressing and genre-bending, *Orlando* (1927), to Virginia Woolf's blacking-up disguise (complete with false beard, caftan and turban) as a member of the entourage of the 'Emperor of Abyssinia', which in 1910 gained access as visiting royalty to the British navy's state-of-the-art man-o'-war, the *Dreadnought*, a hoax fictionalised in a short story by Woolf entitled 'A Society' (1921).[44] Such investigations question a couple of assumptions about the nexus between literature and lying. First, that fiction is an altogether higher class of deception

---

[41] Weintraub, *Victoria*, 535.
[42] Blair, *Confidence Man in Modern Fiction*, 134.
[43] De Grave, *Swindler, Spy, Rebel*; Landay, *Madcaps, Screwballs, and Con Women*.
[44] Kennard, 'Power and Sexual Ambiguity', 150.

than mere deceitfulness. And second, that deceitfulness is a predominantly masculine weakness, attested to by precept in *Much Ado about Nothing* ('men were deceivers ever') and by example in narratives about seduced-and-abandoned heroines like Thomas Hardy's Tess Durberfield.

Since 'crimes' of writing are personalised whenever they are detected, they tend to be treated as isolated instances of individual malpractice rather than as symptomatic of systemic malfunctions in the literary world. If your sympathies happen to lie with the victim, the critical protocol on such occasions is to revile the perpetrator, as Toby Forward was to discover after deceiving Virago Press into publishing his stories as the work of 'Rahila Khan'. But should you happen to sympathise with the perpetrator, you will feel at liberty to revile the victim, as opponents of 'postmodernism' did when they discovered that a cultural studies journal called *Social Text* had been tricked into publishing as genuine what turned out to be a spoof article on science studies written by a physicist, Alan Sokal.[45] Just how successfully this socio-cultural etiquette deflects attention from the institutional shoddiness that permits such incidents to succeed is evident to anybody who reads between the lines of Neal Bowers' account of the 'David Sumner' affair. In *Words for the Taking* (1997), Bowers complains that, 'between 1992 and 1994, a person calling himself David Sumner had two of [Bowers'] poems accepted as his own 20 times at 19 different literary magazines'.[46] Feeling both outraged and victimised by this imposture, Bowers began his 'hunt for [the] plagiarist', aided by a compilation called *Poet's Market*, which lists upwards of two thousand poetry magazines. Tracked down by Bowers' private detective, the plagiarist (a 'sociopathic thief' called David Jones) turned out to have been a primary-school teacher before being jailed for child molestation.[47] Although Bowers does not reveal this fact until late in the book, his narrative constructs it as proleptic: 'pedophilia and plagiarism', he concludes, 'seem to be expressions of [Jones'] need to control'.[48] Like those little girls who testified to Jones' encroachments on their bodies, Bowers feels 'contaminated' by Jones' molestation of the corpus of his poetry.[49] Textual 'molestation', in Edward Said's formulation, is that 'consciousness of one's duplicity' which stems from an awareness

[45] Sokal, 'A Physicist Experiments with Cultural Studies', 62.
[46] Bowers, *Words for the Taking*, 12.
[47] Ibid., 15, 116–17.   [48] Ibid., 124.   [49] Ibid., 128.

(especially common in novelists) that one's 'authority . . . is a sham'.[50] As a poetaster who lacked authority, Jones molested some of Bowers' poems by copying them out and 'improving' them before sending them for publication (as the work of 'David Sumner') to the editors of magazines 'so obscure and ephemeral' as to be 'unobtainable beyond the locale of their production'.[51]

The most disturbing feature in all of this, however, is something not emphasised by Bowers, namely the endemic myopia of those poetry editors who, while indulging their personal tastes in deciding what to print, exhibited no professional obligation to read even the better-known poetry magazines published by other people. The poem that first alerted Bowers to the theft of his intellectual property appeared as the work of 'David Sumner' in the December 1991 issue of the *Mankato Poetry Review*, only three months after the publication of Bowers' original version – not in some obscure and ephemeral poetry magazine but in the most durable and famous of them all, *Poetry* (Chicago). To ask how that could have come about, and why this 'oversight' was repeated by the editors of several other journals, is to focus on high-cultural malpractices that are far more significant than Neal Bowers' personal feelings about what happened to him. David Jones' success in masquerading plagiaristically as 'David Sumner' is a more effective indictment of self-serving little magazines – and poetry journals in particular – than any number of critical articles about editors whose professional shortcomings are highlighted in such episodes.

The production and circulation of spurious texts is a cultural strategy used in the interests of various political agendas, one of which is the invention for nationalistic purposes of an inheritance suppressed by colonisers. Apart from Macphossian, the most impressive of these is the work of the Welsh autodidact, Edward Williams, who in 1788 gave himself the bardic name of 'Iolo Morganwg' (Ned of Glamorgan), on account of his unsubstantiatable conviction that Welsh poets were descendants of the ancient Druids, of which he himself was the last scion.[52] He successfully passed off his creative imitations of the fourteenth-century poet, Dafydd ap Gwilym, as newly discovered originals subsequently incorporated into the very first edition of that poet's work, which was published in

---

50 Said, 'Molestation and Authority in Narrative Fiction', 49.
51 Bowers, *Words for the Taking*, 96.
52 Morgan, *Iolo Morganwg*, 11, 13.

London in 1789 by a group of expatriates with ambitions to revive Welsh literature. And as an inventor of historical lore and neo-Druidic traditions, such as the Gorsedd of Bards (a moot which from 1819 onwards was assimilated into the eisteddfod), Williams was to contribute further fabrications to *The Myvyrian Archaiology of Wales* (1801–07). Yet just as misprision can stimulate creativity – as happened when those sixteenth-century Florentine humanists, the Camarata, inadvertently created modern opera in the mistaken assumption that ancient Greek drama had been sung – so too literary forgery can have positive consequences. The Ossianic controversy stimulated salvage operations in other submerged cultures. These included bilingual samplers such as Edward Jones' *Musical and Poetical Relicks of the Welsh Bards* (1784) and Evan Evans' *Some Specimens of the Poetry of the Antient Welsh Bards* (1764), which nominates Taliesin as the British Homer, and to which Chatterton responded by Ossianising one of its translations.[53] Iolo's multifarious forgeries made him, in Prys Morgan's estimation, 'one of the main influences on Welsh culture in the nineteenth century'. Generated by his 'remarkably precocious sense of Welsh nationhood', Iolo's invented traditions melded so successfully with surviving customs that it took over a century to disentangle fact from fiction. And by sustaining interest in Welsh as a spoken language they helped subvert governmental policies for anglicising Wales.[54]

Literary forgery has long been used much less benignly as a weapon in the arsenal of devices for discrediting political opponents. The most notorious case is *The Protocols of the Elders of Zion*, an anti-Semitic tract that purports to reveal a Jewish conspiracy to achieve world domination. Originating in France, it reached Russia in 1895, two years before the first Zionist Congress was held at Basle.[55] A complete text of the *Protocols* was first published in Russia by Sergei Nilus in 1905, although Europeans remained largely unaware of the book until it was brought to their attention by Russian refugees from the Bolshevik Revolution of 1917. Translated into English as *The Jewish Peril* (1920), the *Protocols* were debated seriously until Herman Bernstein exposed them as a fabrication in *The History of a Lie* (1921), some six months before *The Times* published the complementary revelations by Philip Graves, reprinted in pamphlet form as *The*

---

[53] Groom, *Making of Percy's* Reliques, 97; Donald S. Taylor, *Chatterton's Art*, 275, 279.
[54] Morgan, *Iolo Morganwg*, 88, 90, 89.
[55] Bernstein, *Truth about 'The Protocols of Zion'*, xxx.

Truth about 'The Protocols' – A Literary Forgery (1921). The 'factual' *Protocols* turned out to be not just fictitious but actually fictional in origin. For the allegation that representatives of the twelve tribes of Israel had met secretly to plan a global take-over came from a German novel called *Biarritz* (1868), by 'Sir John Retcliffe'. This was the pseudonym of Hermann Goedsche, who worked as a journalist for a conservative newspaper and began writing novels after being dismissed from the Prussian postal service for his involvement in forged letters designed to incriminate the democratic leader, Benedic Waldeck, in high treason.[56] Goedsche's Gothic imagination represents the Jewish leaders as meeting secretly at night 'in the Jewish Cemetery in Prague', and in a manner 'very similar to the meeting of the Illuminati described by Dumas' at the beginning of *Mémoires d'un médecin: Joseph Balsamo* (1846).[57] In order to write what came to be known as 'The Rabbi's Speech' in that chapter, Goedsche plagiarised a satirical pamphlet published in 1864 by a French lawyer, Maurice Joly. Entitled *Dialogue aux enfers entre Montesquieu et Machiavel*, it was written in the same genre as Landor's *Imaginary Conversations* (1824–29) and directed against Napoleon III, whose behaviour Joly represents as despotically Machiavellian by comparison with the liberalism advocated by Montesquieu. In Goedsche's appropriation of Joly's infernal dialogue, the Jewish leader outlines what anti-Semitic conspiracy-theorists always suspect, namely Machiavellian strategies for achieving global supremacy. Goedsche's chapter about what had happened in Prague's Jewish Cemetery began to be de-fictionalised when the Russian heirs of 'Retcliffe' published it separately in 1872 as a pamphlet, with the rider that although it was fiction it was based on fact.[58] In the final stage of decontextualisation, the fictional frame was eliminated altogether: isolated as a Jewish blueprint for 'world domination, as was promised to our father Abraham', 'The Rabbi's Speech' could circulate independently of Goedsche's novel, and purely as anti-Semitic propaganda.[59]

Sometimes the discrediting of political opponents is achieved by Piltdownistic forgeries, which involve deliberately planting spurious evidence with the intention of having it exhumed by somebody who will think it genuine. The most famous Piltdownist in the visual arts

---

[56] Norman Cohn, *Warrant for Genocide*, 33.
[57] Eco, *Foucault's Pendulum*, 489.
[58] Cohn, *Warrant for Genocide*, 36.   [59] Ibid., 274.

is Michelangelo, who sculpted in marble a 'sleeping Cupid' which was sent to Rome so that it could be buried, dug up and then sold as an antique. Or at least, that is what Giorgio Vasari reports in his *Lives of the Artists* (1550). But since Michelangelo's agency in this affair is uncertain, and the artefact itself has not survived, there is some justification for treating that *dio d'amore dormente* not as a 'lost' work by Michelangelo but as a discursive effect of 'the forgery anecdote', whose generic affinities, Sándor Radnóti argues, are with the picaresque.[60] Piltdownism is named of course after the greatest scientific fraud of the twentieth century, which occurred in 1912 when a respected geologist, Charles Dawson, and an eminent palaeontologist, Arthur Smith Woodward, announced their discovery (in a gravel-pit near Piltdown in Sussex) of the skull of that 'missing link' between ape and human whose existence had been predicted in the evolutionary theories of Charles Darwin and Thomas Ernest Huxley. The skull of the 'Dawn Man of Piltdown' (*Eoanthropus dawsoni*) turned out to have been fabricated from a human cranium and the jawbone of an orang-utan.[61]

Literary studies are equally vulnerable to such activities. Hewlett reports that George Steevens, the eighteenth-century editor of Shakespeare, was a notable Piltdownist who used to 'disseminate fictitious illustrations of Shakespeare's text' – such as Peele's letter to Marlowe about Shakespeare's plagiarism of Alleyn – in the hope of entrapping Malone into adopting them, thereby giving Steevens 'the gratification of correcting the blunder in his next edition'.[62] Literary Piltdownism is fictionalised by Rudyard Kipling in 'Dayspring Mishandled' (1928), which tells how a Chaucer expert was conned into accepting as genuine the forged fragment of a 'lost' Canterbury Tale planted in the binding of a 1485 copy of the Vulgate Bible, and whose Dutch provenance is revealed orthographically in its haunting refrain about wasted youth, 'Daiespringe mishandeelt cometh nat agayne'.[63] But the most interesting case occurred in 1747, when William Lauder – a Jacobite Scot who regarded John Milton as an 'Arch-Traytor and Regicide' – contributed to the *Gentleman's Magazine* five articles, whose cumulative effect was to accuse Milton of having

---

[60] Nobili, *Gentle Art of Faking*, 89; Quint, 'Counterfeit and the Original', 1; Radnóti, *The Fake*, 1–2, 10.
[61] Weiner, *Piltdown Forgery*, 36–53.
[62] Hewlett, 'Forged Literature', 335.
[63] Kipling, *Limits and Renewals*, 12.

plagiarised in *Paradise Lost* (1667) various Latin texts by modern authors, but three in particular: a poem by Jacobus Masenius called *Sarcotis* (1654), Hugo Grotius' tragedy *Adamus Exul* (1601) and Andrew Ramsay's *Poemata Sacra* (1633).[64] Lauder's method was to interpolate into texts by those neo-Latin authors passages from the Latin *paraphrasis poetica* of *Paradise Lost* published by William Hog in 1690, and then quote them as 'evidence' that Milton was a plagiarist. Johnson, who later confessed that he had mistakenly thought Lauder 'too frantic to be fraudulent', was so impressed by these pseudo-revelations that he wrote 'most of the Preface and the Postscript' to Lauder's *Essay on Milton's Use and Imitation of the Moderns in his Paradise Lost* (1749).[65] Michael J. Marcuse, however, finds no other evidence of Johnson's complicity in this deception; indeed, it was Johnson who subsequently dictated the retraction signed by Lauder and published in 1751 as *Letter to the Reverend Mr Douglas*, that is, John Douglas, whose refutation of Lauder's *Essay* had appeared the previous year in a book with the tell-all title, *Milton Vindicated from the Charge of Plagiarism, Brought against Him by Mr. Lauder, and Lauder Himself Convicted of Several Forgeries and Gross Impositions on the Public* (1750).[66] Weakly claiming after the event to be merely a hoaxer who 'never would have drawn Lines' from so obvious a source as Hog's Latin paraphrase if he had 'design'd a lasting Imposition on the Publick', Lauder nevertheless maintained his view that Milton was a plagiarist.[67] This involved repeating the unsubstantiated rumour that Milton had added to a text dubiously attributed to Charles I, *Eikon Basiliké* (1642), a prayer plagiarised from Sir Philip Sidney's *Arcadia* (1590), and had done so in the expectation that as soon as the theft was revealed then the King himself would be discredited as a plagiarist. It was with an eye on Douglas' riposte to his first book, therefore, that Lauder's next attack on Milton was entitled *King Charles I Vindicated from the Charge of Plagiarism, Brought against Him by Milton, and Milton Himself Convicted of Forgery; and a Gross Imposition on the Public* (1754). This episode, which was to influence Johnson's attitude in the 1760s to Macphossian in particular and the Scots in general, turned out to be a *felix culpa* for Milton scholars, since Lauder's unsuccessful attempt at discrediting

---

[64] Marcuse, 'Lauder Controversy and the Jacobite Cause', 45.
[65] Clifford, 'Johnson and Lauder', 354; Marcuse, 'Pre-Publication History of Lauder's *Essay*', 57.
[66] Marcuse, ' "Scourge of Impostors": Douglas and Lauder', 252.
[67] Marcuse, '*Gentleman's Magazine* and the Lauder/Milton Controversy', 183.

Paradise Lost drew attention to 'that massive body of works in prose and verse which provide the direct analogues and most immediate literary context for Milton's Christian epic'.[68]

A conspicuous strength of literary forgery is to expose the politics of people who attack it, which it does by encouraging them to reveal their undeclared partialities in the course of articulating their objections to it. Like good books (in W.H. Auden's aphorism), literary forgeries read *us*, and thereby reveal the crypto-politics of our 'literary' objections to them. Jonathan Bate shows this to be the case in Malone's response to the Ireland forgeries in the 1790s, when he was representing Shakespeare so selectively as to make him sound like Edmund Burke. This no doubt consoled fellow conservatives trying to cope with the consequences of the French Revolution. But as a politically motivated reconstruction of the past, Malone's 'Shakespeare' was a fiction mobilised in order to suppress novelties deemed *ipso facto* spurious.[69] The critical overkill exhibited in Malone's *Inquiry* into Ireland's 'Shakespeare' manuscripts is less puzzling once you realise that he felt obliged to discredit them conclusively because they were symptomatic of the 'detestable doctrines of French Philosophy and the imaginary Rights of Man'.[70] Malone's right-wing construction of England's national poet therefore has affinities with Ireland's cruder strategy of manufacturing documents designed to augment our scanty knowledge of Shakespeare. 'Both the fabricator and the supposedly disinterested scholar', Bate concludes, 'were in fact in the business of *forging their own cultural identity*'.[71]

Misrecognising literary forgeries continues to be an occupational hazard for literary critics, who may be targeted whenever their authority is questioned by a writer whose work they have rejected because it fails to meet currently fashionable criteria. Such episodes merely confirm the acumen displayed in the 'polemical introduction' to Northrop Frye's *Anatomy of Criticism* (1957), which exposes the conceptual vacuousness of evaluative literary criticism by showing how Shakespeare, Milton and Shelley can be promoted or demoted in relation to one another merely by changing the criteria by which

---

68 Marcuse, ' "Scourge of Impostors": Douglas and Lauder', 254.
69 Bate, 'Faking It: Shakespeare and the 1790s', 80, 64.
70 Malone, *Inquiry into the Authenticity of Certain Papers*, 150–51.
71 Bate, 'Faking It: Shakespeare and the 1790s', 80.

they are judged.[72] As a creative way of judging the judges, literary forgery is the *bête noire* of a literary awards system referred to less politely as the 'literature racket', especially by those who think that a literary prize is more of a marketing device for publishers than a public acknowledgement by experts of literary excellence. By selecting the 'best' book from the current year's crop, prize-awarding panels reassure book-buyers in need of guidance that – despite what they may have read in newspapers about the destruction of literature in universities by deconstructionists who celebrate the death of the author – the real world of books and writing is still safely in the hands of literature-loving experts, who can recognise a good book when they see one. Since that cosy relationship between experts who know best and amateur readers who depend on them is shattered by the appearance of prize-winning literary forgeries, it is hardly surprising that those who write them get vilified. As became evident, however, in public discussions of the 'Demidenko' and 'Koolmatrie' cases in the 1990s, the outing of a literary forgery can have salutory consequences for the literary establishment by enabling its members to suspend momentarily their habitual rivalries and factionalism by reaffirming their solidarity in exhibitions of moral superiority at the expense of their transgressive victims. The novels of Darville/ 'Demidenko' and Carmen/'Koolmatrie' were a timely exposure of both the ethical hegemony and critical shortcomings of the gate-keepers of Australian literature in the 1990s, most of whom responded in what Philip Roth would call an 'ecstasy of sanctimony'.[73]

Fears that a prestigious prize will lose all credibility as a result of such a fiasco prove unfounded, however. This is not because people have short memories in postmodern times, but because media attention to a literary scandal raises the public profile of the prize, thus confirming the marketing savvy that even bad publicity is better than no publicity. The major casualty, in fact, is neither the prize nor the hoaxer but the literary awards system as represented by its judges. For whenever a literary forgery wins a literary prize it becomes clear that some other agenda than the putative one of recognising 'literary merit' is being implemented: hence the allegation that 'Demidenko' received the Miles Franklin award for *The*

---

[72] Frye, *Anatomy of Criticism*, 23–24.
[73] Roth, *Human Stain*, 2.

Hand That Signed the Paper 'as a kind of multicultural affirmative action prize'.[74] The ideologies that sustain the twin institutions of literary grants and literary awards are as much a cause of literary forgeries as the mischievousness of those individuals who produce them. Unless affirmative action on behalf of 'minority' writers in a multicultural society is matched by increased funding for the arts, male members of the hegemonic group – who think of themselves simply as writers, untroubled by gender (deemed merely women's business) and unmarked by ethnicity (something only for people from non-English-speaking backgrounds to worry about) – will feel excluded from a grants system increasingly fragmented by such categories as 'women's' or 'ethnic' or 'Aboriginal' writing. They will also suspect that their work is being overlooked by panels of literary judges who are tacitly pressured into exercising affirmative action on behalf of some group they themselves cannot join. At such moments it will appear that the best way of attracting favourable attention from the distributors of cultural kudos is to deceive them into believing that one writes as a member of a currently fashionable minority. And deficiencies in the awards system prove them right to think so. 'Wanda Koolmatrie' wrote neither better nor worse as an Aboriginal woman than her creator, Leon Carmen, did as a Caucasian man. If this episode is symptomatic, then the fact that 'Koolmatrie' was a prize-winning author whereas Carmen was not indicates that 'literary merit' – a criterion which is as sacred to literary judges as it is suspect to literary theorists – plays only a minor role in a highly politicised but ultimately patronising literary awards system that wilfully misrecognises white mediocrity as black excellence.

The 'Koolmatrie' case reveals the efficacy of literary forgery as cultural critique in affronting both the right as an ethical malpractice and the left by its indifference to identity politics. Carmen's refusal to be intimidated by those ethical commandments that forbid men to write as women (and Europeans to write as members of other racial groups) did not evoke memories of the American poet David Dwyer, who while still in his twenties pretended to be a ninety-two-year-old woman called 'Ariana Olisvos', two of whose poems were judged good enough to be published by the feminist journal *Aphra* in its special issue on ageing. Such versatility is frowned upon nowadays; indeed, when reprinting those poems in his Juniper Prize-winning

[74] Goldsworthy, 'Dewogging of Helen Demidenko', 32.

book, *Ariana Olisvos Her Last Works and Days* (1976), Dwyer was obliged
to acknowledge that the editors of *Aphra* had found his 'fraudulent
entry into [their] enclave morally and politically offensive and
artistically distasteful'.[75] Yet he experienced nothing like the outrage
provoked by Kent Johnson's timely invention in 1996 of a Hiroshima
survivor, 'Araki Yasusada', the pseudonym (so Kent Johnson informs
us in his capacity as 'a caretaker of the Yasusada manuscripts') of
'the late Tosa Motokiyu', a writer 'who did not wish to attach his
legal name to the hyperauthorial person he brought into being'.[76]
The hostile reception accorded such inter-ethnic performativity – in
which Japanese otherness perceived under Western eyes generates
ersatz *japonaiserie* – was predictable, since it questioned one of the
dogmas of a then dominant post-colonial criticism: namely, that
since exploration is historically the vanguard of exploitation, the
benign mask of empathy always conceals the rapacity of appropriation.

Literary forgeries, like literature, can be subject to revaluations
conducted for reasons that are never merely aesthetic. Those who
revive interest in a particular literary forgery tend to do so because of
its potential usefulness in implementing agendas of their own.
Macphossian's 'rehabilitation' late in the twentieth century was
motivated by the revival of Scottish nationalism in that period rather
than by a belated recognition of its literary merit. The Romantic
generation of poets which succeeded Chatterton's ignored questions
of provenance when celebrating the neglected genius of that *poète
maudit* who was not so much a faker as a fakir, an indigent but
wonder-working 'marvellous boy', as Wordsworth called him when
subscribing with Coleridge to a new edition of *The Works of Thomas
Chatterton* (1803).[77] And as soon as post-structuralist critics like
Roland Barthes had familiarised the notion that subjectivity is a
discursive effect whose corollary is the 'death' of the author, that
textual *bricolage* which constitutes the complete *oeuvre* of 'Ern Malley'
– and which the American poet Kenneth Rexroth welcomed as an
experiment in collaborative writing – could be reclaimed a mere
half-century after its first publication as a hoax, and showcased by
John Tranter and Philip Mead in their *Penguin Book of Modern*

[75] Dwyer, *Ariana Olisvos*, 8, 60–61.
[76] Kent Johnson, 'Letter to *American Book Review*'; Perloff, 'In Search of the Authentic Other',
passim.
[77] Meyerstein, *Life of Chatterton*, 504, 501.

Australian Poetry (1991) as a postmodern masterpiece ahead of its time.[78]

Like literature, every literary forgery has two lives: first as a cultural intervention, and second as a symptom of the culture into which it intervenes. Ireland's Shakespeare forgeries, Derk Bodde argues, are more than 'mere literary curiosities, because they show what the people of their time conceived Shakspere to be'.[79] Contrary to the desires of those who aim to flush all dreck out of culture, spurious writings do not disappear after their exposure in the way that out-of-favour party-members used to do from the photographic record of Stalinist Russia.[80] Instead, they survive devaluation in one taxonomy (the genuine) by means of revaluation in another (the fake), where their scarcity-value as collectables in a retrochic culture that turns trash into treasure makes them sought after as rarities. Whenever Ireland needed money he became a metaforger. 'He would recopy the 1799 printed version of *Vortigern* into his Shakespeare-hand', Jeffrey Kahan writes, 'and sell it as an original forgery', in addition to making and selling 'endless copies of his supposedly original rough drafts'.[81] Today's *mea culpa* fashion for withdrawing a text from circulation as soon as it is discovered to be a forgery would have struck the publishers of Lauder's account of 'plagiarism' in *Paradise Lost* as a waste of commercial opportunities, since on the very day that Lauder confessed to his malarkey they readvertised his book as 'a Masterpiece of Fraud'.[82] Once detected, Wise's bibliographical spuriosities similarly underwent reclassification as the prized artefacts of a master forger, and were so successful in their new career that by 1967 Wiseana was fetching higher prices in auction rooms than genuine works by the authors he published spurious editions of.[83] An ironic consequence of that reversal of fortune is that whereas wealthy American dupes once constituted a significant market for Wise forgeries, the University of Texas now houses for the benefit of scholars the most comprehensive collection of them anywhere in the world.[84] There the bogus and the genuine

---

[78] Mead, 'Cultural Pathology', 85; Tranter and Mead (eds.), *Penguin Book of Modern Australian Poetry*, 86–100.
[79] Bodde, *Shakspere and the Ireland Forgeries*, 31.
[80] King, *Commissar Vanishes*, 9–13.
[81] Kahan, *Reforging Shakespeare*, 205.
[82] Baines, *House of Forgery in Eighteenth-Century Britain*, 84.
[83] Barker, *Butterfly Books*, 77.
[84] Barker and Collins, *Sequel to 'An Enquiry'*, 13, 148.

occupy the same institutional space, just as the real books and the *trompe-l'oeil* book-spines did in the Reading Room 'designed' by Panizzi for the British Museum, which in 1990 staged its own version of the return of the repressed with a fascinating exhibition whose very title, *Fake?*, questions our confidence in the adequacy of this cultural category.[85]

[85] Jones (ed.), *Fake?*, 16.

Epilogue

Strange all this Difference should be
'Twixt Tweedle-*dum* and Tweedle-*dee*!
John Byron (1725)[1]

The evidence presented in this book to support its argument that literature and literary forgery have more in common than is generally acknowledged is available in the public record. None of it is buried in archives to which access is restricted, nor has a conspiratorial *omerta* obliged scholars to suppress it. The consensus, nevertheless, is that fake literature is an aberration best ignored rather than a critique of the twin institutions of literature and literary studies. Most people who publish, sell, review or judge books think that literary forgeries are an expensive waste of everybody's time. Because critics disapprove of spurious works published inadvertently, literary forgeries feature in histories of literature only if 'serious' writing is affected by them. As Michael Heyward observes, the 'Ern Malley' affair is remembered because it is 'the definitive moment in Australian literary modernism'.[2] In modern American poetry, however, the comparable hoax – uncannily named 'Spectrism' – is relatively unknown, and is either omitted from literary histories or mentioned only *en passant*. Critical of the fashion in an emergent modernism for multiplying '-isms' such as Imagism, Witter Bynner and Arthur Davison Ficke published as 'Emanuel Morgan' and 'Anne Knish' a volume of mock-experimental poems entitled *Spectra* (1916). Prefaced with the obligatory manifesto, this one linking 'Spectric' poetry to Futurist painting, their work was taken as seriously as that of other competing groups until 1918, when Bynner

---

[1] David Nichol Smith (ed.), *Oxford Book of Eighteenth Century Verse*, 223.
[2] Heyward, *Ern Malley Affair*, 237.

195

revealed the hoax.[3] After the appearance of Louis Untermeyer's obituary note on this episode in *The New Era in American Poetry* (1919), 'Spectrism' was forgotten until William Jay Smith exhumed it in *The Spectra Hoax* (1961).

Less conspicuous forgeries sink without trace. Who now remembers the debate about Jane Lowell's pseudo-autobiographical book, *The Cradle of the Deep* (1929), written in the genre of imaginary 'wanderings in the South Seas' that George Shepard Chappell had satirised when, as 'Walter E. Traprock', he described *The Cruise of the Kawa* (1922) to the nonexistent Filbert Islands, famous for their nuts?[4] When Syd Harrex established in 1984 that the frequently reprinted *Letters of an Indian Judge to an English Gentlewoman* (1934), by 'Arvind Nehra', was the work of Dorothy Black, a white with eighty-odd novels to her credit, he was unaware that in 1978 BBC radio had broadcast on this novel an 'inquest' largely ignored by the print media.[5] Interest in Black's book was limited in the 1970s because the critical agenda which would have made it significant had not been formulated. Feminists critical in that decade of male writers who masquerade as female had no polemical use for examples of the reverse process, except as evidence of how the oppressive conditions of patriarchy compel women to 'immasculate' themselves (as Judith Fetterley puts it) and adopt andronyms in order to be heard.[6] Not until Edward Said's *Orientalism* (1978) had enabled the development of a post-colonial criticism whose key-term is 'race' rather than 'gender' could *Letters of an Indian Judge* cease to be merely a literary curiosity and come to be read instead as symptomatic of literature's complicity with colonial exploitation.

To speculate about the cultural consequences of eroding a commonsense distinction between the genuine and the spurious involves imagining how we might have thought otherwise of these matters if we had not inherited a print culture which developed and naturalised a copyright law that privileges origins, authorship and authenticity. Such counterfactual speculations are in my opinion timely, given that we live in what Hillel Schwartz calls *The Culture of the Copy* (1996), increasingly enmeshed in an electronic communications system which is eroding many of the cultural categories reified by print,

---

[3] William J. Smith, *Spectra Hoax*, 77–79.
[4] Colcord and Broun, 'Are Literary Hoaxes Harmful?'; Yapp, *Hoaxers and Their Victims*, 154–55.
[5] Harrex and Hosking, 'Black and Dead Letters', 47, 55–56.
[6] Fetterley, *Resisting Reader*, xx.

including the category of the genuine. I think that literary forgeries are the price we pay for authorising people called creative writers to imagine situations and then write about them. Such cost–benefit analysis is commonly encountered in defences of various phenomena whose advantages are accompanied by disadvantageous side-effects. For instance, should it turn out (as some researchers argue) that schizophrenia is principally a linguistic disorder, then it may come to be considered the high price paid by some so that the rest can enjoy the privileges conferred by language. Similarly, in order to preserve freedom of speech in a liberal democracy, I think we are obliged – notwithstanding arguments to the contrary by Pierre Vidal-Naquet in *Assassins of Memory* (1993) and Deborah Lipstadt in *Denying the Holocaust* (1993) – to debate with Holocaust-deniers who masquerade as historical revisionists, and who believe that the Holocaust is 'a "hoax" perpetrated by Jews ("Zionists") in an attempt to blackmail the rest of the world for sympathy, money, and legitimacy for the state of Israel'.[7] Otherwise, their writings will circulate unchallenged as samizdat texts outside those arenas where debate and refutation take place, and as high-brow versions of rabble-rousing propaganda like Michael A. Hoffman's comic-book, *Tales of the Holohoax*, which advertises a videotape (*Tour of Auschwitz Fakes*) by Ditlieb Felderer, the author of *Anne Frank's Diary – A Hoax* (1979).[8]

The chances of a literary hoax winning any literary prize could be reduced considerably by the introduction of bureaucratic procedures, such as checking the bona fides of short-listed candidates and requiring them to sign statutory declarations. But even if such protocols could be agreed to universally and implemented successfully, to police literary production in this way might be counterproductive. For if, as I have argued, spuriosity is systemic to literature, we could well endanger the very thing such vigilance was designed to protect. Far better, I think, to start with the premise that imaginative writing justifies its existence not by being authentic but by being anarchic. In liberal democracies, however, the anarchic seems doomed to domestication by various containment procedures. In literary studies, this has been achieved by the formalist fiction that the best writers are those who resolve chaos into cosmos by virtue of what Wallace Stevens calls (in his poem, 'The Idea of Order at Key

---

[7] Drobnicki, 'Holocaust-Denial Literature', 157.
[8] Hoffman, *Tales of the Holohoax*, 15.

West') their 'blessed rage for order'. Framed in this way, imaginative writing can be co-opted for socially beneficial purposes, including its educational use in the production of responsible citizens. Those who lead chaotic lives can be given the opportunity to experience order vicariously and come to respect it by learning how to appreciate the so-called 'hidden order' of literary classics.[9] But if, as Wind argued in 1963, art is irredeemably anarchic – which is why Plato excluded artists from his ideal republic – then its driving force may well be what Morse Peckham calls our 'rage for chaos', which confirms Salvador Dalí's view that order is a 'mortuarial' dispensation.[10] In the aftermath of post-structuralism, however, neither cosmos nor chaos characterises the literary work, but instead a hybrid 'chaosmos' (to recall James Joyce's portmanteau word), produced by processes described in Félix Guattari's *Chaosmosis* (1995).

Literary forgeries are even more anarchic than literature because they question those institutions which identify and process the 'genuine' article. This is why their discovery provokes in people with a vested interest in keeping such institutions intact – namely literary pundits and other custodians of an unexamined connoisseurship – the phenomenon first described by Stanley Cohen in 1972 as 'moral panic'. Moral panics emerge, writes Cohen (after reflecting on public attitudes to gang-fights between Mods and Rockers in Britain during the 1960s), whenever something is perceived as 'a threat to societal values and interests' and reported 'in a stylized and stereotypical fashion by the mass media'. Immediately, 'the moral barricades are manned by editors, bishops, politicians and other right-thinking people', and 'socially accredited experts pronounce their diagnoses and solutions'.[11] While the panic lasts, the offending text and its even more offensive author are treated savagely by the literary establishment *pour encourager les autres*. Yet the serial scapegoating of successful literary hoaxers cannot repair the damage they do by exposing weaknesses in those publishing, reviewing and prize-giving practices which constitute the literary world. As a form of cultural critique, the work of literary hoaxers creatively complements that deconstruction of literary criticism by critical theory which characterised English studies in the last quarter of the twentieth century. By castigating critical theory, however, as the means by which postmodernists

---

[9] Ruthven, 'Critics and Cryptomorphs', 106–07.
[10] Peckham, *Man's Rage for Chaos*; Rogerson, *Dalí Scandal*, 182.
[11] Kenneth Thompson, *Moral Panics*, 7–8.

destroy literature, a theorophobic media has deprived non-specialist readers of the conceptual equipment that would enable them at least to understand the games being played by those texts which map the trajectory of literary supercheries from Macpherson's 'Ossian' to Carmen's 'Wanda Koolmatrie', and to ask what makes them different from that legitimate kind of writing which is known as literature.

The line of speculation developed in this book leads me to two possible conclusions. The more moderate would propose both a moratorium on the demonising of literary forgeries and a systematic investigation of what they tell us about the so-called genuine article. The justification for doing so would be that literary hoaxes release creative energies not yet domesticated by those cultural conventions which legitimate literature as a social institution. *Faking Literature* might thus contribute to a more broadly based but not yet conceptualised field of spuriosity studies, which would also investigate not only art forgery but the phenomena surveyed in Fred Fedler's *Media Hoaxes* (1989). These include the television quiz-show scandals of the 1950s, analysed by Kent Anderson in *Television Fraud* (1978), which attracted huge audiences enthralled by a Columbia University teacher of English from a famous literary family, Charles Van Doren, as he sat in his glass-walled contestant's booth with the airconditioning turned off to help him perspire with the mental effort of wrestling with questions he had previously been given the answers to. And another prime site is the broadcast by Orson Welles in 1938 of H.G. Wells' *War of the Worlds* (1898) as a CBS radio news item, done so convincingly that thousands of New Yorkers abandoned their homes in the belief that Martians had invaded the earth.

A more radical conclusion to my enquiries, however, would accord with Susan Gillman's argument that in nineteenth-century America 'imposture' and 'identity' were such 'dark twins' that imposture was second nature to Samuel Clemens, whose twin was Twain, the 'littery man'.[12] In the idiom of Rudyard Kipling, the colonel's lady of literature and the Judy O'Grady of literary forgery are sisters under the skin, and have so much in common that it would be prejudicial to treat them differently. Recollecting Charles Lamb's put-down of Thomas Heywood as 'a sort of *prose* Shakespeare', Oscar Wilde once described the novelist George Meredith – who had been the artist's model when Henry Wallis painted in 1856 his sanitised version of

---

[12] Gillman, *Dark Twins*, 14–52.

'The Death of Chatterton' (draped elegantly on his bed instead of lying in his own vomit) – as 'a prose Browning', before adding, 'and so is Browning'.[13] Seeing that provocation and dissent are the diastole and systole of critical enquiry, I close with a provocation: literary forgery is a sort of spurious literature, and so is literature. Consequently, when we imagine the relationship between literature and literary forgeries, we should not be thinking of Dr Jekyll and Mr Hyde but rather of Tweedledum and Tweedledee.

---

[13] Horst Schroeder, 'Browning Passage in Wilde's "Critic as Artist" ', 63.

Bibliography

Aagaard-Mogensen, Lars, 'Unfakables', *Danish Yearbook of Philosophy*, 15 (1978), 97–104.

Abbott, Craig S., 'The Case of Scharmel Iris', *PBSA*, 77 (1983), 15–34.

Abbott, Frank Frost, 'Some Spurious Inscriptions and Their Authors', *Classical Philology*, 3 (1908), 22–30.

Acker, Kathy, *Blood and Guts in High School: Plus Two* (London, 1984).
In Memoriam to Identity (London, 1990).

Ackroyd, Peter, *Chatterton* (London, 1987).

Adams, Percy G., *Travelers and Travel Liars 1660–1800* (Berkeley, Calif., 1962).

Adams, Timothy Dow, 'The Mock-Biography of Edwin Mullhouse', *Biography*, 5 (1982), 205–14.

Adkins, Nelson F., ' "Chapter on American Cribbage": Poe and Plagiarism', *PBSA*, 42 (1948), 169–210.

'Adoré Floupette' [Gabriel Vicaire and Henri Beauclair], *Les Déliquescences: Poèmes décadents* [1885], intro. N. Richard (Paris, 1984).

Albright, Evelyn May, *Dramatic Publication in England, 1580–1640* [1927] (New York, 1971).

Alcoff, Linda Martín, 'The Problem of Speaking for Others', in *Who Can Speak?*, ed. Roof and Wiegman, 97–119.

Aldington, Richard, *Frauds* (London, 1957).

Alexander, Peter, *Roy Campbell: A Critical Biography* (Oxford, 1982).

Allen, Peter, *Talks with Elizabethans: Revealing the Mystery of 'William Shakespeare'* (London, 1947).

Altrocchi, Rudolph, *Sleuthing in the Stacks* [1944] (Port Washington, N.Y., 1968).

Amirault, Chris, '*Pseudologica Fantastica* and Other Tall Tales: The Contagious Literature of Munchausen Syndrome', *Literature and Medicine*, 14 (1995), 169–90.

Amos, William, *The Originals: Who's Really Who in Fiction* (London, 1985).

Amselle, Jean-Loup, *Mestizo Logics: Anthropology of Identity in Africa and Elsewhere* [1990], trans. Claudia Royal (Stanford, Calif., 1998).

Anderson, Kent, *Television Fraud: The History and Implications of the Quiz Show Scandals* (Westport, Conn., 1978).

Anderson, Perry, *The Origins of Postmodernity* (London, 1998).

Andrews, William L., *To Tell a Free Story: The First Century of Afro-American Autobiography, 1760–1865* (Urbana, Ill., 1986).

'Anne Hughes' [Jeanne Preston], *Anne Hughes: Her Boke*, ed. Mollie Preston, intro. Michael Croucher (London, 1981).

Anon., 'Literary Impostures – Alexandre Dumas', *North American Review*, 78 (1854), 305–45.

Angle, Paul M., 'The Minor Collection: A Criticism', *Atlantic Monthly*, 14 (1929), 516–25.

Arac, Jonathan, 'The Future of English after the Cold War', *Critical Quarterly*, 39 (1997), 8–10.

'Araki Yasusada' [Kent Johnson], 'Doubled Flowering: From the Notebooks of Araki Yasusada', trans. Tosa Motokiyu *et al.*, *American Poetry Review*, 25 (July/August 1996), 23–26.

'Ariana Olisvos' [see Dwyer, David].

Armitt, Lucie, *Theorising the Fantastic* (London, 1996).

Armstrong, Tim, *Modernism, Technology, and the Body: A Cultural Study* (Cambridge, 1998).

Arnau, Frank, *Three Thousand Years of Deception in Art and Antiques* [1959], trans. J. Maxwell Brownjohn (London, 1961).

'Arvind Nehra' [Dorothy Black], *Letters of an Indian Judge to an English Gentlewoman* [1934] (London, 1978).

Asher, Richard, 'Munchausen's Syndrome', *Lancet*, 10 February 1951, 339–41.

Auchter, Dorothy, 'Did Shakespeare Write Shakespeare? A Bibliography of the Authorship Controversy', *BB*, 55 (1998), 63–71.

Auden, W.H., *Collected Shorter Poems 1927–1957* (London, 1966).

Austin, J.L., *How to Do Things with Words* (Oxford, 1962).

'B. Wongar' [Sreten Bozic], *The Track to Bralgu* (London, 1978).

Walg: A Novel of Australia (New York, 1983).

Dingoes Den (Sydney, 1999).

Babcock-Adams, Barbara, ' "A Tolerated Margin of Mess": The Trickster and His Tales Reconsidered', *Journal of the Folklore Institute, 1975* (Bloomington, Ind., 1975), 145–86.

Bacon, Francis, 'The Nature of Poetry', in *English Critical Essays*, ed. E.D. Jones, 104–09.

Bagnani, Gilbert, 'On Fakes and Forgeries', *Phoenix*, 14 (1960), 228–44.

Baine, Rodney M., *Daniel Defoe and the Supernatural* (Athens, Ga, 1968).

Baines, Paul, ' "Ward in Pillory": Alexander Pope and the Case of Forgery', *Literature and History*, 12 (1986), 195–214.

'Literary Forgery and the Ideology of Detection', *SVEC*, 303 (1992), 597–600.

' "Putting a Book out of Place": Johnson, Ossian and the Highland Tour', *Durham University Journal*, n.s., 53 (1992), 235–48.

'The Macaroni Parson and the Marvellous Boy: Literature and Forgery in the Eighteenth Century', *Angelaki*, 1.2 (1994), 95–112.

The House of Forgery in Eighteenth-Century Britain (Aldershot, 1999).

Ball, Robert J. and J.D. Ellsworth, 'The Emperor's New Clothes: Hyper-reality and the Study of Latin', *Modern Language Journal*, 80 (1996), 77–84.

Banfield, Edward C., 'Art versus Collectibles: Why Museums Should Be Filled with Fakes', *Harper's Magazine*, 1587 (August 1982), 28–34.

Baridon, Michel, 'Ruins as a Mental Construct', *Journal of Garden History*, 5 (1985), 84–96.

Barker, Nicolas, *The Butterfly Books: An Enquiry into the Nature of Certain Twentieth Century Pamphlets* (London, 1987).

and John Collins, *A Sequel to 'An Enquiry into the Nature of Certain Nineteenth Century Pamphlets': The Forgeries of H. Buxton Forman and T.J. Wise Re-Examined* (London, 1983).

'The Forgery of Printed Documents', in *Fakes and Frauds*, ed. Robyn Myers and Michael Harris (Winchester, 1989), 109–23.

Barnes, Julian, *England, England* (London, 1998).

Barnum, P.T., *The Humbugs of the World: An Account of Humbugs, Delusions, Impositions, Quackeries, Deceits and Deceivers Generally, in All Ages* (New York, 1866).

Barth, John, 'The Literature of Exhaustion [1967]', in *The Novel Today*, ed. Malcolm Bradbury (Glasgow, 1990), 71–85.

Barthes, Roland, 'The Reality Effect [1968]', in *The Rustle of Language*, trans. Richard Howard (New York, 1986), 141–48.

'The Death of the Author [1968]', in *Image Music Text*, trans. Stephen Heath (Glasgow, 1977), 142–48.

S/Z [1970] (New York, 1974).

Bate, Jonathan, 'Faking It: Shakespeare and the 1790s', *Essays and Studies*, 46 (1993), 63–80.

'The Authorship Controversy', *The Genius of Shakespeare* (London, 1997), 65–100.

Bate, Walter Jackson, 'Percy's Use of His Folio Manuscript', *Journal of English and Germanic Philology*, 43 (1944), 337–48.

The Burden of the Past and the English Poet (Cambridge, Mass., 1970).

Bates, Susannah, *The Pendex: An Index of Pen Names and House Names in Fantastic, Thriller, and Series Literature* (New York, 1981).

Baudelaire, Charles, *Baudelaire as a Literary Critic*, trans. Lois Boe Hyslop and Francis E. Hyslop (Pittsburgh, 1964).

Baudrillard, Jean, *Simulations* [1991], trans. Paul Fosse *et al.* (New York, 1983).

The Gulf War Did Not Take Place [1991], trans. Paul Patton (London, 1995).

Bauer, Dale M., 'The Politics of Collaboration in *The Whole Family*', in *Old Maids to Radical Spinsters*, ed. Laura L. Doan (Urbana, Ill., 1991), 107–22.

Baym, Nina, 'Delia Bacon: History's Odd Woman Out', *NEQ*, 69 (1996), 223–49.

Beckett, Alice, *Fakes: Forgery and the Art World* (London, 1995).

Bédoyère, Guy de la, 'John Evelyn and the Art of Quoting', *TLS*, 8 September 1995, 16.

Bendix, Regina, *In Search of Authenticity: The Formation of Folklore Studies* (Madison, Wis., 1997).

Benjamin, Mary A., 'The Forger and His Work', *Autographs* [1946], rev. ed. (New York, 1963), 87–110.

Benjamin, Walter, *Illuminations* [1955], trans. Harry Zohn (London, 1973).

Bennett, Tony and Janet Woollacott, *Bond and Beyond: The Political Career of a Popular Hero* (London, 1987).

Bentley, Gerald Eades, 'Authenticity and Attribution in the Jacobean and Caroline Drama', *English Institute Annual: 1942* (1943), 101–18.

Berek, Peter, 'The "Upstart Crow", Aesop's Crow, and Shakespeare as Reviser', *Shakespeare Quarterly*, 35 (1984), 205–07.

Berne, Eric, *Games People Play: The Psychology of Human Relationships* [1964] (London, 1966).

Bernstein, Herman, *The Truth about 'The Protocols of Zion'* [1935], intro. Norman Cohn (New York, 1971).

Blair, John G., *The Confidence Man in Modern Fiction: A Rogue's Gallery with Six Portraits* (London, 1979).

Bloom, Harold, *The Anxiety of Influence* (New York, 1973).

— *et al.*, 'Plagiarism: A Symposium', *TLS*, 9 April 1982, 413–15.

Blumenthal, Walter Hart, *False Literary Attributions: Works not Written by Their Supposed Authors, or Doubtfully Ascribed* (Lexington, Ky, 1965).

Bodde, Derk, *Shakspere and the Ireland Forgeries* (Cambridge, Mass., 1930).

Boller, Paul F. and John George, *They Never Said It: A Book of Fake Quotes, Misquotes, and Misleading Attributions* (New York, 1989).

Boorstin, Daniel J., *The Image: A Guide to Pseudo-Events in America* [1961] (New York, 1964).

Borges, Jorge Luis, *Labyrinths* [1956–60], ed. Donald A. Yates and James E. Irby (Harmondsworth, 1970).

Bormann, Ernest G., 'Ethics of Ghostwritten Speeches', *Quarterly Journal of Speech*, 47 (1961), 262–67.

Bose, Mihir and Cathy Gunn, *Fraud: The Growth Industry of the Eighties* (London, 1989).

Bouchard, Norma, ' "Critifictional" Epistemes in Contemporary Literature: The Case of *Foucault's Pendulum*', *Comparative Literature Studies*, 32 (1995), 497–513.

Bowers, Neal, 'A Loss for Words: Plagiarism and Silence', *ASch*, 63 (1994), 545–55.

— *Words for the Taking: The Hunt for a Plagiarist* (New York, 1997).

Boyes, Georgina, *The Imagined Village: Culture, Ideology and the English Folk Revival* (Manchester, 1993).

Bracey, Robert, *Eighteenth-Century Studies and Other Papers* (Oxford, 1925).

Bredius, Abraham, 'A New Vermeer: Christ and the Disciples at Emmaus', *Burlington Magazine*, 71 (November 1937), 10–11.

Brinton, Daniel G., 'The Curious Hoax of the Taensa Language', *Essays of an Americanist* (Philadelphia, 1890), 452–67.

Bristol, Michael D., 'Shakespeare the Myth', in *A Companion to Shakespeare*, ed. David Scott Kastan (Oxford, 1999), 489–502.

Bronson, Bertrand H., *Joseph Ritson: Scholar-at-Arms*, 2 vols. (Berkeley, Calif., 1938).

Brooke, Christopher, 'Approaches to Medieval Forgery [1968]', *Medieval Church and Society* (London, 1971), 100–20.

Browne, Sir Thomas, *Religio Medici* [1643], ed. James Winny (Cambridge, 1963).

Browning, Robert, *The Complete Works of Robert Browning*, ed. Roma A. King et al., 11 vols. (Athens, Ohio, 1969–98).

'Essay on Chatterton [1842]', *Complete Works*, vol. III, 161–79.

'Essay on Shelley [1852]', *Complete Works*, vol. V, 137–51.

Brunazzi, Elizabeth, 'The Question of Colette and Collaboration', *TSWL*, 13 (1994), 281–91.

Burkett, B.G. (with Glenna Whitley), *Stolen Valor: How the Vietnam Generation Was Robbed of Its Heroes and Its History* (Dallas, 1999).

Burroughs, William S., 'Les Voleurs', *The Adding Machine* (New York, 1986), 19–21.

Burton, Sarah, *Impostors: Six Kinds of Liar* (London, 2000).

Buruma, Ian, *Voltaire's Coconuts, or Anglomania in Europe* (London, 1999).

Butler, Judith, *Gender Trouble: Feminism and the Subversion of Identity* (New York, 1990).

Excitable Speech: A Politics of the Performative (New York, 1997).

Byron, Lord, *Complete Poetical Works*, ed. Jerome McGann, 9 vols. (Oxford, 1980–93).

Letters and Journals, ed. Rowland E. Prothero, 6 vols. (London, 1922).

Caillois, Roger, *Man, Play and Games* [1958], trans. Meyer Barash (New York, 1961).

Callaghan, Dympna, 'The Vicar and Virago: Feminism and the Problem of Identity', in *Who Can Speak?*, ed. Roof and Wiegman, 195–207.

Cameron, Anne, *Daughters of Copper Woman* (Vancouver, B.C., 1981).

Camille, Michael, 'The *Très Riches Heures*: An Illuminated Manuscript in the Age of Mechanical Reproduction', *Critical Inquiry*, 17 (1990), 72–107.

Carcaterra, Lorenzo, *Sleepers* (London, 1995).

Carpenter, Frederic I., 'The Vogue of Ossian in America: A Study in Taste', *American Literature*, 2 (1930–31), 405–17.

Carroll, David, 'Freud and the Myth of Origin', *NLH*, 6 (1974–75), 513–28.

Carter, John and Graham Pollard, *An Enquiry into the Nature of Certain Nineteenth Century Pamphlets* (London, 1934).

Catterall, Lee, *The Great Dalí Art Fraud and Other Deceptions* (Fort Lee, N.J., 1992).

Caviness, Madeline Harrison, ' "De convenientia et cohaerentia antiqui et novi operis": Medieval Conservation, Restoration, Pastiche and

Forgery', in *Intuition und Kunstwissenschaft*, ed. Peter Bloch *et al.* (Berlin, 1973), 205–21.

Cescinsky, Herbert, *The Gentle Art of Faking Furniture* (New York, 1931).

Chambers, E. K., *The History and Motives of Literary Forgeries* (Oxford, 1891).

Chapman, R.W., 'Blair on Ossian', *RES*, 7 (1931), 80–83.

Chatterton, Thomas, *The Complete Works of Thomas Chatterton*, ed. Donald S. Taylor and Benjamin Lee Hoover, 2 vols. (Oxford, 1971).

The Rowley Poems 1794, intro. Jonathan Wordsworth (Oxford, 1990).

Chestnut, Mary, *A Diary from Dixie*, ed. Ben Ames Williams, foreword Edmund Wilson (Cambridge, Mass., 1980).

Cifali, Mireille, 'The Making of Martian: The Creation of an Imaginary Language', in Théodore Flournoy, *From India to the Planet Mars* [1899], ed. Sonu Shamdasani (Princeton, N.J., 1994), 269–87.

Clanchy, M.T., *From Memory to Written Record: England 1066–1307* [1979], 2nd ed. (Oxford, 1993).

Clark, Carol Lea, 'Charles A. Eastman (Ohiyesa) and Elaine Goodale Eastman: A Cross-Cultural Collaboration', *TSWL*, 13 (1994), 271–80.

Clark, Kenneth, 'Forgeries', *HisT*, 29 (1979), 724–33.

Clifford, James L., 'Johnson and Lauder', *PQ*, 54 (1975), 342–56.

Cohn, Dorrit, *The Distinction of Fiction* (Baltimore, 1999).

Cohn, Norman, *Warrant for Genocide: The Myth of the Jewish World-Conspiracy and the Protocols of the Elders of Zion* (London, 1967).

Colcord, Lincoln and Heywood Broun, 'Are Literary Hoaxes Harmful? A Debate', *Bookman*, 69 (June 1929), 347–54.

Cole, Sonia, *Counterfeit* (London, 1955).

Colgan, Maurice, 'Ossian: Success or Failure for the Scottish Enlightenment?', in *Aberdeen and the Enlightenment*, ed. Jennifer J. Carter and Joan H. Pittock (Aberdeen, 1987), 344–49.

Collins, John, *The Two Forgers: A Biography of Harry Buxton Forman and Thomas J. Wise* (Aldershot, 1992).

Combs, Richard, 'Orson Welles's *F for Fake* [1976]', in *Imagining Reality*, ed. Kevin Macdonald and Mark Cousins (London, 1996), 221–24.

Constable, Giles, 'Forgery and Plagiarism in the Middle Ages', *Archiv für Diplomatik*, 29 (1983), 1–41.

Coombe, Rosemary J., *The Cultural Life of Intellectual Properties* (Durham, N.C., 1998).

Cooney, Seamus, 'Scott's Anonymity – Its Motives and Consequences', *SSL*, 10 (1973), 207–19.

Cosgrove, Stuart, 'In Praise of Plagiarism', *New Statesman and Society*, 1 September 1989, 38–39.

Coward, Rosalind, 'Looking for the Real Thing', *New Statesman*, 1 April 1988, 20–22.

Crawford, Robert, 'Post-Cullodenism', *LRB*, 3 October 1996, 18.

Critchley, Simon, *The Ethics of Deconstruction: Derrida and Levinas* (Oxford, 1992).

Crowley, John W., 'The Whole Famdamnily', *NEQ*, 60 (1987), 106–13.

Culler, Jonathan, *Framing the Sign: Criticism and Its Institutions* (Oxford, 1988).

Cyr, Helen W., *The Shakespeare Identity Crisis: A Reference Guide* (Baltimore, 1986).

Davis, Bertram H., *Thomas Percy: A Scholar-Cleric in the Age of Johnson* (Philadelphia, 1989).

Davis, Leith, ' "Origins of the Specious": James Macpherson's Ossian and the Forging of the British Empire', *ECent*, 34 (1993), 132–50.

Davis, Whitney, *Replications: Archaeology, Art History, Psychoanalysis* (University Park, Penn., 1996).

Dawson, George, 'Literary Forgeries and Impostures', *Shakespeare and Other Lectures*, ed. George St Clair (London, 1888), 142–53.

Debord, Guy, *Society of the Spectacle* [1967] (Detroit, 1977).

Comments on the Society of the Spectacle [1988], trans. Malcolm Imrie (London, 1990).

De Graef, Ortwin, 'Dead Herrings: "You Must Have Mistaken the Author" ', *Textual Practice*, 8 (1994), 239–54.

De Grave, Kathleen, *Swindler, Spy, Rebel: The Confidence Woman in Nineteenth-Century America* (Columbia, Miss., 1995).

De Grazia, Margreta, *Shakespeare Verbatim: The Reproduction of Authenticity and the 1790 Apparatus* (Oxford, 1991).

Deleuze, Gilles, 'The Powers of the False', *Cinema 2: The Time-Image* [1985], trans. Hugh Tomlinson and Robert Galeta (London, 1989), 126–55.

'The Simulacrum and Ancient Philosophy', *The Logic of Sense* [1969], trans. Mark Lester, ed. Constantin V. Boundas (London, 1990), 253–79.

Difference and Repetition [1968], trans. Paul Patton (London, 1994).

and Félix Guattari, *A Thousand Plateaus: Capitalism and Schizophrenia* [1980], trans. Brian Massumi (Minneapolis, 1987).

Deloria, Philip J., *Playing Indian* (New Haven, Conn., 1998).

Del Renzio, Toni, 'Multiple Authenticity', *Art and Artists*, 9 (July 1974), 22–27.

De Plaen, Guy, 'Authenticity: An Uncertain Concept', *Museum*, 41 (1989), 127–28.

De Quincey, Thomas, '*Walladmor*: A Pseudo-Waverley Novel', *The Collected Writings of Thomas De Quincey*, ed. David Masson, vol. XIV (Edinburgh, 1890), 132–45.

Derrida, Jacques, *Of Grammatology* [1967], trans. Gayatri Chakravorty Spivak (Baltimore, 1976).

'Signature Event Context', *Glyph*, 1 (1977), 172–97.

Acts of Literature, ed. Derek Attridge (New York, 1992).

Given Time: 1. Counterfeit Money [1991], trans. Peggy Kamuf (Chicago, 1992).

'Force of Law: The "Mystical Foundation of Authority" [1989]', in *Deconstruction and the Possibility of Justice*, ed. Drucilla Cornell *et al.* (New York, 1992), 3–67.

Dickinson, Emily, *The Poems of Emily Dickinson*, ed. Thomas H. Johnson, 3 vols. (New York, 1955).

Disraeli, Isaac, *Curiosities of Literature*, ed. Benjamin Disraeli, 3 vols. (London, 1881).

Doctorow, E.L., 'False Documents', *American Review*, 26 (November 1977), 215–32.

Doody, Margaret Anne, *The Daring Muse: Augustan Poetry Reconsidered* (Cambridge, 1985).

Dorson, Richard M., 'Folklore and Fake Lore', *American Mercury*, 70 (1950), 335–49.

Folklore and Fakelore (Cambridge, Mass., 1976).

Douglas, Mary, *Purity and Danger: An Analysis of Concepts of Pollution and Taboo* (London, 1966).

Dovey, Kimberly, 'The Quest for Authenticity and the Replication of Environmental Meaning', in *Dwelling, Place and Environment*, ed. David Seamon and R. Mugerauer (The Hague, 1986), 33–49.

Dow, Steve, 'Sins of the Mothers', *Australian*, 15–16 May 1999, Magazine, 14–16.

Drabble, Margaret (ed.), *The Oxford Companion to English Literature*, new ed. (Oxford, 1985).

Drewe, Robert, 'Solved: The Great B. Wongar Mystery', *Bulletin Literary Supplement*, 21 April 1981, 2–7.

Drobnicki, John A. *et al.*, 'Holocaust-Denial Literature: A Bibliography', *BB*, 51 (1994), 17–14; 53 (1996), 259–68; 55 (1998), 157–68.

Dryden, John, 'An Essay of Dramatic Poesy [1668]', in *English Critical Essays*, ed. E. D. Jones, 122–206.

Durham, Scott, *Phantom Communities: The Simulacrum and the Limits of Postmodernism* (Stanford, Calif., 1998).

Dwyer, David, *Ariana Olisvos Her Last Works and Days* (Cambridge, Mass., 1976).

Dyer, Carolyn Stewart and Nancy Tillman Romalov (eds.), *Rediscovering Nancy Drew* (Iowa City, 1995).

Dyer, Geoff, *Out of Sheer Rage: In the Shadow of D.H. Lawrence* (London, 1997).

Eco, Umberto, *Faith in Fakes*, trans. William Weaver (London, 1986); repr. as *Travels in Hyperreality* (London, 1987).

Foucault's Pendulum, trans. William Weaver (London, 1989).

'Forgeries, Originals and Identity', in *Signs of Humanity / L'homme et ses signes*, ed. Michel Balat and Janice Deledall-Rhodes, vol. II (Berlin and New York, 1992), 605–18.

'The Force of Falsity', *Serendipities*, trans. William Weaver (New York, 1998), 1–21.

Ede, Lisa and Andrea Lunsford, *Singular Texts / Plural Authors: Perspectives on Collaborative Writing* (Carbondale, Ill., 1990).

Edwards, W.A., *Plagiarism: An Essay on Good and Bad Borrowing* (Cambridge, 1933).

Ehrsam, Theodore G., *Major Byron: The Incredible Career of a Literary Forger* (London, 1951).

Eliot, T.S., *Selected Prose of T.S. Eliot*, ed. Frank Kermode (London, 1975).

Ellison, Ralph, *Invisible Man* (New York, 1952).

Emerson, Ralph Waldo, 'Quotation and Originality [1876]', in *Ralph Waldo Emerson*, ed. Richard Poirier (Oxford, 1990), 427–39.

'Ern Malley' [James McAuley and Harold Stewart], *Collected Poems* (Pymble, N.S.W., 1993).

Fagan, Louis, *The Life of Sir Anthony Panizzi, K.C.B.* [1880], 2 vols. (New York, 1970).

Fairer, David, 'The Poems of Thomas Warton the Elder?', *RES*, 26 (1975), 287–300, 395–406.

Farrer, J.A., *Literary Forgeries*, intro. Andrew Lang (London, 1907).

Fay, Stephen *et al.*, *Hoax: The Inside Story of the Howard Hughes – Clifford Irving Affair* (London, 1972).

Feather, John, 'The Book Trade in Politics: The Making of the Copyright Act of 1710', *Publishing History*, 8 (1980), 19–44.

Federman, Raymond, *Critifiction: Postmodern Essays* (Albany, N.Y., 1993).

Fedler, Fred, *Media Hoaxes* (Ames, Iowa, 1989).

Feifer, Maxine, *Going Places: The Ways of the Tourist from Imperial Rome to the Present Day* (London, 1985).

Ferguson, Niall (ed.), *Virtual History: Alternatives and Counterfactuals* (London, 1998).

'Fernandes de Briao' [Joyce Carol Oates], 'Plagiarized Material', *The Poisoned Kiss and Other Stories from the Portuguese* (New York, 1975), 159–81.

Fetterley, Judith, *The Resisting Reader: A Feminist Approach to American Fiction* (Bloomington, Ind., 1978).

Finney, Brian, 'Peter Ackroyd, Postmodernist Play and *Chatterton*', *Twentieth Century Literature*, 38 (1992), 240–61.

Fitzgerald, F. Scott, *The Bodley Head Scott Fitzgerald*, intro. J.B. Priestley, vol. 1 (London, 1958).

Flowers, Amy, *The Fantasy Factory: An Insider's View of the Phone Sex Industry* (Philadelphia, 1998).

Foley, Frederic J., *The Great Formosan Impostor* (St Louis, Miss., 1968).

Folkenflik, Robert, 'Macpherson, Chatterton, Blake and the Great Age of Literary Forgery', *Centennial Review*, 18 (1974), 378–91.

'Forrest Carter' [Asa Carter], *The Education of Little Tree* [1976], intro. Rennard Strickland (Albuquerque, 1986).

Forster, E.M., 'Anonymity: An Enquiry [1925]', *Two Cheers for Democracy* (London, 1951), 87–97.

Forward, Toby, 'Diary', *LRB*, 4 February 1988, 21.

Feminine Parts: A Book of Milesian Tales (London, 1992).

Foucault, Michel, 'What Is an Author? [1968]', *Language, Counter-Memory, Practice*, ed. and intro. Donald F. Bouchard (Oxford, 1977), 113–38.

Discipline and Punish: The Birth of the Prison [1975], trans. Alan Sheridan (Harmondsworth, 1979).

Franzen, Christine, *The Tremulous Hand of Worcester: A Study of Old English in the Thirteenth Century* (Oxford, 1991).

Freud, Sigmund, *The Standard Edition of the Complete Psychological Works of Sigmund Freud*, ed. and trans. James Strachey *et al.*, 24 vols. (London, 1966–73).

Frow, John, 'Repetition and Limitation: Computer Software and Copyright Law', *Screen*, 29 (1988), 4–20.

'Intertextuality and Ontology', in *Intertextuality*, ed. Michael Worton and Judith Still (Manchester, 1990), 45–55.

Fruman, Norman, *Coleridge, the Damaged Archangel* (New York, 1971).

Frye, Northrop, 'Towards Defining an Age of Sensibility', *ELH*, 23 (1956), 144–52.

Anatomy of Criticism (Princeton, N.J., 1957).

Fuegi, John, *The Life and Lies of Bertolt Brecht* (London, 1994).

Furbank, P.N. and W.R. Owens, *Defoe De-Attributions* (London, 1994).

'The Defoe That Never Was: A Tale of De-Attribution', *ASch*, 66 (1997), 276–84.

Gaddis, William, *The Recognitions* [1955] (London, 1985).

Galsworthy, John, 'Conscience [1922]', *Caravan* (London, 1925), 817–25.

Ganzel, Dewey, *Fortune and Men's Eyes: The Career of John Payne Collier* (Oxford, 1982).

Garber, Marjorie, *Shakespeare's Ghost Writers: Literature as Uncanny Causality* (New York, 1987).

Garbus, Martin and Richard Kurnit, 'Libel Claims Based on Fiction Should Be Lightly Dismissed', *BrLR*, 51 (1985), 401–23.

Gary, Romain, *Vie et mort d'Emile Ajar* (Paris, 1981).

Gaskill, Howard, ' "Ossian" Macpherson: Towards a Rehabilitation', *Comparative Criticism*, 8 (1986), 113–46.

'Ossian in Europe', *Canadian Review of Comparative Literature / Revue Canadienne de Littérature Comparée*, 21 (1994), 643–78.

(ed.), *Ossian Revisited* (Edinburgh, 1991).

Gates, Henry Louis, Jr, ' "Authenticity", or the Lesson of Little Tree', *NYTBR*, 24 November 1991, 1, 26–30.

Geertz, Clifford, *The Interpretation of Culture* (New York, 1973).

Genette, Gérard, *Paratexts: Thresholds of Interpretation* [1987], trans. Jane E. Lewin (Cambridge, 1997).

Gibson, H.N., *The Shakespeare Claimants: A Critical Survey of the Four Principal Theories Concerning the Authorship of Shakespeare's Plays* [1962] (New York, 1971).

Gide, André, *Les Faux-Monnayeurs* [1926], ed. J.C. Davies (London, 1986).

Gilbert, Sandra Caruso Mortola and Susan Dreyfuss David Gubar, 'Ceremonies of the Alphabet: Female Grandmatologies and the Female Authorgraph', in *The Female Autograph*, ed. Domna C. Stanton (Chicago, 1987), 21–48.

Gillman, Susan, *Dark Twins: Imposture and Identity in Mark Twain's America* (Chicago, 1989).

Ginsberg, Elaine K. (ed.), *Passing and the Fictions of Identity* (Durham, N.C.: 1996).

Goldberg, Jonathan, *Writing Matter: From the Hands of the English Renaissance* (Stanford, Calif., 1990).

Goldsworthy, Peter, 'The Dewogging of Helen Demidenko [1996]', *Navel Gazing* (Ringwood, Vic., 1998), 26–42.

Goodman, Ellen, 'The Doris Lessing Hoax [1984]', in *Critical Essays on Doris Lessing*, ed. Claire Sprague and Virginia Tiger (Boston, Mass., 1986), 212–13.

Goux, Jean-Joseph, *The Coiners of Language* [1984], trans. Jennifer Curtiss Gage (Norman, Okla, 1994).

Grace, Sherrill E., 'Respecting Plagiarism: Tradition, Guilt, and Malcolm Lowry's "Pelagiarist Pen"', *ESC*, 18 (1992), 461–82.

Grafton, Anthony, *Forgers and Critics: Creativity and Duplicity in Western Scholarship* (Princeton, N.J., 1990).

Gray, Thomas, *Correspondence of Thomas Gray*, ed. Paget Toynbee and Leonard Whibley, 3 vols. (Oxford, 1935).

Grebanier, Bernard, *The Great Shakespeare Forgery: A New Look at the Career of William Henry Ireland* (London, 1966).

Green, J.C.R., *Fernando Pessoa: The Genesis of the Heteronyms* (Portree: Isle of Skye, 1982).

Greene, David, *Makers and Forgers* (Cardiff, 1975).

Griffin, Robert J., 'Anonymity and Authorship', *NLH*, 30 (1999), 877–95.

Groom, Nick, 'Forgery or Plagiarism? Unravelling Chatterton's Rowley', *Angelaki*, 1.2 (1994), 41–54.

'Thomas Chatterton Was a Forger', *Yearbook of English Studies*, 28 (1998), 276–91.

The Making of Percy's Reliques (Oxford, 1999).

Guattari, Félix, *Chaosmosis: An Ethico-Aesthetic Paradigm* [1992], trans. Paul Bains and Julian Pefanis (Bloomington, Ind., 1995).

Gudeman, Alfred, 'Literary Frauds among the Greeks', in *Classical Studies in Honour of Henry Drisler* (London, 1894), 52–74.

'Literary Frauds among the Romans', *Transactions of the American Philological Association*, 25 (1894–95), 140–64.

Gunew, Sneja, 'Culture, Gender and the Author-Function: "Wongar's" *Walg* [1987]', in *Australian Cultural Studies*, ed. John Frow and Meaghan Morris (St Leonards, N.S.W., 1993), 3–14.

'The Demidenko Show and Its Gratifying Pathologies', *AusFS*, 11 (1996), 53–63.

Guy, Josephine M., 'Self-Plagiarism, Creativity and Craftsmanship in Oscar Wilde', *English Literature in Transition*, 41 (1998), 6–23.

Hacking, Ian, *Rewriting the Soul: Multiple Personality and the Sciences of Memory* (Princeton, N.J., 1995).

212 *Bibliography*

Haddy, Richard I., 'The Münchhausen of Munchausen Syndrome', *Archives of Family Medicine*, 2 (1993), 141–42.

Hagstrum, Jean, *The Sister Arts: The Tradition of Literary Pictorialism and English Poetry from Dryden to Gray* (Chicago, 1958).

Haldeman, Joe, *The Hemingway Hoax* (London, 1990).

Hall, Max, *Benjamin Franklin and Polly Baker: The History of a Literary Deception* [1960] (Pittsburgh, 1990).

Hallahan, William H., *The Ross Forgery* (London, 1977).

Hallgren, Gary, 'T.S. Eliot's *Wasteland*', in Henry Beard *et al.*, *The Book of Sequels* (New York, 1991), 126–27.

Hamburger, Käte, 'Authenticity as Mask: Wolfgang Hildesheimer's *Marbot*', in *Neverending Stories*, ed. Ann Fehn *et al.* (Princeton, N.J., 1992), 87–97.

Hamilton, Charles, *The Robot that Helped to Make a President: A Reconnaissance into the Mysteries of John F. Kennedy's Signature* (New York, 1965).

Harker, Dave, *Fakesong: The Manufacture of British 'Folksong' 1700 to the Present Day* (Milton Keynes, 1985).

Harrex, Syd and Susan Hosking, 'Black and Dead Letters: Some Lessons Learned from Bogus Autobiography', in *Raj Nostalgia*, ed. Annie Greet *et al.* (Adelaide, 1992), 47–59.

Harris, P.R., *A History of the British Museum Library 1753–1973* (London, 1998).

Harris, Patricia R., *The Reading Room* (London, 1979).

Harris, Robert, *Selling Hitler: The Story of the Hitler Diaries* (London, 1986).

Harrison, Wilson R., 'Forged Signatures', *Suspect Documents: Their Scientific Examination* (London, 1966), 373–426.

Harvey, Sir Paul and J.E. Heseltine, *The Oxford Companion to French Literature* (Oxford, 1959).

Haugen, Kristine Louise, 'Ossian and the Invention of Textual History', *Journal of the History of Ideas*, 59 (1998), 309–27.

Haverkamp-Begemann, Egbert with Carolyn Logan, *Creative Copies: Interpretative Drawings from Michelangelo to Picasso* (New York, 1988).

Hayes, Julie C., 'Plagiarism and Legitimation in Eighteenth-Century France', *ECent*, 34 (1993), 115–31.

Haywood, Ian, *The Making of History: A Study of the Literary Forgeries of James Macpherson and Thomas Chatterton in Relation to Eighteenth-Century Ideas of History and Fiction* (Rutherford, N.J., 1986).

Faking It: Art and the Politics of Forgery (Brighton, Sussex, 1987).

Hazen, Allen T., 'Literary Forgeries and the Library', *Columbia Literary Columns*, 22 (1972), 6–13.

Hebborn, Eric, *Drawn to Trouble: Confessions of a Master Forger* (New York, 1991).

The Art Forger's Handbook (London, 1997).

'Helen Demidenko' [Helen Darville], *The Hand That Signed the Paper* (St Leonards, N.S.W., 1994).

Heller, Joseph, *Picture This* (London, 1988).

Hellmann, John, 'JFK: The Author and the Text', *American Literary History*, 2 (1990), 743–55.

Hewlett, Henry G., 'Forged Literature', *Nineteenth Century*, 29 (1891), 318–38.

Heyward, Michael, *The Ern Malley Affair* (St Lucia, Queensland, 1993).

Hobsbawm, Eric and Terence Ranger (eds.), *The Invention of Tradition* (Cambridge, 1983).

Höfele, Andreas, 'Die Originalität der Fälschung: Zur Funktion des Literarischen Betrugs in England 1750–1800', *Zeitschrift für Sprach- und Literaturwissenschaft*, 18 (1986), 75–95.

Hoffman, Michael A., *Tales of the Holohoax: A Journal of Satire*, vol. 1 (Temecula, Calif., 1989).

Hogle, Jerrold E., 'The Gothic Ghost of the Counterfeit and the Progress of Abjection', in *A Companion to the Gothic*, ed. David Punter (Oxford, 2000), 293–304.

Holmes, Richard, 'Thomas Chatterton: The Case Re-Opened', *Cornhill Magazine*, 178 (1970), 203–49.

Holstein, Mark, 'A Five-Foot Shelf of Literary Forgeries', *Colophon*, 2 (1937), 550–67.

Home, Stewart (ed.), *Plagiarism: Art as Commodity and Strategies for Its Negation* (London, 1988).

Honan, William H., 'Into an Age of Fake: A Very Real Quandary', *New York Times*, 3 September 1991, C14.

Hope, Warren and Kim Holston, *The Shakespeare Controversy: An Analysis of the Claimants to Authorship, and Their Champions and Detractors* (Jefferson, N.C., 1992).

Hopkins, Gerard Manley, *The Poetical Works of Gerard Manley Hopkins*, ed. Norman H. MacKenzie (Oxford, 1990).

Hoving, Thomas, *False Impressions: The Hunt for Big-Time Art Fakes* (New York, 1996).

Howard, Rebecca Moore, 'Plagiarisms, Authorships, and the Academic Death Penalty', *College English*, 57 (1995), 788–806.

Huck, Peter, 'A Fraction too Much Fiction?', *Age Good Weekend*, 7 February 1998, 28–32.

Huizinga, Johan, *Homo Ludens: A Study of the Play Element in Culture* [1938] (London, 1970).

Hustvedt, Sigurd Bernhard, *Ballad Criticism in Scandinavia and Great Britain during the Eighteenth Century* (New York, 1916).

Hutcheon, Linda, 'Literary Borrowing . . . and Stealing: Plagiarism, Sources, Influences, and Intertexts', *ESC*, 12 (1986), 229–39.

Hutchinson, Peter, *Games Authors Play* (London, 1983).

Huxtable, Ada Louise, *The Unreal America: Architecture and Illusion* (New York, 1997).

Ingleby, C. Mansfield, *The Shakspeare Fabrications, or, The MS. Notes of the Perkins Folio Shown to Be of Recent Origin* (London, 1859).

Irving, Clifford, *Fake! The Story of Elmyr de Hory* [1969] (London, 1970).

The Hoax [1972] (Sagaponack, N.Y., 1981).

Iser, Wolfgang, 'Representation: A Performative Act', *Prospecting: From Reader Response to Literary Anthropology* (Baltimore, 1989), 236–48.

Jackson, H.J., 'Sterne, Burton, and Ferriar: Allusions to the *Anatomy of Melancholy* in Volumes Five to Nine of *Tristram Shandy*', *PQ*, 54 (1975), 457–70.

'Jacob D'Ancona' [David Selbourne], *The City of Light*, trans. and ed. David Selbourne (New York, 1997).

'James Tiptree, Jr' [Alice Sheldon], *Warm Worlds and Otherwise*, intro. Robert Silverberg (New York, 1975).

Jardine, Lisa and Alan Stewart, *Hostage to Fortune: The Troubled Life of Francis Bacon* (London, 1998).

Jenkins, David C., 'The Search for the J.P. Collier Ink Syndrome', *Literary Research*, 13 (1988), 95–122.

Jenkins, Henry, *Textual Poachers: Television Fans and Participatory Culture* (New York, 1992).

Jenks, Chris (ed.), *Core Sociological Dichotomies* (London, 1998).

Jeppson, Lawrence, *The Fabulous Frauds: Fascinating Tales of Great Art Forgeries* (New York, 1970).

Johns, Alessa, 'Mary Hamilton, Daniel Defoe, and a Case of Plagiarism in Eighteenth-Century England', *English Language Notes*, 31 (1994), 25–33.

Johnson, Barbara, *The Critical Difference: Essays in the Contemporary Rhetoric of Reading* (Baltimore, 1980).

Johnson, Kent, 'Letter to *American Book Review* [on Yasusada]', *Jacket*, no. 5, 1998 (http:www.jacket.zip.com.au/jacket05).

Johnston, Arthur, *Enchanted Ground: The Study of Medieval Romance in the Eighteenth Century* (London, 1964).

Jones, Edmund D. (ed.), *English Critical Essays: Sixteenth, Seventeenth and Eighteenth Centuries* (London, 1922).

Jones, Mark (ed.), *Fake? The Art of Deception* (London, 1990).

'Do Fakes Matter?', *Why Fakes Matter: Essays on Problems of Authenticity*, ed. Mark Jones (London, 1992), 7–11.

Jost, John *et al.* (eds.), *The Demidenko File* (Kingswood, Vic., 1996).

Judd, Alan, *Ford Madox Ford* (London, 1990).

Judd, Catherine A., 'Male Pseudonyms and Female Authority in Victorian England', in *Literature in the Marketplace*, ed. John O. Jordan and Robert L. Platten (Cambridge, 1996), 250–68.

Kahan, Jeffrey, *Reforging Shakespeare: The Story of a Theatrical Scandal* (London, 1998).

Kamuf, Peggy, *Signature Pieces: On the Institution of Authorship* (Ithaca, N.Y., 1988).

Kaplan, Louise J., *The Family Romance of the Impostor-Poet Thomas Chatterton* (New York, 1988).

Kaplan, Carey and Ellen Cronan Rose, 'Strange Bedfellows: Feminist Collaboration', *Signs*, 18 (1993), 547–61.

Keating, Tom, *The Fake's Progress: Being the Continuing History of the Master Painter and Simulator Mr. Tom Keating* (London, 1977).

Keats, John, *Letters of John Keats*, ed. Frederick Page (Oxford, 1954).

Kellett, E.E., *Literary Quotation and Allusion* (Cambridge, 1933).

Keneally, Thomas, 'The Soul of Things', *NYTBR*, 25 June 1978, 14–15.

Kennard, Jean E., 'Power and Sexual Ambiguity: The *Dreadnought* Hoax, *The Voyage Out*, *Mrs Dalloway* and *Orlando*', *Journal of Modern Literature*, 20 (1996), 149–64.

Kennedy, James *et al.* (eds.), 'Notes on Anonymity and Pseudonymity', *Dictionary of Anonymous and Pseudonymous English Literature*, 3 vols. (Edinburgh, 1926), vol. I, xi-xxiii.

Kennedy, John F., *'Let the Word Go Forth': The Speeches, Statements, and Writings of John F. Kennedy*, intro. Theodore C. Sorensen (New York, 1988).

Kenner, Hugh (ed.), *Seventeenth Century Poetry: The Schools of Donne and Jonson* (New York, 1964).

   The Counterfeiters: An Historical Comedy [1968] (Baltimore, 1985).

Kerrigan, Michael, *Bluff Your Way in Literature* (London, 1987).

Kewes, Paulina, 'Gerard Langbaine's "View of *Plagiaries*": The Rhetoric of Dramatic Appropriation in the Restoration', *RES*, 48 (1997), 2–18.

King, David, *The Commissar Vanishes: The Falsification of Photographs and Art in Stalin's Russia* (Edinburgh, 1997).

Kinzie, Mary, ' "Irreference": The Poetic Diction of John Ashbery', *Modern Philology*, 84 (1986–87), 267–81, 382–400.

Kipling, Rudyard, *Limits and Renewals* (London, 1932).

Klotz, Irving M., 'Munchausen Syndromes: Hoaxes, Parodies, and Tall Tales in Science and Medicine', *Perspectives in Biology and Medicine*, 36 (1992), 139–54.

Knowlson, James R., 'George Psalmanaazaar: The Fake Formosan', *HisT*, 15 (1965), 871–76.

Koestenbaum, Wayne C., *Double Talk: The Erotics of Male Literary Collaboration* (New York, 1989).

Korn, Eric, 'Remainders', *TLS*, 1–7 April 1988, 357.

Kristeva, Julia, *Powers of Horror: An Essay on Abjection* [1980], trans. Leon S. Roudiez (New York, 1982).

Kruse, Horst H., 'Literary Old Offenders: Mark Twain, John Quill, Max Adeler and Their Plagiarism Duels', *Mark Twain Journal*, 29.2 (1991), 10–27.

Lang, A[ndrew], 'Literary Forgeries', *Contemporary Review*, 44 (1883), 837–49.

Landay, Lori, *Madcaps, Screwballs, and Con Women: The Female Trickster in American Culture* (Philadelphia, 1998).

Lanham, Richard A., *A Handlist of Rhetorical Terms*, 2nd ed. (Berkeley, Calif., 1991).

Lanza, Joseph, *Elevator Music: A Surreal History of Muzak, Easy-Listening, and Other Moodsong* (New York, 1994).

Lausberg, Heinrich, *Handbook of Literary Rhetoric: A Foundation for Literary Studies*, ed. David E. Orton and R. Dean Anderson (Leiden, 1998).

Lawless, Emily, 'A Note on the Ethics of Literary Forgery', *Nineteenth Century*, 41 (1897), 84–95.

(ed.), *With Essex in Ireland: Being Extracts from a Diary Kept in Ireland during the Year 1599 by Mr. Henry Harvey* (London, 1890).

Leader, Zachary, *Revision and Romantic Authorship* (Oxford, 1996).

Leavitt, David, *While England Sleeps* (New York, 1993).

Arkansas: Three Novellas (Boston, Mass., 1997).

Lee, Sidney, 'Psalmanazar, George', in *Dictionary of National Biography*, ed. Sidney Lee, vol. 10 (London, 1909), 439–42.

Leeming, David, *Stephen Spender: A Life in Modernism* (New York, 1999).

Lejeune, Philippe, *On Autobiography*, ed. Paul John Eakin, trans. Katherine Leary (Minneapolis, 1989).

Lem, Stanislaw, *Imaginary Magnitude*, trans. Marc E. Heine (London, 1985).

Lessing, Doris, *The Diaries of Jane Somers* (London, 1984).

Levinson, Marjorie, *The Romantic Fragment Poem: A Critique of a Form* (Chapel Hill, N.C., 1986).

Lewis, Roger C., *Thomas James Wise and the Trial Book Fallacy* (Aldershot, 1995).

Lewis, Wyndham, *The Revenge for Love* [1937], ed. Reed Way Dasenbrock (Santa Rosa, Calif., 1991).

Lindberg, Gary, *The Confidence Man in American Literature* (New York, 1982).

Lindey, Alexander, *Plagiarism and Originality* (New York, 1952).

Lisboa, Eugenio with L.C. Taylor (eds.), *A Centenary Pessoa* (Manchester, 1995).

Lönnrot, Elias (comp.), *The Kalevala or Poems of the Kaleva District*, trans. and intro. Francis Peabody Magoun (Cambridge, Mass., 1963).

Love, Harold (ed.), *The Works of John Wilmot, Earl of Rochester* (Oxford, 1999).

Lowenthal, David, 'Counterfeit Art: Authentic Fakes?', *International Journal of Cultural Property*, 1 (1992), 79–103.

Lynn, Kenneth S., *The Air-Line to Seattle: Studies in Literary and Historical Writing about America* (Chicago, 1983).

Lyotard, Jean-François, *The Postmodern Condition: A Report on Knowledge* [1979], trans. Geoff Bennington and Brian Massumi (Minneapolis, 1984).

McCabe, Cynthia Jaffee *et al.*, *Artistic Collaboration in the Twentieth Century* (Washington, 1984).

Macdonald, Dwight, 'Annals of Crime: The First Editions of T.J. Wise', *NY*, 10 November 1962, 169–205.

McDonald, Gerald D., 'Forgeries in the Library', *Bulletin of the New York Public Library*, 41 (1937), 623–28.

MacDougall, Curtis D., *Hoaxes* [1940] (New York, 1958).

McEwan, Ian, *Enduring Love: A Novel* [1997] (New York, 1998).

'Shocking Attempted Fraud', *Psychiatric Bulletin*, 23 (1999), 508.

McGann, Jerome J., 'The Infatuated Worlds of Thomas Chatterton', in *Early Romantics*, ed. Thomas Woodman (London, 1998), 233–41.

McGrady, Mike, *Stranger Than Naked; or, How to Write Dirty Books for Fun and Profit: A Manual* (New York, 1970).

McGrail, Mary Ann, 'From Plagiaries to Sources', *Poetica*, 48 (1997), 169–85.

Mackenzie, Henry (ed.), *Report of the Committee of the Highland Society of Scotland, Appointed to Inquire into the Nature and Authenticity of the Poems of Ossian* (Edinburgh, 1805).

McManaway, James G., *The Authorship of Shakespeare* (Washington, 1962).

Macpherson, James, *The Poems of Ossian and Related Works*, ed. Howard Gaskill, intro. Fiona Stafford (Edinburgh, 1996).

Mailer, Norman, *Armies of the Night* (New York, 1968).

——— *Marilyn: A Biography* (New York, 1973).

Mair, John, *The Fourth Forger: William Ireland and the Shakespeare Papers* [1938] (Port Washington, N.Y., 1972).

Maitland, Sara and Micheline Wandor, *Arky Types* (London, 1987).

Mallon, Thomas, *Stolen Words: Forays into the Origins and Ravages of Plagiarism* (New York, 1989).

Malone, Edmond, *Cursory Observations on the Poems Attributed to Thomas Rowley* (London, 1782).

——— *An Inquiry into the Authenticity of Certain Miscellaneous Papers and Legal Instruments* [1796], intro. Arthur Freeman (London, 1970).

Mankowitz, Wolf, *Exquisite Cadaver* (London, 1990).

Manne, Robert, *The Culture of Forgetting: Helen Demidenko and the Holocaust* (Melbourne, 1996).

Marberry, M.M., *Splendid Poseur: The Story of a Fabulous Humbug* (London, 1954).

Marcus, Laura, *Auto/biographical Discourses: Theory, Criticism, Practice* (Manchester, 1994).

Marcuse, Michael J., 'The Lauder Controversy and the Jacobite Cause', *Studies in Burke and His Time*, 18 (1977), 27–47.

——— 'The Pre-Publication History of William Lauder's *Essay on Milton's Use and Imitation of the Moderns in His Paradise Lost*', *PBSA*, 72 (1978), 37–57.

——— 'The *Gentleman's Magazine* and the Lauder/Milton Controversy', *Bulletin of Research in the Humanities*, 81 (1978), 179–209.

——— ' "The Scourge of Impostors, the Terror of Quacks": John Douglas and the Exposé of William Lauder', *Huntington Library Quarterly*, 42 (1978–79), 231–61.

Marder, Louis, 'Shakespearean Frauds and Forgeries', *His Exits and His Entrances* (Philadelphia, 1963), 212–32.

'Marichiko' [Kenneth Rexroth], 'The Love Poems of Marichiko, trans. Kenneth Rexroth', in Kenneth Rexroth, *'Flower Wreath Hill': Later Poems* (New York, 1978), 103–44.

Martin, Laura, ' "Eskimo Words for Snow": A Case Study in the Genesis and Decay of an Anthropological Example', *American Anthropologist*, 82 (1986), 418–23.

Martin, Peter, *Edmond Malone, Shakespearean Scholar: A Literary Biography* (Cambridge, 1995).

Masson, David, *Edinburgh Sketches and Memories* (London, 1892).

Masson, Sophie, *The Hoax* (Milsons Point, N.S.W., 1997).

Masten, Jeffrey, *Textual Intercourse: Collaboration, Authorship, and Sexualities in Renaissance Drama* (Cambridge, 1997).

Mathews, Nieves, *Francis Bacon: The History of Character Assassination* (New Haven, Conn., 1996).

Mead, Philip, 'Cultural Pathology: What Ern Malley Means', *Australian Literary Studies*, 17 (1995), 83–87.

Medawar, P.B., *The Art of the Soluble* (Harmondsworth, 1969).

Meltzer, Françoise, *Hot Property: The Stakes and Claims of Literary Originality* (Chicago, 1994).

Metzger, Bruce, 'Literary Forgeries and Canonical Pseudepigrapha', *Journal of Biblical Literature*, 91 (1972), 3–24.

Meyers, Jeffrey, *Hemingway: A Biography* (London, 1987).

Meyerstein, E.H.W., *A Life of Thomas Chatterton* (London, 1930).

Michaels, Eric, *Bad Aboriginal Art: Tradition, Media, and Technological Horizons*, foreword Dick Hebdige, intro. Marcia Langton (St Leonards, N.S.W., 1994).

Miller, Edward, *Prince of Librarians: The Life and Times of Antonio Panizzi of the British Library* (London, 1967).

Miller, Keith D., 'Composing Martin Luther King, Jr.', *PMLA*, 105 (1990), 70–82.

Miller, Nancy K., *French Dressing: Women, Men and Ancien Régime Fiction* (New York, 1995).

Mills, Gary B. and Elizabeth Shown Mills, '*Roots* and the New "Faction": A Legitimate Tool for Clio?', *Virginia Magazine of History and Biography*, 89 (1981), 3–26.

Morgan, Prys, *Iolo Morganwg* (Cardiff, 1975).

Morrissette, Bruce, *The Great Rimbaud Forgery: The Affair of 'La Chasse spirituelle'* (St Louis, Miss., 1956).

Mossner, Ernest Campbell, *The Forgotten Hume: Le Bon David* (New York, 1943).

'Mudrooroo Nyoongah' [Colin Johnson], *Wild Cat Falling* (Sydney, 1965).

Muecke, Stephen and Noel King, 'On Ficto-Criticism', *Australian Book Review*, October 1991, 13–14.

Nagel, James, 'The Early Composition History of *Catch-22*', in *Biographies of Books*, ed. James Barbour and Tom Quirk (Columbia, Miss., 1996), 262–90.

Needham, Rodney, *Exemplars* (Berkeley, Calif., 1985).

Nelson, William, 'From Fraud to Fiction', *Fact or Fiction: The Dilemma of the Renaissance Story Teller* (Cambridge, Mass., 1973), 11–37.

Nettell, Stephanie, 'Sex Scandal', *TLS*, 13–19 November 1987, 1250.

Nichol, Don, 'Rewriting Plagiarism', *Angelaki*, 1.2 (1994), 13–21.

Nicholl, Charles, 'Into the Dark Heart', *TLS*, 9 January 1998, 32.

Nichols, Marie Hochmuth, *Rhetoric and Criticism* (Baton Rouge, La, 1963).

Nobili, Riccardo, *The Gentle Art of Faking: A History of the Methods of Producing*

Imitations and Spurious Works of Art from the Earliest Times up to the Present Day (London, 1922).

Nolan, Maggie, 'The Absent Aborigine [B. Wongar]', *Antipodes*, 12 (1998), 7–13.

Nordloh, David J., 'First Appearances of Henry James's "The Real Thing": The McLure Papers as a Bibliographical Resource', *PBSA*, 78 (1984), 69–71.

O'Connell, Kylie, '(Mis)Taken Identity: Helen Demidenko and the Performance of Difference', *AusFS*, 11 (1996), 39–52.

Ogburn, Charlton, *The Mysterious William Shakespeare: The Myth and the Reality* (New York, 1984).

O'Halloran, Clare, 'Irish Re-Creations of the Gaelic Past: The Challenge of Macpherson's Ossian', *Past and Present*, 124 (1989), 67–95.

'Olphar Hamst' [Ralph Thomas], *Handbook of Fictitious Names* (London, 1868).

Orvell, Miles, *The Real Thing: Imitation and Authenticity in American Culture, 1880–1940* (Chapel Hill, N.C., 1989).

'Ossian' [see Macpherson, James].

Osteen, Mark, 'The Money Question at the Back of Everything: Clichés, Counterfeits and Forgeries in Joyce's "Eumaeus"', *Modern Fiction Studies*, 38 (1992), 821–43.

Ousby, Ian, *The Englishman's England: Taste, Travel and the Rise of Tourism* (Cambridge, 1990).

Ozick, Cynthia, *Portrait of the Artist as a Bad Character* (London, 1996).

Painter, George D., 'Introduction to the New Edition', *The Vinland Map and the Tartar Relation* [1965], ed. R.A. Skelton *et al.* (New Haven, Conn., 1995), ix-xix.

Palmer, Herbert, *Post-Victorian Poetry* (London, 1938).

Parker, David, 'The Turn to Ethics', *Critical Review*, 33 (1993), 3–14.

Parmet, Herbert S., *Jack: The Struggles of John F. Kennedy* (New York, 1980).

Parsons, Coleman O., *Witchcraft and Demonology in Scott's Fiction* (Edinburgh, 1964).

Parsons, Nicholas T., *The Joy of Bad Verse* (London, 1988).

Partington, Wilfred, *Thomas J. Wise in the Original Cloth: The Life and Record of the Forger of the Nineteenth-Century Pamphlets* (London, 1946).

Pask, Kevin, *The Emergence of the English Author: Scripting the Life of the Poet in Early Modern England* (Cambridge, 1996).

'Paul Radley' [Jack Radley], *Jack Rivers and Me* (Sydney, 1981).

Paull, H.M., *Literary Ethics: A Study in the Growth of the Literary Conscience* (London, 1928).

Peacock, Thomas Love, *Paper Money Lyrics* [1837], in *The Works of Thomas Love Peacock*, ed. H.F.B. Brett-Smith and C.E. Jones, vol. VII (New York, 1967).

Pearson, Edmund Lester, 'The Literary Hoax, I'; 'The Literary Hoax, II', *Books in Black or Red* (New York, 1923), 3–15, 19–37.

Peckham, Morse, *Man's Rage for Chaos: Biology, Behavior and the Arts* (New York, 1965).

Percy, Thomas, *Reliques of Ancient English Poetry*, intro. Nick Groom, 3 vols. (London, 1996).

Perloff, Marjorie, 'In Search of the Authentic Other: The Araki Yasusada "Hoax" and What It Reveals about the Politics of Poetic Identity', *Boston Review* (http://www-polisci.mit.edu/BostonReview/BR22.2/Perloff.html).

Pessoa, Fernando, 'The Heteronyms', in *A Centenary Pessoa*, ed. Lisboa with Taylor, 214–31.

Peterson, Richard A., *Creating Country Music: Fabricating Authenticity* (Chicago, 1997).

Pethica, James, ' "Our Kathleen": Yeats's Collaboration with Lady Gregory in the Writing of *Cathleen ni Houlihan*', *Yeats Annual*, 6 (1988), 3–31.

Phillips, Patricia, *The Adventurous Muse: Theories of Originality in English Poetics 1650–1760* (Uppsala, 1984).

Plant, Sadie, *The Most Radical Gesture: The Situationist International in a Postmodern Age* (London, 1992).

Poe, Edgar Allan, *The Complete Edgar Allan Poe Tales* (London, 1984).

The Brevities, ed. and intro. Burton R. Pollin (New York, 1985).

Posey, Carl A. *et al.* (eds.), *Hoaxes and Deceptions* (Alexandria, Va, 1991).

Powell, Sian, 'Mysterious Case of the Contentious Heritage', *Australian*, 17 June 1996, 12.

Prokosch, Frederic, *The Missolonghi Manuscript* (London, 1968).

The Protocols of the Meetings of the Learned Elders of Zion, trans. Victor E. Marsden (n.p., 1934).

Psalmanazar, George, *A Historical and Geographical Description of Formosa* (London, 1704).

Memoirs of ****, Commonly Known by the Name of George Psalmanazar (London, 1764).

Pullum, Geoffrey K., *The Great Eskimo Vocabulary Hoax: And Other Irreverent Essays on the Study of Language* (Chicago, 1991).

Quérard, M.J.M., *Les Supercheries littéraires dévoilés*, 4 vols. (Paris, 1847).

Quint, David, 'The Counterfeit and the Original', *Origin and Originality in Renaissance Literature* (New Haven, Conn., 1983), 1–31.

Quintilian, *The 'Institutio Oratoria' of Quintilian*, trans. H.E. Butler, 4 vols. (London, 1921).

Radnóti, Sándor, *The Fake: Forgery and Its Place in Art*, trans. Ervin Dunai (Lanham, Md, 1999).

'Rahila Khan' [Toby Forward], *Down the Road, Worlds Away* (London, 1987).

Redfern, Walter, *Clichés and Coinages* (Oxford, 1989).

Remensnyder, Amy G., 'Legendary Treasure at Conques: Reliquaries and Imaginative Memory', *Speculum*, 71 (1996), 884–906.

Rhodes, Henry T.F., 'Literary Forgeries', *The Craft of Forgery* (London, 1934), 234–55.

'Richard Allen' [James Moffat], *Skinhead* (London, 1970).

'Richard Llewellyn' [Vivian Lloyd], *How Green Was My Valley* (London, 1939).

Richardson, Darrell C., 'The Life and Works of Max Brand', in *The Max Brand Companion*, ed. Jon Tuska and Vicki Piekarski (Westport, Conn., 1996), 436–48.

Ricks, Christopher, 'The Case of the Crooked Bookman', *NYRB*, 28 February 1985, 34–36.

Riemer, Andrew, *The Demidenko Debate* (St Leonards, N.S.W., 1996).

Rintoul, M.C., *Dictionary of Real People and Places in Fiction* (London, 1993).

Riviere, Joan, 'Womanliness as Masquerade [1929]', in *Formations of Fantasy*, ed. Victor Burgin *et al.* (London, 1986), 35–44.

Rogers, Pat, 'Defoe as Plagiarist: Camden's *Britannia* and *A Tour thro' the Whole Island of Great Britain*', *PQ*, 52 (1973), 771–74.

  Grub Street: Studies in a Subculture (London, 1972).

Rogerson, Mark, *The Dalí Scandal: An Investigation* (London, 1987).

Romney, Jonathan, 'Forgery and Economy in Gide's *Les Faux-Monnayeurs*', *Neophilologus*, 71 (1987), 196–209.

Roof, Judith and Robyn Wiegman (eds.), *Who Can Speak? Authority and Critical Identity* (Urbana, Ill., 1995).

Rosenbach, A.S.W., 'Some Literary Forgeries', *Books and Bidders* (Boston, Mass., 1927), 98–133.

Rosenthal, Laura J., *Playwrights and Plagiarists in Early Modern England: Gender, Authorship, Literary Property* (Ithaca, N.Y., 1996).

Roth, Philip, *The Human Stain* (New York, 2000).

Roughead, William, *The Riddle of the Ruthvens and Other Studies* [1919], new rev. ed. (Edinburgh, 1936).

Rue, Loyal, *By the Grace of Guile: The Role of Deception in Natural History and Human Affairs* (New York, 1994).

Rushkoff, Douglas, *Cyberia: Life in the Trenches of Hyperspace* (New York, 1995).

Russell, Jeffrey Burton, *Inventing the Flat Earth*, foreword David Noble (New York, 1991).

Russett, Margaret, 'The "Caraboo" Hoax: Romantic Woman as Mirror and Mirage', *Discourse*, 17 (1994–95), 26–47.

Ruthven, K.K., *Critical Assumptions* (Cambridge, 1979).

  'Critics and Cryptomorphs: Observations on the Concept of Hidden Form', *Southern Review*, 15 (1982), 92–110.

  Ezra Pound as Literary Critic (London, 1990).

Ryals, Clyde de L., 'Thomas Carlyle and the Squire Forgeries', *Victorian Studies*, 30 (1986–87), 495–518.

Said, Edward, 'Molestation and Authority in Narrative Fiction', in *Aspects of Narrative*, ed. J. Hillis Miller (New York, 1971), 47–68.

  Beginnings: Intention and Method (New York, 1975).

  The World, the Text, and the Critic (London, 1984).

Samuel, Raphael, *Theatres of Memory, Volume 1: Past and Present in Contemporary Culture* (London, 1994).

Sartiliot, Claudette, *Citation and Modernity: Derrida, Joyce, and Brecht* (Norman, Okla., 1993).

Saunders, David, *Authorship and Copyright* (London, 1992).

Saussure, Ferdinand de, *Course in General Linguistics*, trans. Roy Harris (London, 1983).

Savage, George, *Forgeries, Fakes and Reproductions: A Handbook for the Collector* (London, 1963).

Schama, Simon, *Dead Certainties (Unwarranted Speculations)* (London, 1991).

Schauer, Frederick, 'Liars, Novelists, and the Law of Defamation', *BrLR*, 51 (1985), 233–67.

Scher, Richard B., 'Percy, Shaw and the Ferguson "Cheat": National Prejudice in the Ossian Wars', in *Ossian Revisited*, ed. Gaskill, 207–45.

Schiller, Friedrich, *On the Aesthetic Education of Man* [1795], ed. Elizabeth M. Wilkinson and L.A. Willoughby (Oxford, 1967).

Schoenbaum, S., *Shakespeare's Lives* [1970], new ed. (Oxford, 1991).
William Shakespeare: Records and Images (London, 1981).
Shakespeare and Others (London, 1985).

Scholes, Robert, *Semiotics and Interpretation* (New Haven, Conn., 1982).

Schroeder, Andreas, *Cheats, Charlatans, and Chicanery: More Outrageous Tales of Skulduggery* (Toronto, 1997).

Schroeder, Horst, 'The Robert Browning Passage in Oscar Wilde's "The Critic as Artist"', *ELN*, 32 (1994–95), 62–65.

Schüller, Sepp, *Forgers, Dealers, Experts: Adventures in the Twilight of Art Forgery* [1959], trans. James Cleugh (London, 1960).

Schwartz, Hillel, *The Culture of the Copy: Striking Likenesses, Unreasonable Facsimiles* (New York, 1996).

Schwartz, Joel S., 'Alfred Russel Wallace and "Leonainie": A Hoax That Would Not Die', *Victorian Periodicals Review*, 17 (1984), 3–15.

Schwartz, John Burnham, 'Masked Memoir: Bringing a Famous Geisha back to Life', *NY*, 29 September 1997, 82–83.

Scott, Sir Walter, *Rob Roy*, ed. and intro. Ian Duncan (Oxford, 1998).

Scouten, Arthur H., 'The Warton Forgeries and the Concept of Preromanticism in English Literature', *Etudes Anglaises*, 40 (1987), 434–47.

Searle, John, *Speech Acts* (Cambridge, 1969).

Seaver, Kirsten A., *The Frozen Echo: Greenland and the Exploration of North America, ca. A.D. 1000–1500* (Stanford, Calif., 1996).

Selbourne, David, 'Jacob d'Ancona and Literary Hoaxes', *TLS*, 21 November 1997, 17.

Sergeant, Philip W., *Liars and Fakers* (London, 1925).

Seymour-Smith, Martin, 'Laura Riding's "Rejection of Poetry"', *Review*, 23 (1970), 10–14.

Sharrad, Paul, 'Does Wongar Matter?', *Kunapipi*, 41 (1982), 37–50.

Shattuck, Roger, 'The Threat to Proust', *NYRB*, 18 March 1999, 10–12.

Shaw, Eva, *Ghostwriting: How to Get into the Business* (New York, 1991).

Shaw, Peter, 'Plagiary', *ASch*, 51 (1981–82), 325–37.

Shell, Marc, *The Economy of Literature* (Baltimore, 1978).

Sherman, Sandra, *Finance and Fictionality in the Early Eighteenth Century: Accounting for Defoe* (Cambridge, 1996).

Shindo, Charles, J. *Dust Bowl Migrants in the American Imagination* (Kansas, 1997).

Shortland, Michael, 'Robert Southey's *The Doctor &C*: Anonymity and Authorship', *ELN*, 31 (June 1994), 54–63.

Sidney, Sir Philip, 'An Apology for Poetry [1580]', in *English Critical Essays*, ed. E.D. Jones, 1–64.

The Poems of Sir Philip Sidney, ed. William A. Ringler, Jr (Oxford, 1962).

Siegel, Lee, *Love in a Dead Language: A Romance* (Chicago, 1999).

Silverman, Kenneth, *Edgar A. Poe: Mournful and Never-Ending Remembrance* (New York, 1991).

Silverton, Pete, 'Publish and Be Shammed', *Punch*, 10–16 April 1991, 30–34.

Skeat, Walter W., 'Essay on the Rowley Poems', *The Poetical Works of Chatterton*, vol. II (London, 1871), vii-xlvi.

Skipp, Francis E., '*Of Time and the River*: The Final Editing', *PBSA*, 64 (1970), 313–22.

Slepian, Barry, 'The Ironic Intention of Swift's Verses on His Own Death', *RES*, 14 (1963), 249–56.

Smart, J.S., *James Macpherson: An Episode in Literature* (London, 1905).

Smith, David Nichol (ed.), *The Oxford Book of Eighteenth Century Verse* (Oxford, 1926).

Smith, Donald B., *Long Lance: The True Story of an Impostor* (Toronto, 1982).

Smith, Robert Metcalf, *The Shelley Legend* (New York, 1945).

Smith, William Jay, *The Spectra Hoax* (Middletown, Conn., 1961).

Snyder, Edward D., *The Celtic Revival in English Literature 1760–1800* (Cambridge, Mass., 1923).

Sobran, Joseph, *Alias Shakespeare: Solving the Greatest Literary Mystery of All Time* (New York, 1997).

Sokal, Alan, 'A Physicist Experiments with Cultural Studies', *Lingua Franca*, 6 (May/June 1996), 62–64.

Spender, Dale, *The Writing or the Sex? Or Why You Don't Have to Read Women's Writing to Know It's No Good* (New York, 1989).

Spender, Stephen, *World within World* (London, 1951).

Stafford, Fiona J., *The Sublime Savage: A Study of James Macpherson and the Poems of Ossian* (Edinburgh, 1988).

Stagl, Justin, *A History of Curiosity: The Theory of Travel 1550–1800* (Switzerland, 1995).

Steele, Hunter, 'Fakes and Forgeries', *British Journal of Aesthetics*, 17 (1977), 254–58.

Steiner, George, *Language and Silence: Essays 1958–1966* [1967] (Harmondsworth, 1969).

Steinhauer, Yvette, 'Jack Higgins: If He's Said It Once, He's Said It a Thousand Times', *Age Good Weekend*, 24 June 1988, 51–55.

Stern, J.P., 'Sweet Sin', *LRB*, 5–18 August 1982, 3, 5–6.

Stewart, Susan, *Crimes of Writing: Problems in the Containment of Representation* (New York, 1991).

Stillinger, Jack, *Multiple Authorship and the Myth of Solitary Genius* (New York, 1991).

Stivale, Charles J., *The Two-Fold Thought of Deleuze and Guattari: Intersections and Animations* (New York, 1998).

Stoker, Bram, *Famous Impostors* (London, 1910).

Stoll, Clifford, *The Cuckoo's Egg: Tracking a Spy through the Maze of Computer Espionage* (New York, 1989).

Sullivan, Jane, 'Regarding Henry', *Age*, 24 February 1996, Extra, 5.

Swan, Jim, 'Touching Words: Helen Keller, Plagiarism, Authorship', in *The Construction of Authorship*, ed. Martha Woodmansee and Peter Jaszi (Durham, N.C., 1994), 57–100.

Syme, Ronald, 'Fraud and Imposture', in *Pseudepigrapha I*, ed. Kurt von Fritz (Genève, 1972), 3–21.

Szyliowicz, Irene L., *Pierre Loti and the Oriental Woman* (London, 1988).

Taylor, Donald S., *Thomas Chatterton's Art* (Princeton, N.J., 1978).

Taylor, Mark C., *Kierkegaard's Pseudonymous Authorship: A Study of Time and the Self* (Princeton, N.J., 1975).

Thody, Philip *et al.*, *Faux Amis and Key Words* (London, 1985).

Thomas, Alan G., 'First Editions, Fakes and Forgeries', *Great Books and Book Collectors* (London, 1975), 234–51.

Thomas, Max W., 'Eschewing Credit: Heywood, Shakespeare, and Plagiarism before Copyright', *NLH*, 31 (2000), 277–94.

'Thomas Rowley' [see Chatterton, Thomas].

Thompson, Kenneth, *Moral Panics* (London, 1998).

Thompson, Michael, *Rubbish Theory: The Creation and Destruction of Value* (Oxford, 1979).

Thomson, Derick S., *The Gaelic Sources of Macpherson's 'Ossian'* (Edinburgh, 1952).

'Bogus Gaelic Literature c.1750–c.1820', *Transactions of the Gaelic Society of Glasgow*, 5 (1958), 172–88.

'"Ossian" Macpherson and the Gaelic World of the Eighteenth Century', *Aberdeen University Review*, 40 (1963), 7–20.

'Macpherson's *Ossian*: Ballads to Epics', in *The Heroic Process*, ed. Bo Almquist *et al.* (Dublin, 1987), 243–64.

Tietze, Hans, *Genuine and False: Copies, Imitations, Forgeries* (London, 1948).

Todd, Dennis, *Imagining Monsters: Miscreations of the Self in Eighteenth-Century England* (Chicago, 1995).

Todd, Janet and Elizabeth Spearing (eds.), *Counterfeit Ladies: The Life and Death of Mal Cutpurse; The Case of Mary Carleton* (London, 1994).

Tolstoy, Nikolai, 'The Diary of Nobody at All: Penguin, the BBC and a Spurious Documentary', *Encounter*, 58 (May 1982), 32–39.

Tout, T.F., 'Mediæval Forgers and Forgeries', *John Rylands Library Bulletin*, 5 (1919), 208–34.

Tranter, John and Philip Mead (eds.), *The Penguin Book of Modern Australian Poetry* (Ringwood, Vic., 1991).

Trevor-Roper, Hugh, *A Hidden Life: The Enigma of Sir Edmund Backhouse* (London, 1976).

Turkle, Sherry, *Life on the Screen: Identity in the Age of the Internet* (New York, 1995).

Turner, Frank M., 'The Homeric Question', in *A New Companion to Homer*, ed. Ian Morris and Barry Powell (Leiden, 1997), 123–45.

Twain, Mark, *Is Shakespeare Dead? From My Autobiography* (New York, 1909).

Veblen, Thorstein, *The Theory of the Leisure Class* [1899] (New York, 1994).

Vickers, Brian, 'Plato's Attack on Rhetoric', *In Defence of Rhetoric* (Oxford, 1988), 83–147.

Wadsworth, Frank W., *The Poacher from Stratford: A Partial Account of the Controversy over the Authorship of Shakespeare's Plays* (Berkeley, Calif., 1958).

'Walter E. Traprock' [George Shepard Chappell], *The Cruise of the Kawa: Wanderings in the South Seas* (London, 1922).

Walton, Douglas, *Appeal to Expert Opinion: Arguments from Authority* (University Park, Penn., 1997).

'Wanda Koolmatrie' [Leon Carmen], *My Own Sweet Time* (Broome, Western Australia, 1994).

Wark, McKenzie, 'The Demidenko Effect', *The Virtual Republic* (St Leonards, N.S.W., 1997), 119–53.

Warneminde, Martin, 'Fakes: The Futile Fight', *Bulletin*, 8 October 1991, 36–41.

Warren, Murray, *A Descriptive and Annotated Bibliography of Thomas Chatterton* (New York, 1977).

Wasserstein, Bernard and David Wasserstein, 'Jacopo Spurioso', *TLS*, 14 November 1997, 15–16.

Weinbrot, Howard D., *Britannia's Issue: The Rise of British Literature from Dryden to Ossian* (Cambridge, 1993).

Weiner, J.S., *The Piltdown Forgery* [1955] (New York, 1980).

Weinsheimer, Joel, 'Conjectures on Unoriginal Composition', *ECent*, 22 (1981), 58–73.

Weintraub, Stanley, *Victoria: Biography of a Queen* (London, 1987).

Weiss, Jeffrey, *The Popular Culture of Modern Art: Picasso, Duchamp and Avant-Gardism* (New Haven, Conn., 1994).

Welcher, Jeanne K., 'Gulliver in the Market-place', *SVEC*, 217 (1983), 129–39.

Wellek, René, *The Rise of English Literary History* (Durham, N.C., 1941).
Discriminations: Further Concepts of Criticism (New Haven, Conn., 1970).

Weschler, Lawrence, *Boggs: A Comedy of Values* (Chicago, 1999).

West, Harry, *Fraud: The Growth Industry* (London, 1987).

Whibley, Charles, 'Of Literary Forgers', *Cornhill Magazine*, n.s., 12 (Jan.-June 1902), 624–36.

Whistler, James McNeill, *The Gentle Art of Making Enemies* (London, 1892).

White, Harold Ogden, *Plagiarism and Imitation during the English Renaissance* (Cambridge, Mass., 1935).

Whitehead, John, *This Solemn Mockery: The Art of Literary Forgery* (London, 1973).

Whiteley, Opal, *The Singing Creek Where the Willows Grow: The Rediscovered Diary of Opal Whiteley*, ed. Benjamin Hoff (New York, 1986).

Whitman, Walt, *Leaves of Grass*, ed. Emory Holloway (London, 1947).

Wilkomirski, Binjamin, *Fragments: Memories of a Wartime Childhood* (New York, 1996).

Williams, Ian Kennedy, *Malarky Dry* (Sydney, 1990).

Williams, Raymond, *Keywords: A Vocabulary of Culture and Society* (Glasgow, 1976).

Wilson, Harriet E., *Our Nig* [1859], intro. Henry Louis Gates (New York, 1983).

Wilson, Robert A., 'Fakes, Forgeries, and Facsimiles', *Modern Book Collecting* (New York, 1980), 191–200.

Wilson, Vivian Deborah, 'The Law of Libel and the Art of Fiction', *Law and Contemporary Problems*, 44 (1981), 27–50.

Wimsatt, W.K. and Margaret H. Wimsatt, 'Self-Quotations and Anonymous Quotations in Johnson's Dictionary', *ELH*, 15 (1948), 60–68.

Wind, Edgar, *Art and Anarchy* [1963], intro. John Bayley (Evanston, Ill., 1985).

Wispé, Lauren, 'History of the Concept of Empathy', in *Empathy and Its Development*, ed. Nancy Eisenberg and Janet Strayer (Cambridge, 1987), 17–37.

Wittgenstein, Ludwig, *Philosophical Investigations* [1953], trans. G.E.M. Anscombe, 3rd ed. (Oxford, 1968).

Wolfe, Tom, *The New Journalism* (New York, 1973).

Wood, Frances, *Did Marco Polo Go to China?* (London, 1995).

Wood, Gordon S., 'Novel History', *NYRB*, 27 June 1991, 12, 14–16.

Woodring, Carl, 'Lamb's Hoaxes and the Lamb Canon', *Charles Lamb Bulletin*, 10–11 (1975), 39–41.

Wordsworth, William, *The Poems of Wordsworth*, ed. Thomas Hutchinson (London, 1926).

Wright, Christopher, *The Art of the Forger* (London, 1984).

Wright, Louis B., 'The Anti-Shakespeare Industry and the Growth of Cults', *Virginia Quarterly Review*, 35 (1959), 289–303.

Yapp, Nick, *Hoaxes and Their Victims* (London, 1992).

Yeats, W.B., *The Collected Poems* (London, 1950).

Young, Edward, *Conjectures on Original Composition* [1759], in *English Critical Essays*, ed. E. D. Jones, 315–64.

Zucker, Paul, 'Ruins – an Aesthetic Hybrid', *Journal of Aesthetics and Art Criticism*, 20 (1961–62), 119–30.

Zug, Charles G., 'Sir Walter Scott and the Ballad Forgery', *SSL*, 8 (1970), 52–64.

Index of names

Index of subjects

appropriation
  cultural, 9, 27–8, 61, 78
  textual, 125, 126, 136, 138
  'textual poaching', 127
  see also plagiarism
art forgery, 87, 126, 162, 172, 173
attribution, 93, 104, 129–30, 153, 160
  'de-attribution', 130
  stylometrics and, 130
  see also authorship
authenticity, 4, 25, 34, 146–70
  aesthetics and, 10, 29, 62, 65, 66, 163, 179
  aura and, 85, 160
  authentication and, 22, 162–3
  authenticatory devices, 149–50
  'authentic reproductions', 68
  context-dependent, 163
  as criterion of literary value, 15
  as discursive effect, 74, 149
  fabricated, 68
  as guarantee of exchange-value, 161
  inauthenticity and, 65–6, 161, 169
  irrelevance of, 179, 192
  performance and, 78
  print-culture and, 12, 160
  provenance myths and, 13, 18, 23, 39, 43, 176, 179
  signature and, 153, 156
  slave-narratives and, 101
  spuriosity, relation to, 72, 84
  tourism and, 169
authorship, 91–120
  allonymity and, 104–6
  alterity and, 68, 72, 79
  alters and, 109–10
  anonymity and, 92, 101–3
  antonymity and, 103
  anxieties of, 114
  auctor v. *scriptor*, 112
  aura and, 153, 158
  Bardolatry and, 6, 115, 118
  communal, 74

'devilling' and, 100
as discursive effect, 74
doubles and, 109
empathy and, 25–7
as fictional construct, 111
franchising of, 92, 113–14
ghostwriting and, 99–100
heteronyms and, 110–11
as hoax, 92
of 'Homer', 42, 93
homonymity and, 103
imputed, 15, 92, 103–6
as institution, 90
intellectual property and, 112–13, 139 (*see also* copyright)
mononymity and, 103, 113
orthonymity and, 103, 106
personae and, 92, 107–8
polyonomasia and, 107
pseudonyms and, 34, 73, 107, 179–80
Romantic ideology of, 56, 91, 92, 96, 98, 111
of 'Shakespeare', 93–4, 114–20
substylistic traces of, 130
textual authority and, 15, 35, 92, 98, 103
see also attribution, collaboration, subjectivity
autobiography, pseudo-, 55, 70–1, 87, 157, 178, 196
  'autobiographical pact', 44
  as 'autofiction', 67
  indexicality and, 150
  see also first-person narratives, unreliability of

ballads, 7, 9, 11, 16, 17, 42
  forgeability of, 17, 178
  forgery of, 17, 45, 105
  'scandals' of, 17
bibliographical forgery, 53, 58, 165–6, 171
  'association copies' and, 161
  restoration and, 129